Haunted
Kansas

Haunted Kansas

Ghost Stories and Other Eerie Tales

Lisa Hefner Heitz

UNIVERSITY PRESS OF KANSAS

© 1997 by the University Press of Kansas
All rights reserved

Published by the University Press of Kansas (Lawrence, Kansas 66045), which was
organized by the Kansas Board of Regents and is operated and funded by Emporia State
University, Fort Hays State University, Kansas State University, Pittsburg State University,
the University of Kansas, and Wichita State University

Library of Congress Cataloging-in-Publication Data
Heitz, Lisa Hefner.
Haunted Kansas : ghost stories and other eerie tales / Lisa Hefner Heitz.
p.   cm.
Includes bibliographical references and index.
ISBN 978-0-7006-0865-2 (alk. paper)
ISBN 978-0-7006-0930-7 (pbk.)
1. Ghosts—Kansas.   I. Title.
BF1472.U6H445   1997
133.1'09781—dc21   97-17327

British Library Cataloguing in Publication Data is available.

Printed in the United States of America

10   9   8   7

To the memory of my parents,
Gene and Reeselynn Hefner

"I have always been interested in witchcraft and superstition, but have never had much traffic with ghosts, so I began asking people everywhere what they thought about such things, and I began to find out that there was one common factor—most people have never seen a ghost, and never want or expect to, but almost everyone will admit that sometimes they have a sneaking feeling that they just possibly *could* meet a ghost if they weren't careful—if they were to turn a corner too suddenly, perhaps, or open their eyes too soon when they wake up at night, or go into a dark room without hesitating first."
  — Shirley Jackson, from "Experience and Fiction," a lecture, 1958

"Ghosts, it is advanced, either do not exist at all, or else, like the stars at noonday, they are there all the time and it is we who cannot see them."
  — Oliver Onion, from "Credo," *The Collected Ghost Stories,* 1935

" 'Ay, but there's this in it,' said the landlord. 'There's folks, i' my opinion, they can't see ghos'es, not if they stood as plain as a pikestaff before 'em. And there's reason i' that. For there's my wife, now, can't smell, not if she'd the strongest o' cheese under her nose. I never see'd a ghost myself but then I says to myself, "Very like I haven't got the smell for 'em." And so, I'm for holding with both sides; for, as I say, the truth lies between 'em.' "
  — George Eliot, *Silas Marner,* 1861

"From ghoulies and ghosties and long-leggety
    beasties
And things that go bump in the night, Good
    Lord, deliver us!"
    — Cornish prayer

Contents

School and Theater Ghosts   61

Graveyard Ghosts   91

Ghosts on the Range   113

Ghostly Oddities   141

The Most Haunted Town in Kansas: Atchison 157

Acknowledgments

I am grateful to my family and friends for their support and encouragement during the research and writing phases of this project. I especially want to thank my husband, Mark, and my daughter, Kara, for their constant love and understanding.

Thanks to my editor, Michael Briggs, for his expert advice and his patience in guiding me, beginning to end, through the long and heretofore unfamiliar process that ultimately resulted in this book.

Without the help of numerous people throughout the state, this collection of stories would not have been possible. I appreciate the assistance of everyone who responded to my queries or helped me find answers; those who provided me with information or steered me to other sources; everyone who talked to me, wrote to me, called me, and shared stories with me; all who helped introduce me to the ghosts of Kansas and their legends. Many of these individuals are named in the "Notes and Sources" section of this book, and I thank them.

Some people merit special recognition for their particular assistance or encouragement: Tom Averill, Jennie Chinn, Gene DeGrusan, Henry A. Ford, Pat Garwood, Susie Haver, Nancy Hopkins, Dr. James Hoy, Cindy Jones-Blanton, Marci Penner, Susan Sutton, Beccy Tanner, and Barbara Ulrich-Hicks. In addition, my gratitude to certain intrepid individuals who accompanied me on some of my "ghost hunt" trips around the state: Marta Barron, Becky Bruning, Junie Davis, Kara Heitz, Shelly Kelley, Steffie and Stu McFarlane, Gina Sanders, and Clayton Senne.

I also want to thank Dr. Robert Smith, retired professor of anthropology at the University of Kansas, Lawrence, for sparking my interest in the study of legends and folklore and Dr. Norman Yetman, my graduate adviser at the University of Kansas, for his unfailing support of my academic progress and his interest in this project.

Finally, to the legendary ghosts of Kansas, my thanks for allowing me to find them and capture them between the covers of this book.

Introduction

The crowd began gathering on the sidewalk shortly after 11:00 P.M., standing in the dark beneath an ancient elm tree. People in groups of two or three, whispering or giggling behind their hands, hastened down the street as midnight approached. The moon hovered just over the top of the elm tree, casting fingers of dark shadows out over the yard, shadows that reached and touched the faces of the residents of Gaylord, Kansas, lined up along the sidewalk in front of the abandoned, and quite haunted, house.

At 12:00 A.M., the spectral show they had all come to see began. Night after night, rerun after rerun, the same ghastly performance played out. First, the lights. Colored lights—red, blue, green, yellow—began to dimly glow from behind the cracked and dust-streaked windows on the second story. Gradually increasing in magnitude, the glow became a radiance behind the glass, the colors flashing and dancing in a spectacular rainbow show.

Next, the silhouettes. Framed in one of the brilliantly lit windows, the darkened outlines of two figures appeared facing one another. Slowly it became obvious that one shape was that of a woman; the other was that of a man. Motionless at first, the figures began to move and weave and, finally, struggle.

Last, and most anticipated by the crowd, the moans began. Low and nearly inaudible at first, the moaning quickly escalated into groaning, the groans finally becoming shrieks. After several shrieks had died on the wind, the people thronging below the windows, with one unconscious movement, huddled more closely together in anticipation of the finale. A long, blood-curdling scream issued from the house as the dark silhouettes in the window struggled together, the shadow of the woman trying to escape the strangling hands of the shade that had her in a fatal embrace. With a last strangled scream, the figures began to fade, and the carnival-like lights dimmed. Within seconds, the windows were without light, and the house was silent.

The crowd on the sidewalk was as silent as the house. Individual voyeurs began breaking from the group and walking away. Couples clung together, and families left the scene in small bunches. Some people would be back the next night, part of tomorrow's crowd on the sidewalk. Some people would be too frightened or horrified by what they had seen to return. But regardless of who was and who was not there to watch them, the phantoms of the Gaylord haunted house would repeat their ghoulish performance the following night at midnight, to the horror and delight of the crowd gathered below.

Legend holds that in the late 1800s, the tiny town of Gaylord, just south of Smith Center in north-central Kansas, was home to the haunted house that produced this nightly spook show. The legend doesn't tell us if the events enacted by the phantoms were echoes of a real struggle and strangulation that had occurred in the house when it was occupied by living beings. Some people do believe that apparitions are psychic imprints left at the scene of a violent or tragic event. This legend also doesn't tell us how long the apparitions continued their nightly show or if a rational explanation could be made for this event. Perhaps some local jokesters wanted to liven things up in Gaylord, or some charlatan spiritualists wanted to stir up interest in the supernatural and scare up some business. Or maybe it is all just a story—a good ghost story that started on a Halloween night one hundred years ago and has been added to and embellished over the generations as one person has told it to another and another.

The haunted house in Gaylord is gone now, and its ghosts are presumably gone, too. But though the phantoms of Gaylord may no longer be around, plenty of other ghosts still do reside in Kansas—more than almost anyone can imagine. One doesn't even have to believe in ghosts to see that they live among us in their stories and legends. And like the ghosts of Gaylord, they can come back for performance after performance whenever their stories are told.

In 1995 I began the research that would result in this book, traveling to many parts of the state, visiting "haunted" sites, learning of stories of ghosts and monsters, listening to personal tales of experiences with the paranormal.

I stood on a haunted bridge north of Valley Center and waited for the ghost of Theorosa to come flying up from the creek bed below and try to throw me into the water—a stunt, I had been told, for which she was known. I walked through the rubble of the empty third floor of an old hotel building in Wichita, peering down a dimly lit hallway to try and see the luminous blue form of the Blue Handkerchief Ghost. I listened carefully for the clatter of the dragging saber of Custer's Ghost on the stairway at the Custer House at Fort Riley. I drove through the Sandhills State Park north of Hutchinson, looking for the shanty of the infamous Hamburger Man, and I climbed down to the edge of St. Jacob's Well south of Dodge City, looking for any signs of the cowboy ghost and his ghost horse who were rumored to still drink at the natural well some one hundred years after they had drowned in it. In Concordia, I toured the Brown Grand Theatre and scanned the balcony for the apparition of Earl, a benevolent ghost who had supposedly materialized in front of a balcony window in the past. In Atchison, I ventured into Jackson Park and tried to sense the presence of the legendary ghost of Molly, a poor restless spirit reputed to still roam near the place where she was hanged in Molly's Hollow.

In every instance, I saw nothing, I heard nothing, I felt nothing—nor did I expect to. I was (and for the most part still am) a ghost skeptic. I have no reason to believe in ghosts but really no reason to disbelieve. I simply have not seen any, nor have I witnessed any direct personal proof of the paranormal, ghosts or otherwise. My search for these Kansas ghosts began, and continues, primarily because of a love of stories and legends. I was in pursuit of legendary tales in Kansas, not necessarily the real ghosts of Kansas. My experiences by and large bore out my belief that the stories keep the ghosts alive, not vice versa. "Do *you* believe in ghosts?" I am often asked. I believe in ghost *stories,* I usually respond.

My initial interest in local supernatural or ghost legends began with the Albino Woman, a particularly vivid legend cycle that had been around my hometown of Topeka for generations. For a paper in a folklore class at the University of Kansas and later for a thesis for a graduate degree in American studies ("The Albino Woman of Topeka: A Local Belief Legend as Cultural Prism"), I first drew upon my own memories of "legend tripping" (a phrase coined by noted folklorist Jan Harold Brunvand) with my high school friends in the late 1960s, when we would drive to Rochester Cemetery in North Topeka and search for a ghostly woman in white, a vaporous pale presence in long flowing robes. We never found her, but other teenagers claimed to have seen her luminous figure floating among the tombstones and her red eyes gleaming from the midst of the trees surrounding the cemetery. (A condensation of the large number of stories and legend variants collected on the Albino Woman can be found in the Graveyard Ghosts chapter in this book.)

The Albino Woman and the other Kansas ghosts included in this volume have many reasons for being in their respective communities, and they fulfill numerous functions that contribute to their longevity and status as local legends. Ghost stories can serve as ways to express social concerns and parental control. ("Don't go parking on Lover's Lane in the cemetery, or [insert name of local ghost or monster] will get you!") The telling of specific ghost stories can serve as a bonding ritual in a fraternity, sorority, or college dorm (such as the George and the Night Nurse and Virginia, the Ghost of Sigma Nu stories in this book) or even in a neighborhood that shares a haunted house or a location near a legend site. Stories are a way to share family history and folklore (see the Phantom Cat) and can serve as a relief from tedium as well as a bonding experience for employees who might work in a building haunted by the legend of a ghost (see the Emporia Country Club Ghosts).

Individual psychological or social concerns or fears can be reflected in other ghost tales (such as the Hamburger Man story). Often such tales are based on historical events or actual persons, and the legendary stories that arise may become an odd type of oral history that commemorates an incident or individual for many years after, but with a supernatural twist. (Examples from this book would be Custer's Ghost, the Ghost of Ida Day, and the Ghost of Kate Coffee and Her Ghouls.)

A legendary ghost also can function as a tie to a specific landscape or landscape element, contributing to a "mystic sense of place" that settles in around a ghost's supposed haunt. (See the Theorosa's Bridge and St. Jacob's Well stories.) Or a ghost story may arise simply to fill a need to explain what might appear to be a supernatural event in a natural world. (This is evident in both the Caretaker Ghosts and the Ghostly Trumpeter of Paola High School.)

Folklorist Linda Degh, in her essay "The 'Belief Legend' in Modern Society," presumes that young people who legend trip and share local ghost legends do so to participate in ritualized dating behavior, engage in initiation rites, or join in a ritual fear-inducing activity that is also part of teen social behavior. (The legend cycles of the Albino Woman and Theorosa's Bridge aptly demonstrate this function.)

Different legends in this book illustrate all of the functions outlined above. In some cases the legends have multiple reasons for being and perform several functions for the community of folk, the unified group of individuals, that tells and retells a particular story. However, some of the tales are stories based on a personal experience with the supernatural or paranormal, stories that are known just within a particular family or neighborhood or workplace rather than throughout the community. These accounts are not public legends but may become so in time if they are told and passed on to others to retell. Regardless of their genesis or their function, all of the stories in this collection have one element in common: They are Kansas stories told about Kansas ghosts by Kansas people.

When I began the research for this book, I was hoping to uncover fifty or sixty legends throughout the state that would be similar to the legend I was most acquainted with—the Albino Woman legend. To my surprise, with the help of numerous individuals in libraries, museums, universities, high schools, visitors' centers, Chamber of Commerce offices, and a number of other source locations as well as the assistance of many friends, acquaintances, and interested individuals around the state who were willing to share stories with me, I was able to unearth and catalog over 250 legends and stories of the supernatural, dealing with everything from run-of-the-mill ghosts (including a ghost who haunts a mill!) to monsters to sea serpents to unidentified flying objects. Obviously, this book only scratches the surface of the great treasure trove that is legendary Kansas and simply presents a sampler of the colorful collection of ghosts and local ghost legends haunting the Kansas landscape.

Deciding how to organize and categorize the legends was a major challenge, but eventually patterns began to emerge, and the chapters evolved somewhat naturally. The first obvious pattern proved that, for the most part, clusters of legends echo population clusters. The more people there are to tell stories, the more stories there are. Therefore, the heaviest concentration of legends can be found in northeast and south-central Kansas. The legends are fewer and farther between in other parts of the state, although each region is represented in this book. But the legends to which I refer in this volume are only the stories that I have found or heard about so far; I am convinced there are still dozens (if not hundreds) of stories out there that I just don't know about . . . yet. And they are everywhere.

There are historical legends, no longer active, that may only be referenced in an old newspaper story or in dusty folklore archives or told by a few old-timers. During my research, I found many ghost (and monster) legends and stories that had been actively told thirty, fifty, even one hundred years ago but that seem to have died with their tellers. For instance, archival stories tell of a "beast" or "giant" who attacked and murdered a family of three, as well as slashing the throat of their horse, as they all traveled on the old Military Road between Fort Scott and Baxter Springs. This incident supposedly occurred "on a drizzling chilly morning" in April

1896. The giant came charging out from a grove of trees and ambushed the family about four miles outside of Pittsburg, breaking the father's neck "with one blow." The mother was struck in the face, and "she crumpled to the wet, soggy, roadbed." The baby in his cradle was "flung into the deep trench that bordered the road." According to a rendition of the story collected nearly forty years ago, the gruesome crime was never solved, and the giant beast was never caught. No further reference to this story has surfaced so far.

There are no doubt current, active legends that are well known in a certain town or area that are waiting to be discovered and added to the list. Adults may not always be familiar with these stories—they may not be cross-generational. But if any ghost stories are to be found in an area, local teenagers and young people are often the best sources and usually have the most vivid renditions or versions of a tale. They can also be quite convincing in their belief that the stories are "true" or "real."

But adults can also be convincing in their portrayals of contemporary ghosts they feel they have encountered. In downtown Wichita, in the old Carey House Square building, the Blue Handkerchief Ghost (described more fully in the House Ghosts chapter) is a very vividly drawn and reportedly active spirit. Many stories are in circulation about this ghost and have been for years. Rose Mason, who at one time owned a restaurant in the building, called the ghost Julie and said that she was a young prostitute murdered by a client in a room on the third floor. According to Rose, Julie died in the 1920s or 1930s when the Carey House was evidently a hotel notorious for housing "ladies of the evening."

There are legends in the making in some locations—legends derived from a recent event, usually connected with violence or a tragedy—where stories of ghosts and supernatural occurrences are just beginning to circulate. The most arresting legend in the making I have found concerns Rocky Ford Bridge in Emporia. Students at Emporia State University have told me that the bridge is now commonly known throughout town as "Bird Bridge," a reference to the death of Sandra Bird, who plunged to her death off the bridge a few years back. She was one victim of a murderous liaison between her minister husband and his church secretary, both of whom are now serving time in prison.

No ghost has yet been reported at the scene, but the Emporia State students talk of legend tripping to the site. They indicate that a popular activity among high school and college students in Emporia is to go in groups out to the bridge at night, where it has been reported that blood will appear on the ground under the bridge near where Sandra Bird's car went into the water the night of her death, and screams and moans can sometimes be heard. Adding to the popular fascination with the crime and the location is the fact that a made-for-television movie about the case, "Murder Ordained," was filmed in and around Emporia and used local people as extras. Now popular interest in the incident seems to be fixed on the overt symbol of the crime—the bridge—and it is spawning a supernatural legend that is sure to acquire more elements, more details, and more versions as time goes on and increasing numbers of individuals make ritualized journeys to the site and tell stories of their experiences there. One would expect that sometime soon, if not already, someone will begin telling of seeing the ghost of a woman near the water or on the bridge.

As exemplified by bridge ghosts, well ghosts, hill ghosts, and hollows ghosts, many of the ghosts of Kansas are tethered to the landscape by a connection to a geographic feature or constructed element of the landscape. Specific reference points and explicit descriptions of the terrain or the environment of the legend enhance the story and provide a shared experience for legend trippers who physically visit the site as well as for others who hear the stories and can relate to them because they are aware of the geographic landmarks of their community. These elements or references also contribute to an overall sense of the supernatural, of a mystical place, within the community or its outlying areas.

But often one wonders if a certain hill or a certain bridge or a certain cemetery has been perceived as being "eerie" or "creepy" just since the birth of a legend there. Or do certain locations attract ghosts and legend? Which came first, the place or the ghost? According to Kent C. Ryden in his book, *Mapping the Invisible Landscape,* "Migratory legends . . . often become attached to real features in the local landscape because they confirm lurking feelings that local residents already have about those places. Occasionally, though, they may settle on places perfectly innocently, because they demand a certain setting and one just happens to be on hand in the local scene; once they become so anchored, however, they may change forever the way that people feel about those places" (pp. 83–84).

It is difficult to decide whether a legend has attached itself to a specific area or place because of inherent "lurking feelings" in the local landscape or because this particular ghost/legend demanded this certain setting. But regardless of whether a ghost or its haunt came first, the landscape or setting is one of the most important elements in any ghost story and particularly in Kansas ghost stories. Ryden again expresses this so well: "Stories—and folklore in general—are inextricably linked with landscapes, overlying them snugly, bound to them and coloring them like paint on a barn wall. They are a central means by which people organize their physical surroundings" (p. 56).

People in Kansas, especially in western Kansas, have a lot of space in which to organize their physical surroundings, and generally their ghosts have a lot of space in which to roam. This spaciousness is one element that provides legends in Kansas with a unique link to the landscape on which they exist, a link that becomes an integral part of a community or local region legend. Although similar legends may exist in other states, a specific landscape legend in Kansas has indigenous elements that make it a legend of the plains rather than a legend of the mountains or a legend of the seashore.

The first three chapters of this book deal with stories about ghosts that primarily inhabit or haunt structures: houses and public buildings, forts, schools, and theaters. One might argue that a haunted house in Kansas is not profoundly different from a haunted house in Louisiana or Maine or New Mexico. But the story of the Old Stone House built of large blocks of Kansas sandstone out in the country between Neal and Toronto in southeast Kansas and the legend of the Haunted Farm near Ellinwood and Great Bend in south-central Kansas both have immediate descriptive elements ("imposing slabs of rock guarding the house"; "a beautiful native sandstone two-story house"; "a pitchfork"; "an orchard fence") and surrounding landscape features that couldn't be found in a mossy mansion on the bayous of Louisiana, a wooden shingled house on the rugged coast of Maine, or an old adobe ranch house in New Mexico.

The fourth chapter introduces Graveyard Ghosts of Kansas. Again, the landscape features of many cemeteries, haunted or otherwise, in this state differ from those of cemeteries in Boston or Los Angeles, and the cultural and historical climates are worlds apart. The ghosts in Kansas graveyards may be similar to those in some stories in other areas, but they won't be exactly the same because they are determined and defined by their surrounding terrain and the culture of their surrounding communities. The Caretaker Ghosts tend their nineteenth-century graves on an isolated hill in rural Nemaha County near the town of Seneca. These ghosts are a far cry from the legend of the ghost of Paul Revere in a seventeenth-century cemetery in Boston or the spirit of a deceased movie star who reputedly haunts a cemetery in California.

The legends in the next chapter, Ghosts on the Range, contain the ghosts most defined by the Kansas landscape, in particular the wide-open aspects of its terrain. These ghosts are more free ranging, not confined to a building or structure, liberated to walk and wander, hunt and run, fly and ride horses. They may be associated with a landscape feature (a river, a creek, a hill, a hollow) or a man-made structure (a bridge, a shack), but essentially they are as free as the cows that roam the range. Or in the case of St. Jacob's Well in the Big Basin area south of Dodge City and north of Ashland in southwest Kansas, they (a cowboy ghost and his ghost horse) are as free as the buffalo that graze the hills and mounds of the basin area that protects and guards the natural spring-fed well that is the source of the legends in that region.

The sixth chapter offers a collection of Ghostly Oddities that defy categorization with any of the other chapters in the book. Mystic Cow Lights, a phantom cat, an angel in the clouds over Greensburg, a haunted mattress, a haunted hayloft, and a ballad-singing ghost that sits in a tree—all might easily be included in a book called *Eccentric Kansas*. The legendary mystic lights near Wallace in northwest Kansas and their supposed source definitely tell a tale of the rural plains of Kansas. The other oddities might not be quite as landscape linked, but they do reveal the quirky nature of many Kansas stories.

Finally, the last chapter awards Atchison with the title of the Most Haunted Town in Kansas. Atchison is a northeastern Kansas river town, and its glut of haunted house legends reflects the cultural concerns and architectural makeup of the town. Atchison celebrates its colorful history as a railroad town on the bluffs of the Missouri River and takes pride in its abundance of beautifully restored Victorian mansions (and the ghosts that cohabit them with the living owners). A prominent version of the predominant legend in Atchison, the Legend of Molly's Hollow in Jackson Park, relates a story from the era of Bleeding Kansas in Civil War times, a story that is indigenous to a Kansas border town that struggled with the issues of slavery, statehood, and civil unrest and disorder during the most turbulent times in the state's history.

Whether or not one considers the designation as the Most Haunted Town in Kansas to be a desirable accolade, it must be noted that several other Kansas towns could just as easily have been chosen for this dubious honor. Emporia and Hutchinson both can claim a myriad of monsters and ghosts, and Leavenworth and Fort Leavenworth have enough ghosts to populate a small ghost town. Topeka, Lawrence, Manhattan, Wichita, and the metropolitan Kansas City area are large centers of population; therefore they are also populated by a large number of ghost legends. Atchison won this admittedly subjective "contest" because of its efforts to preserve its folkloric history and ghost legends by way of its popular yearly Haunted Atchison Trolley Tour and because of its status as a small town that must have the most ghosts per capita in the state.

Following the stories is a comprehensive "Notes and Sources" section that details for each legend additional information to enhance the stories and provides a bibliographic listing of all sources consulted for each individual story. An "Additional Resources" section at the end of the book provides suggestions for further reading in the subject area, including some titles of other state collections of ghost lore, collections of American ghost lore, and general reference works dealing with ghost lore and paranormal phenomena. A final shortlist of viewing recommendations mentions some noteworthy movies (all on video) dealing with ghosts and hauntings.

Throughout the state, all these native stories taken as a whole offer a part of a varied tapestry that is Kansas legend and lore. I believe it is important to collect these stories and all types of legends to compile and preserve a repository of Kansas folklore that has been largely overlooked or ignored. Although some of the stories are historical and no longer "alive" as oral folklore, and some are personal memories or narratives of individual experiences with the supernatural, many of the ghosts in the book are actively kept alive and haunting by the stories that flesh them out and allow them to evolve through numerous retellings through the years, or even generations.

Although this book broaches the world of folklore because of the very nature of its subject as well as a certain attention to details of theme, function, motif elements, and a necessary regard for identification of sources and source materials, this book is a far cry from a true folkloristic treatment of legend and storytelling events and is not meant to be such. Legends by their very nature are loosely structured, and each individual's version of a traditional legend story is "a re-creation of the story by the teller using the basic elements of its traditional content," according to Jan Harold Brunvand (*The Study of American Folklore*, pp. 158–159). These re-creations can vary from extensive, fully developed narratives to "mere fragments of rumor and hearsay," again according to Brunvand (*The Study of American Folklore*, p. 159).

Linda Degh indicates in "The 'Belief Legend' in Modern Society" that "one often has to piece together a legend widely circulating in a given region where it lives and functions in variable forms. Some are lengthy, well-polished versions; others are independent, loosely connected stories or short accounts of facts and simple statements of knowledge of a fact of belief. . . . The greater the popularity of a legend within a group, the more functional it becomes, and the more and more conspicuous its incompleteness becomes" (p. 62).

A true scholarly treatment of the legends collected in this book would demand printing only verbatim texts of story versions and story fragments; taking careful note of the participants in a storytelling session, the setting, and the situation; and piecing together the legend like a jigsaw puzzle. Careful analysis of the story variants and the storytelling event itself with its associated actions and reactions would also be included. But, as Brunvand admits in his book, *The Vanishing Hitchhiker,* "the live telling that is dramatic, fluid, and often quite gripping in actual folk performance before a sympathetic audience may seem stiff, repetitious, and awkward on the printed page" (p. 9).

To avoid this pitfall, I have taken journalistic and literary license with the legends to form them into my own re-creations of the stories. Except for instances where it is made clear that a portion of a story or a retelling of a story is taken from verbatim text quoted from a named or identified source, I have rewritten all narratives using information either gleaned from original sources such as personal interviews, personal letters, attendance at storytelling events, and so on or taken from such secondary sources as newspaper articles, folklore archives, and museum and library holdings and/or publications.

The stories in this book are simply that—stories. They are not necessarily meant to be accepted as fact or, alternatively, as complete fiction. They exist, like the ghosts, in a netherworld somewhere in between. The first-hand accounts of personal experiences from named sources were told to me as fact. Like me, you have to make up your own mind about the viability of these ghosts. With some stories, I seized upon the believable or fact-based center of the legend and from it spun an expanded or modified version of the story to most accurately convey the "spirit" of the legend as I understood it from the various story variants or fragments I had collected. Always I tried to stay as close to verbatim or quoted renditions of the legends as I possibly could, adding little of fiction or fancy that wasn't already present. Although I have often presented the legends in a cohesive story form that appears factual or fact based, that may not always be the case.

In the "Notes and Sources" section that follows, the veracity of the so-called facts of the legend should be specifically addressed or be made obvious.

My aim is to present Kansas ghost legends in a fashion that is accessible to anyone interested in legends, stories, ghosts, Kansas history, or Kansas folklore. Or all of the above. Although a complement of five dozen ghosts comes with this book, rational Kansans need not fear that their state is being overrun with spooks and spirits and monsters. Mostly the state is inhabited by legends, stories, and imaginative storytellers.

A caution: Although I make general references to the locations of most of the legend sites in the book, I usually omit specific directions to a site. Of course, I made exceptions in the case of public buildings or public access areas (a public library, a public park) or in instances where a legend has been well publicized previously in the media and attention is welcomed (the St. Jacob's Well site, the Brown Grand Theatre). Some sites are generally accessible only to residents, students and staff, or members (fraternity houses, schools, country clubs), and they may not welcome curiosity seekers or ghost hunters. Private residences are not specifically identified so as to protect the privacy of their owners or residents, except in the cases of some older historical legends where the structures no longer exist.

Fort Scott is a national historic site and welcomes visitors at all times it is open. Fort Riley and Fort Leavenworth are active military installations, and although the grounds are generally open to visitors, only specific buildings are open to the public for touring. Some of the fort ghosts share quarters with active military personnel in what amount to private homes, and they should be respected as such.

Range ghosts are generally in areas that are accessible to the public, but neighbors and private property owners in the immediate vicinity may be leery (and many are) of visitors to the area who disregard property boundaries, No-Trespassing signs, and the rights to quiet and privacy, even in a rural neighborhood or area. The exception here is St. Jacob's Well, which is part of the Big Basin Prairie Reserve and owned and managed by the Kansas Department of Wildlife and Parks. The site is open to the public.

Finally, a word about cemeteries. Although ghost stories and legends all over the world have been associated with graveyards and burial grounds, cemeteries are places of inviolate sanctity held sacred by the families and friends of those buried there. Vandalism and desecration are very real problems for communities and caretakers where partying legend trippers and disrespectful visitors have wreaked havoc in or near a cemetery. (The Demonic Church story in the Graveyard Ghosts section of this book addresses this issue and illustrates what can happen to a little rural town when a local legend attracts unwanted and destructive elements.) As a result of problems like this in the past, many urban as well as rural cemeteries have security guards to monitor the grounds and enforce strict rules about being in the cemetery past sundown or after closing hours, especially on or near Halloween.

Sixty legends are included in this book. But around 200 (at last count) have been left out. Some of the prominent legends still haunting my files include the Ghost of the Columbian Theatre (Wamego), the Blue Light Lady (Hays), the Phantom of Sauer Castle (Kansas City), Sinkhole Sam (lurking outside Inman), and the Spooksville Triangle Spook Light (a legend of southeast Kansas, southwest Missouri, and northeast Oklahoma). Also, ghost legends of Native American Kansans and representative legends exclusive to other ethnic and cultural groups in the state remain to be explored, perhaps in a future endeavor.

Kansas, like other states, is possessed of its own distinctive ghost story tradition. All these legends—of public and private ghosts, of past, present, and future ghosts—haunt the geographic and cultural terrain of the plains, hills, and valleys of the state, fading in and out of our communities, weaving spectral patterns that present a whole varied phantasmic tapestry of Kansas legends. Whether one believes the Albino Woman and others of her kind in the Kansas landscape have been conjured up by impressionable minds or are actual manifestations of restless spirits, the fact remains that the appeal of ghosts and their stories is an irrefutable and universal feature of human experience.

Local legends like the Albino Woman legend of Topeka or the Theorosa's Bridge legend of Valley Center are about stories—patterns of stories told to children, told to teenagers, told to neighbors, told to friends. They are exciting stories and scary stories, a multitude of stories wrapped up in one package—a benign Pandora's box. Each individual adds a story to the box, and when the lid is opened the ghost steps out, fleshed out with substance and meaning, connected to a community through the landscape and lore of the area, tied by generations of oral storytelling tradition.

Which brings me back to my question: Which comes first, the place or the ghost? The geography and topography of Kansas, together with our cultural landscape, form a specific "sense of place" for the state and allow the placement of legends on the physical landscape. Ultimately, then, I believe the place has drawn the ghost, and the ghost has further defined the place. In the process, both the landscape and the lore have been validated.

In *The Oxford Book of the Supernatural,* the editor, D. J. Enright, notes:

"One thing is certain, that the supernatural has this in common with nature: you may drive it out with a pitchfork, but it will constantly come running back" (p. 1).

Another thing is certain: All the pitchforks in Kansas couldn't drive out all the ghosts in Kansas. And even if they could, the ghosts would keep coming back in the stories.

House Ghosts
(Haunted Houses
& Buildings)

aunted houses are what most people think of when they think of ghosts. Many legends of haunted houses in a particular community are not widely known outside of a certain family who may have experienced a ghostly presence in their home or outside of a certain neighborhood where neighbors or area young people may share stories of "the spooky old house on the corner." Other houses or some public buildings have become locally famous for a resident ghost or an odd "supernatural" occurrence that has been the impetus for a thriving local legend cycle that often persists for many years, even generations.

Carey House Square in downtown Wichita and the old Koett farmstead outside of Ellinwood are examples of haunted locations that have become locally famous for their respective ghosts, spawning numerous stories and legend versions. The ghost of Ida Day in Hutchinson, however, is a library phantom whose reputation mainly resides, along with the ghost, inside the library. The Country Club Ghosts in Emporia are just as reclusive as Ida Day, prompting stories mainly among employees and members of the club.

The Haunted Duplex story is a first-person account of a very personal supernatural experience. This story is not known outside of the family who encountered their very own resident ghost, but each member of the family has a story to tell.

These and more stories of haunted houses and other public and private buildings with resident ghosts are all an integral part of the legends that make up haunted Kansas.

The Old Stone House

The story of the old stone house in Greenwood County is a personal ghost story—one family's experience with the paranormal. Whatever ghosts the old stone house contained perished with the demolition of the house in 1957. Forty years later, however, Mrs. Cummings readily recalled the unexplainable occurrences that remain vivid in her memory and in her family's collection of familial legend and lore.

Marcella Benson Cummings and her husband, William H. Cummings, moved into the stone house in 1947, shortly after the birth of their first daughter. According to Mrs. Cummings, it was a "beautiful native sandstone two-story house, built just south of Walnut Creek in Pleasant Grove Township." The house was located five miles west of the town of Toronto and about the same distance southeast of Neal. Mr. and Mrs. Cummings researched the history of the house when they moved in and determined that it had originally been built in the 1880s.

The L-shaped house had three rooms up and three rooms down. An enormous retaining wall on two sides of the front yard framed the lovely old house with more native stone—imposing slabs of rock guarding the house and protecting the yard from erosion. In the summertime, the house would get uncommonly hot by afternoon because of the heat-retaining qualities of the stone.

The first indication that more than just heat was retained within the walls came soon after the Cummings family moved in. "We dearly loved our old stone house," recalled Mrs. Cummings, "but strange things were heard. Faint voices were often heard, but one couldn't quite make out what was being said. I had told my husband about the voices, but he thought it was only my imagination, and didn't hesitate to tell me so! One day he came in from work and soon after asked me why I had turned off the radio. I assured him the radio had not been on and reminded him of the voices I had also been hearing."

Several years after this incident, Mr. and Mrs. Cummings and their three-year-old daughter were downstairs in the dining room having dinner. A new baby, also a daughter, was asleep upstairs in her bedroom. Mrs.

Cummings related what happened next: "Suddenly a baby cried out quite loud. The sound came from the buffet in the corner of the dining room. We all looked at one another without saying a word when the three-year-old said, 'There is a baby in the buffet.' We checked the buffet and I went upstairs to find our baby daughter sleeping peacefully, totally undisturbed. The sound certainly had not come from upstairs nor had it sounded that way. Another mystery."

On another occasion, Mrs. Cummings was sitting in the dining room with the door into the hallway closed. It was wintertime, and she wanted the door closed to keep warmth in the room. As Mrs. Cummings sat, absorbed in her task, she heard the dining room door open quietly, "wide enough for someone to enter." She then heard the door, just as quietly, close. According to Mrs. Cummings, a natural explanation for this episode would be difficult: "The house had settled through the years, and the door from the dining room into the hallway had to be propped open or it would automatically go closed. . . . All I saw was the door open and close . . . a door that could not do so on its own because of the settling of the floors. Strange!"

Strange indeed. Also mystifying for the Cummings family was a disturbance that took place in the middle of the night during the ten years they resided in the house. Mrs. Cummings related: "Our daughters slept in the southwest bedroom over the dining room, and Bill and I slept in the bedroom directly to the right at the head of the stairway. One night I was wakened to hear heavy footsteps coming up the stairs in the middle of the night. I was petrified and couldn't make a sound. They came to the top of the stairs and turned down the hall toward the girls' room. By this time I was shaking Bill to waken him and about that time Barbara screamed, 'Someone is in my room!' We ran down the hall, but there was not a soul to be seen. It was impossible for anyone to go back downstairs without our knowing, because he or she would have had to pass us in the hallway."

With the start of construction of the Toronto Reservoir in 1957, the government commenced blasting rock in the vicinity of the Cummings house. "In the middle of one night," said Mrs. Cummings, "a loud crack woke us and we discovered a large crack in the wall of the bedroom above the kitchen where the girls were sleeping at the time." Soon after, the family discovered that the mortar between the native stones that made up their house had seriously deteriorated and was no longer adhering to the stone. The old stone house was structurally unsound and had to be torn down.

The house was demolished in 1957 and replaced with a new structure.

The Cummings family continued to live in their new house on the same homesite until the spring of 1990, when they moved to Eureka. According to Mrs. Cummings, "The mysterious happenings ceased when the stone house was destroyed." Whatever entities had coexisted with the Cummings family in the old stone house for ten years were obliterated with the razing of the original structure or were released from the stone boundaries of their earthly confinement.

"I wouldn't have believed in ghosts at all if this had not happened," Mrs. Cummings recently said. "I am not the kind of person to normally believe this kind of thing. At the time it was frightening, particularly when they went into my daughter's room and she screamed. We lived a strange life there," she reflected. "We have never experienced anything like that since, and all the strange experiences stopped after we tore the old house down."

Mrs. Cummings recently mused about the origins of their ghostly housemates: "What did I hear coming up the stairs that also wakened our daughter? What made the baby cry in the buffet, or at least in that corner of the dining room that we all heard? What opened the dining room door so quietly and closed it the same way, and who talked so softly we could not quite hear what was being said? We will never know, but I do know they were all harmless. . . . If there were souls trapped there, they must have been released with the destruction of their domain. May they forever rest in peace."

The Haunted Farm

If it had been possible to obtain a restraining order against a ghost, Fred Koett would have done it. Instead, he appealed to the Barton County attorney for protection. After the family's pet dog was found stabbed to death with a pitchfork in its back, Koett obtained the services of several deputies from the sheriff's office to help guard his farm from his spectral stalker. No arrests were made, but even the deputies agreed that strange things were happening at the Koett farm that summer of 1927.

For months, "hair-raising activities" had been occurring at the Koett place eight miles northeast of Ellinwood. Initially, the incidents were benign: All the pictures in the house were found turned to the wall; a small religious statue of the Virgin Mary was moved by an unseen hand; curious noises were heard throughout the farmhouse. The ghost then graduated to more frightening activities: Bold thumping sounds emanated from various rooms at night; a hired hand opened a closet door to investigate a noise and was punched in the nose by an invisible attacker. The culmination was the gruesome murder of the dog.

Koett's problems with his unfriendly phantom became public knowledge in June 1927 when he contacted the county attorney in Great Bend the day after he had seen the "thing." According to an article in the *Great Bend Tribune*, the farmer and five other men, including Mrs. Koett's brother, Samuel Waddel, and four hired hands, fired their guns at a "wraithlike form" that was spotted in the orchard near the farmhouse. The macabre shade "disappeared over an orchard fence like a slow motion picture of a pole vaulter," according to Waddell. As the form vaulted the fence, it appeared to "vanish into space."

Waddell, a decorated veteran of World War I and a member of the U.S. Marines, was described in the same article in the *Great Bend Tribune* as "an expert marksman." Waddell fired at the ghostly form with a single-barrel shotgun, "more than one shot." He indicated to the *Tribune* reporter that he could "shoot four shells in a single-barrelled shotgun almost as quickly as any other man can handle a repeater," but he was unable to hit the phantom, try as he might.

Things became deadly serious when the dog was discovered impaled on the pitchfork. The sheriff's deputies arrived at the farm and stayed to guard the house and its inhabitants for three nights. Noises, items moving, pictures switching—these things continued to occur while the deputies were in residence, but nothing violent took place. By the fourth day, Koett paid off the deputies and sent them home.

Within the week, Koett and his family returned home from an outing to find an overwhelming odor permeating their house. Mrs. Koett's mother, Mrs. Waddell, who was visiting the family that summer, described the noxious odor: "It smelled like medicine. . . . I think it was tear gas." Things did not get better at the Koett farm. "Then another night," continued Mrs. Waddell, "as we were leaving the house we heard a whispering voice that said, 'get out, get out.'"

The family didn't need any more convincing. "I [can't] stand it any longer," Koett told the reporter. "I don't know what it is that has caused so many mysterious happenings, but I've experienced things that are hardly believable and I have withstood it longer than any other man would." Koett, forty-one years old at the time of the haunting, determined to move his eighteen-year-old wife, his infant son, his mother-in-law, and his brother-in-law and his wife out of the house. Arrangements were made for a public sale at the farm, and Koett sold off all of his family belongings and stock with the exception of a few personal and household effects and the horses and feed needed to get himself, his wife, and his son out of Kansas, "possibly to Oklahoma or Arkansas."

Some neighborhood gossip had focused suspicion on the Waddells as the instigators of the mysterious terrorizing behavior visited upon the Koett farm. The speculation was that Koett's in-laws were trying to scare him off the place so that they could take over the farm. "That's a lie," responded Samuel Waddell. "He has a life interest in the farm and cannot dispose of it. When he does, it will go to the children of his first wife. None of us will get any part of it."

Mrs. Waddell's own personal theory of the identity of the terrorizing spirit placed the ghost within the family circle. "You see, the ghost first started working in Mr. Koett's father's room upstairs in the southwest corner. The mysterious things started to happen in the road below it where he died, and later in the northwest room downstairs where his body lay." Fred Koett's father had owned the farm for years, and Fred had been born in the house. Mrs. Waddell told the *Great Bend Tribune* reporter that she remained convinced that Fred's father's ghost was behind the disturbances: "He wants to tell Fred something and until he has delivered his message," she said, "mysterious things will continue to happen." One wonders, if Mrs. Waddell was correct, just exactly what kind of message old Mr. Koett was trying to deliver by slaughtering the family dog with a pitchfork.

The Koett family spent several weeks packing up their belongings and making their preparations to leave, but they had already vacated the haunted farm. They refused to spend any more nights there and had made arrangements for temporary quarters a half-mile away at the granary. When they returned to the farm each morning to continue sorting and packing, they still had to contend with the ghost and its interference. Crates and furniture would be moved about, and packed items would be unpacked.

Fred Koett was unhappy to be deserting his family farm but resigned to the fact that he had no choice but to leave the farm to the "spooks." Before he left, he did manage to rent the place to a neighbor. Koett claimed that he did not believe that the ghost would follow his family out of state, but just in case, he was vague about their final destination. The *Tribune* article described Koett as being "broken in health as a result of the visitations of the ghostlike figure" and expressed the concern that "if it should continue to haunt him, it may cause his fatal illness."

Perhaps the ghost did follow Fred to Oklahoma or Arkansas, because no additional reports of the malevolent ghost that drove Koett and his family off their farm near Ellinwood were posted. The story of the pitch-fork ghost and the haunted farm, however, remained "Barton County's fa-vorite mystery story" for many years.

The Blue Handkerchief Ghost
of Carey House Square

In the mid-1990s, dinner at the Dine and Roses restaurant in the historic Carey House Square in downtown Wichita often included dessert, a chat with the owner, and sometimes a date with a ghost. Rose Mason has since closed her restaurant, but during the time she owned the Dine and Roses and managed the Carey House and the variety of small shops that used to dot two floors of the old building, she developed an odd relationship with a phantom she called Julie. Legend has it that Julie is the ghost of a young prostitute who lived and worked in the Carey House sometime in the 1920s or 1930s when it was a downtown hotel. Julie was reputedly found murdered in her room on the third floor of the hotel. The murder was never solved, but the story assumes that Julie's killer was one of her "clients."

Rose and others who have encountered Julie at Carey House found her to be most active around the middle of each month. That is when the ghost was most likely to materialize on the stairs between the second and third floors or take a noisy stroll around the third floor. Often she would brush past unsuspecting shoppers in the jewelry shop next to the restaurant, leaving a sudden cold draft that chilled the room.

The Dine and Roses was located on the second floor of the building. Other spaces on the first and second floors were leased to a variety of spe-cialty shops selling everything from arts and antiques to clothing and crafts. The third floor remained empty and unused except for some stor-age. The third-floor rooms were numbered as they would be in a hotel, and the general condition and decor of the third floor were reminiscent of a rundown hotel of sixty years ago or so.

Immediately after Rose moved into her space and started remodeling her restaurant, she began experiencing paranormal experiences that left her shaken. The first time she climbed to the third floor to store some materials in an empty room, she said she "felt something different," particularly in one room. Downstairs, she encountered "cold spots" where the temperature momentarily dropped, unexplained noises, and pranks such as a phone continually being found off the hook when no one else was around. Strange odors also were encountered from time to time, especially the strong smell of roses in the second-floor hallway. Rose found the connection between her name, the name of the restaurant, and the odd intermittent smell of roses in the building amusing at first, and she wallpapered the hallway into her restaurant in a rose print. However, when she discovered after the fact that the third-floor room where Julie supposedly met her demise still had vestiges of the original 1920s-era wallpaper in scraps on the peeling walls—a faded pink print covered with full-blown roses—what had been amusing became definitely creepy. Julie's room—the number "20" still discernible as lighter areas in the aged and grimy wood door where numerals once were affixed—was the only room on the third floor with painted woodwork and wallpaper on the wall.

When the ghost became bold enough to start throwing loaves of bread off the shelves in the pantry and continuously tromping up and down the wooden stairs between the second and third floors, Rose had to admit the building had a serious ghost problem. Her second and final visit to the third-floor storage area resulted in Rose's only visual experience with the ghost. After that experience, Rose refused to set foot on the third floor.

What did she see? Looking down the long barren hallway lined with heavy wooden doors, Rose saw an apparition of a beautiful woman all in blue, floating just above the floor. Rose described the ghost: "It didn't walk—it floated. It wasn't like seeing another human being—I could see right through it. I knew it was an image. The figure was in baby blue—it was absolutely gorgeous. There is no way to describe it. It looked like mounds and mounds of handkerchief material; it literally floated just off the floor, moving down the hall. It was dressed in blue: it looked like a pile of blue handkerchiefs."

Although Rose described the apparition as beautiful, she said that it had no discernible face or features. Her husband experienced the same type of apparition on the third floor, too. Several vendors in the building felt that they had encountered the blue handkerchief ghost as well. The owner of a jewelry shop on the second floor claimed that she had seen the ghost—reflected in a mirror in her shop. What she saw was pale, blue, and floating. She also reported mysterious prankish incidents in her shop, such as jewelry flung off walls into the center of the room and stick-on price cards moved around on pictures. Once, in a shop room next door to her store, she and two other women experienced a sudden episode of dizziness and a "compression" feeling upon entering the room, and the room began whirling about her. All three women claimed to have shared the same frightening experience simultaneously. They thought it was Julie.

However, Rose said she didn't think Julie was evil or mean, just mischievous. In fact, Rose claimed that she felt "protective" of Julie, experiencing what she described as almost a maternal feeling toward the young girl's spirit. She said she did not know why Julie's ghost was there in the building but concluded that it must have had something to do with the unsolved nature of the crime that robbed Julie of her life. Rose speculated that the "unfinished business" of the ghost kept it lingering there, near the scene of the crime. One of Rose's encounters with Julie occurred on an early morning in the summer of 1995. She was in the kitchen, and someone called her name. She responded absentmindedly but heard nothing. "It dawned on me then," said Rose, "that I was completely alone in the building, yet someone had spoken my name. It had to be Julie."

Sightings and tales of the ghost predate the 1990s. Stories are told of a previous vendor in the building who would put a sign of the cross in oil each morning outside the threshhold of her shop to prevent the ghost from entering. In 1982, radio station KFH was a tenant in the building (a large board sign with the slogan KFH Is #1! in orange lettering can still be found discarded, leaning against a splintered wall on the third floor), and the news director, Steve McIntosh, would commonly arrive for work early before the rest of the staff to read his mail and prepare his newcasts. One morning he climbed the stairs to his office on the second floor and began making his way down the dark hallway. As he passed the stairway leading up to the third floor, he was startled by a fleeting impression of the figure of a person standing on the stairs. In an interview with the *Wichita Eagle* newspaper on October 31, 1993, McIntosh recalled, "I really felt that I had seen somebody there. The hair on the back of my neck stood up. Well, I thought, I've seen the ghost."

Rose saw the ghost, too. Although Rose coexisted peacefully with Julie while she shared space with Julie at Carey House, Rose did tire of Julie's antics at times. Rose claimed that the ghost and the pranks did not frighten her, but she always refused to go up to the third floor where Julie roamed the halls in her powder blue dress.

Newspaper articles, radio interviews, and television news segments featuring tales of the ghost of Carey House Square have given Julie the status of Wichita's most famous ghost; thus, the legends of Julie have moved out of the exclusive realm of oral folklore and storytelling into the world of mass media. Julie has become a media celebrity, but shared stories about her continue to reveal a fascinating and classic instance of a colorful ghost legend that echoes the equally colorful history of its hometown.

Herbie the Bakery Ghost

It was time to make the doughnuts back in 1973 at Swanson's Bakery in Manhattan. The bakery operated at 2nd and Poyntz Streets in the heart of the city's downtown, where the Manhattan Town Center mall would later be built.

Kathy was dusting doughnuts with powdered sugar, helping her boss get ready for the morning rush. Patting the excess sugar off her hands onto her apron, she hurried to start the coffeemaker percolating, then stepped into the employees' bathroom to wash her hands.

She turned on the water and pumped the soap dispenser. She glanced into the crackled mirror hanging above the sink and checked her reflection. Using her damp fingers, she was smoothing down some flyaway tendrils of hair when she suddenly felt someone blow on the back of her neck. The cool puff of air ruffled her hair and sent cold shivers down her spine. She spun around in the small bathroom to confront this bold voyeur. Seeing no one, she jerked the bathroom door open and stepped out to see if she could catch sight of the person who had so rudely and suggestively invaded her privacy. She could not.

A customer and Swannie, her boss and owner of the bakery, looked up from the bakery display case when she came around the corner from the bathroom. "She was as white as a ghost," recalled Swannie in an interview with the *Kansas State Collegian* in 1985. "She said, 'Somebody was blowing on my neck.' I told her there was nobody in there."

Swannie did his best to reassure his employee, but not wanting to alarm her even more, he did not mention to her that he, too, had felt a presence in the bathroom at times, as had other employees. Additional strange things had been happening at the bakery as well, such as pans and cooking utensils being moved around and left in unusual places. But the pranks had never been mean-spirited, just playful.

According to Swannie, as time went on he and his staff became accustomed to this ghostly "presence" in the bakery. They even named it Herbie. Why Herbie? "Herbie is just a name that would apply to someone friendly," said Swannie in the *Kansas State Collegian* interview. "Have you ever heard of anybody mean named Herbie?" The ghost's favorite tricks continued to be harmless, but "Herbie's weirdest trick" remained his little bathroom blowing-on-the-neck routine, which he tried out on women and men alike. Perhaps the ghost's amorous side contributed to the decision to name him Herbie. The Disney movie *Herbie, the Love Bug* was popular at the time; Swanson's Bakery now had its own Herbie, the love ghost.

The owner came to believe that a ghost did indeed inhabit the bakery. He also believed that the ghost was most likely to be encountered in the bakery's "long, dark place" of a basement, as Swannie put it. Swannie's employees also knew the ghost liked to hang out in the basement, so they uniformly refused to descend to the lower regions of the bakery for any reason or on any errand. The owner had no choice but to personally take on any task that required a trip to the basement.

In the *Collegian* article, Swannie described some of Herbie's antics: "I put some things in the basement, such as special pans that I use only once every two or three years, . . . and when I go down to get them they're not there or they've been moved to a different place." Swannie also reported that he and a friend had seen Herbie, but in the bakery's back room, not the basement. Quite late one night, he and the friend were talking in the back room when, at the same instant, they looked into the next room and "saw somebody standing there." His friend wondered aloud, "Who's that?," and they walked into the next room to investigate. Not finding anyone there, they searched the bakery, but it was empty—no other people, no employees, the doors locked. The only solid thing there besides the two men was their combined certainty that they had both seen the "medium-sized figure of a man" standing in the middle room between the back room and the front of the bakery. Perplexed, the men eventually wrote the episode off as another one of Herbie's escapades.

Herbie continued his pranks and his flirtatious bathroom behavior until the bakery closed and was demolished to make way for the new downtown mall. Before his bakery closed, Swannie was quoted as saying that he hoped Herbie would live in the new mall.

No reports of Herbie sightings have come from Manhattan Town Center in the years since its opening, but who knows how many individuals have been trying on clothes in a dressing room at Dillard's and suddenly felt a strange, cool breath on the backs of their necks or how many people have been standing at the sink in a bathroom only to be startled by someone blowing softly in their hair. Maybe someone has caught a brief glimpse of a shadow, not too tall and not too short, the shade of a man who vanishes as quickly as he is seen. Maybe it's Herbie, the amorous ghost, evicted from his bakery home and compelled to haunt the Manhattan mall instead.

The Ghost of Ida Day

Shortly after the young reference librarian had started her job at the Hutchinson library, she was sent down to the basement, alone, to shelve some documents in the stacks. Humming to herself, she began slipping several volumes in between other books on the large document shelves in the southwest corner of the basement. After a few moments, someone spoke to her, and she stopped shelving and turned around to see who was there. An imposing, rather stern older woman stood in the shadows below the stairs. "What are you doing?" the woman asked, her voice sharp and imperious.

The young librarian furrowed her brow and squinted in an effort to better see who was questioning her from the dark spot behind the staircase. "I'm shelving documents," she replied, and took a step forward toward the indistinct figure addressing her. "I'm sorry," she added, "I'm new here—are you with the library?" The woman in the shadows did not respond. Instead, she seemed to slip deeper into the dark behind the stairs until she disappeared from sight altogether. The librarian was puzzled—where had the old woman gone? She moved forward to look behind the stairs when she distinctly heard footsteps walking away, behind her, down the narrow corridor between the shelving units. She turned around but could see nothing—no woman, no figure, no form. Just the looming shelves, heavy with books and documents, casting deep shadows on the basement floor.

On Halloween in 1975, the *Hutchinson News* ran an article under the headline, "Ida Day Returns to Hutch: Does a Ghost Haunt the Library?" According to the article, Mrs. Ida Day Holzapfel, head librarian at the Hutchinson Public Library from 1915 to 1925 and again from 1947 to 1954, may have taken up permanent residence at her beloved library, even though she died shortly after resigning from her position early in 1954.

Ida Day arrived in Hutchinson in 1915 and quickly established her reputation as a dedicated and often difficult library administrator. She worked first at the old library building at Fifth and Main Streets until a move out of town with her family caused her to leave her position. She moved back to Hutchinson in 1947 and began a second term as head librarian at the new library building at Ninth and Main.

One former coworker summed up Ida Day's personality and her dedication to her position in nine words: "She was a librarian twenty-four hours a day." She seems to have been a very prim and proper woman, the epitome of the stereotypical old-school librarian, a woman who was known to have reduced an employee to tears more than once because of her harshness. According to the newspaper, Ida Day insisted on having formal tea with her employees every afternoon promptly at three o'clock. Only on days when she was absent did the employees dare to send out for hamburgers and other such vulgar foodstuffs in lieu of Ida Day's proper tea.

Older residents of Hutchinson who knew the librarian verified her reputation as a stern taskmaster and an omniscient presence in the library who would chastise anyone for disturbing the silence rule in the library and readily eject young people who were giddy enough to laugh or cause a disturbance within the walls of her sanctuary for books. One woman reported, "Yes, indeed, we were afraid of her. You didn't dare talk or act silly in her library."

Ida Day stepped down from her administrative duties at the Hutchinson library early in 1954 to take a less demanding position as a reference librarian in Visalia, California. But she never had the chance to share tea with her fellow employees in California. She was killed in a car accident in California on the first day of her new job.

Not long after her death, former employees and coworkers of Ida Day began reporting strange incidents, sounds, and even ghostly apparitions around the library. Voices were heard in rooms that were empty; footsteps were heard where no one was walking. The stacks area in the southwest corner of the basement became notorious as the place where Ida Day was most likely to materialize as a cold or chilly spot, a disembodied voice, or a hazy, indistinct form.

The young librarian who had encountered the arrogant and inquisitive shade in the basement did not know who Ida Day was, nor had she yet heard the stories about her. After her experience, she described the illusory figure that had questioned her to longtime employees of the library. One woman exclaimed, "Well, then, you're describing Ida Day!"

Other individuals have reported feeling a "presence" at certain times in certain areas of the library, and some employees don't care to go down to the basement alone or in the evening. One individual explained her concern: "When it's dark and someone has to go down to the basement, then every sound they hear, they think it's Ida Day. At night, I don't like to step down there either." Another former employee who had worked with Ida Day stressed the validity of these fears, even though she herself did not have firsthand experience with the ghost: "I know different people have different experiences and just because I haven't had any doesn't mean that others don't."

The tales of Ida Day when she was alive are evidently enough to scare the fainthearted—the image of Ida Day as a stern and watchful ghost determined to keep an eye on things in "her" library is truly intimidating! According to the October 31, 1975, piece in the *Hutchinson News*, "It has also become an office joke that whenever anything at the library is misplaced or missing, they blame it on Ida Day." The newspaper also reports: "The feeling, both seriously with some and lightly with others, is that Ida Day Holzapfel has returned to watch over the library and sometimes rebels when she doesn't think it is being run right."

A special publication marking the ninetieth anniversary of the Hutchinson Public Library in 1991 also recounted the story of Ida Day and the reports of library workers who reported seeing and/or hearing a ghost in the library, a ghost assumed to be Ida Day.

Current librarians and Friends of the Library volunteers are familiar with the stories of Ida Day and her continued surveillance of the library in ghostly form. Odd occurrences and unexplained sounds are still sometimes attributed to Ida Day and her now eternal (infernal?) dedication to the library she loved. And no one likes to work in the basement alone after dark.

Oddly, an article published in the *Hutchinson News* in 1954 regarding Ida Day's resignation from the library to take a new job in California may have offered an eerie foreshadowing of Ida Day's ghostly residence in her beloved library. A quote from that article (reproduced in the 1975 Halloween story) reads: "[Mrs. Holzapfel] plans to retain ownership of her home at 430 East 12th and will eventually return to Hutchinson. . . ."

Evidently, Ida Day is home to stay.

The Emporia Country Club Ghosts

At most country clubs a foursome refers to a group of golfers. The most prominent foursome at Emporia Country Club, however, is a group of four individual ghosts—a chef, a golfer, and two former managers—reputed to haunt the nearly ninety-year-old structure located on the northern outskirts of town, just south of the Neosho River.

Don Blaylock is the current general manager of the club. Before becoming manager in 1995, he was a member of the country club for fifteen years. During that time, he said in an interview, he heard "a number of members make comments about the place being haunted." Stories also have circulated for years among the club's employees—stories of strange sounds, strange lights, weird feelings, and odd occurrences.

Many of the stories center around the third floor of the club building, an area now used for storage. For most of the club's history, the third floor was an apartment or suite of rooms that was often used as living quarters for the club's managers or rented out to employees or other tenants. Blaylock explained: "Part of the ghost thing is that the upstairs has always been considered haunted. This is an intriguing old building, built in 1911. It was built as a country club, not used for anything else, but years ago the upstairs was rented out to boarders or roomers. For example, one time a bridegroom rented the rooms for a short time prior to his wedding at the country club, so he would have a place to stay and get ready. Some employees probably used the space or lived there for a time, as did several managers."

According to Blaylock, a Mrs. Flowers managed the club along with her husband some thirty or forty years ago. The couple lived in the upstairs apartment, spending the nights on the third floor and their days and evenings tending to their duties on the lower two floors. Some of the older members blame any purported "ghostly" activity around the club on Mrs. Flowers.

Other members and a significant number of employees attribute any unexplained disturbances to Buck, another former manager of the club. Buck and his wife also resided in the third-floor rooms until the club was remodeled about twenty-five years ago. At that time the couple moved off the premises because updated building codes and zoning ordinances did not allow anyone to live in the upstairs apartment, particularly since it lacked any utilities. Buck, now deceased, left the club in the early 1980s and moved to another town in Kansas to manage another club.

According to Don Blaylock, "The upstairs is not wired or plumbed— that means no heating, no electricity, no plumbing. Some of the stories told about the 'ghosts' mention lights being seen upstairs at night. I have never seen that. If there is a light upstairs then it definitely is a ghost because there is not electricity up there."

Oddly enough, indications are that when Buck and his wife lived at the country club, they believed that a poltergeist was present in the building. Sometimes things appeared to have been moved around the club. One time a chair from the first floor was found broken to bits on the second floor. According to an employee from that time, Buck "was a sensible man who did not joke around about these types of things," and when no other rational explanation could be found, the possibility of a resident poltergeist was raised.

Although ghostly happenings in the building predate Buck's death, still some employees believe that their "friendly spirit" is Buck and that "he has come back to the club because he cared so much for it when he was alive." They also point to a series of "knocking" episodes, odd unexplained thumpings coming from inside a storage closet, that began shortly after Buck died.

Another phantom that might be found lounging around the clubhouse or hanging out at the pro shop is the ghost of a member who supposedly died of a heart attack following a golf tournament at the country club. But the oldest specter in residence at the building is most likely lurking in the kitchen. Referred to only as "the chef," this ghost in his mortal state was the head chef at the country club during the depression years. Legend has it that he died in his sleep while napping in the upstairs apartment.

Employees of the club are the individuals most actively involved in swapping stories about this ghostly foursome. Tradition decrees that new employees are introduced to the tales, not just to "scare" them but to "share experiences" and to "prepare each other for possible visits" from a ghost or ghosts.

These "visits" have taken a variety of forms over the years. At various times, strange momentary power outages have been reported, sometimes just lasting a matter of seconds. Other times, lights would seemingly come back on of their own accord after having been shut off by an employee. On one occasion, a husband and wife who were members of the club asked the manager if the old apartment upstairs was being remodeled. The manager replied in the negative and asked what had prompted them to think so. The couple replied that several nights before they had driven by the club around midnight and "all of the lights were on upstairs." "Impossible," replied the manager. "There is no electricity up there."

Two employees were locking up the clubhouse late one evening. Before exiting the front doors, one woman looked down the hallway and thought she glimpsed a figure standing in the shadows. When she looked again the figure was gone. Her companion, another young woman, indicated she had not seen anything, so the two locked and bolted the doors and exited the building. Before they headed down the sidewalk toward the parking lot, they double-checked the doors from the outside, pushing on them to make certain they were secure. One of the women described her companion's test of the doors, and what happened next: "She pushed them and they did not move. She and I got halfway down the sidewalk and the doors made a sound like a great force was trying to push them open. We ran to our cars as fast as we could. Every night [after that] when the two of us would lock up together, we would say 'good-night' [to the ghost]." The other young woman confirmed her companion's version of this story and gave this description of their experience outside the front of the building: "The doors we had just locked slammed outward as if some invisible person had body-slammed them from the inside. We took off in a hurry."

One evening two children came into the bar area and informed an employee that they had seen a dead man on a couch in front of the fireplace. An immediate check could locate no body, dead or otherwise, in the parlor. On other occasions, individuals coming into the club have mentioned looking up and noticing "people standing in the top floor windows just looking out." Footsteps have been heard trudging across the floors upstairs and heavy furniture has been found moved, all at times when the building was supposed to have been empty.

Evidence of a ghostly party in the bar was heard one Sunday night by three employees who were cleaning up after the club closed. One employee was working in a room next to the bar. Hearing footsteps in the bar, she checked, but the room was empty. Unnerved when she again heard the footsteps, she went to find the chef and his wife in the kitchen. On their way back to the bar area, all three employees distinctly heard the sound of ice tinkling in glasses, voices murmuring together, and more footsteps. According to the employee who first heard the footsteps, "It sounded like a bartender fixing drinks for a few people sitting at a table in front of the bar. We could also hear music."

The chef asked if a table of members was still in the bar. "No," replied the woman. The chef's wife asked, "Well, who's out there then?" "Nobody," replied the woman. "Aw, come on," said the incredulous chef, "someone is there." The three proceeded into the bar and "everything fell silent." Not surprisingly, "we followed each other around very closely the rest of the evening," asserted the woman employee.

Don Blaylock mentioned an incident that he had recently experienced: "The other day I was sitting in the dining room with my head waitress. We both saw a sudden movement and realized at the same instant that 'something' had set the light to swaying. In the next instant we saw that it was a squirrel [evidently an unwanted invader into the dining room] that had run across the top of the light." Blaylock mentioned this episode as an example of how something perfectly explainable can start a story of ghostly visitations.

Every unexplained episode at the Emporia Country Club may indeed have a logical interpretation, but the weaving of stories over many years has introduced a ghostly group of honorary members in the club who often liven up gatherings of real members and employees with their illusory goings-on. An employee began another tale: "One evening I was sitting in the West room in the dark eating dinner when I looked up at the curtains and they were moved back as if someone was holding them back to look out. When I looked again the curtains were shut and no one was there. . . ." No doubt the phantom country club foursome—Buck, Mrs. Flowers, the old golfer, and the chef—were peering out the window to make sure the parking lot was empty and the coast was nearly clear for them to begin another little ghostly-members-only cocktail party in the bar.

The Haunted Duplex

The subdivision spreads out, fingerlike, over ground that once was part of a farm. It contains a block of duplexes built sometime in the 1970s when the subdivision was new. The homes on the street are uniform, neat, well-maintained: a "Brady Bunch"–type of neighborhood. Across the street is a small cemetery, the only piece of land in the area that has resisted takeover by the sprawl of modern construction.

A new family moves into one of the duplexes on the quiet street. Two boys, ages nine and eleven, play basketball in the driveway and ride their skateboards on the sidewalk. The boys tell their mother that they have heard that an old man used to live in the duplex. He's dead now. Maybe he's buried across the road in the pretty little cemetery. Everything's great in this tidy duplex until the boys start talking about hearing "sounds." Then their mother begins to think she hears odd sounds, too: breathing behind her, scratches in the wall, sighs that brush past her ear and drift up above her head like warm air rising in a cool room.

One afternoon the older son rushes into the house from the garage and says that he saw a man sitting in the car in the garage. The woman's husband is at work, the outside garage door is down. Frightened, she shuts and locks the interior garage door to the kitchen and calls the police. When they arrive, they check the garage, but no one is there. The boy gives a description to the police of an older man, dressed in dark clothes, who silently stared at him from the driver's seat of his mother's car when the boy entered the garage from the kitchen to retrieve some sports equipment. "I opened the door," he says, "and this man was sitting in the car." Later, her sons tell the woman that they think that a ghost "lives in our garage."

At first the woman thinks the idea of a ghost in the garage is funny. But over time, her amusement becomes concern as her sons report additional sightings of the old man in the garage. On some level, she begins to accept the idea of the ghost in the garage as reality.

The master bedroom is in the basement of the duplex. After several more months, strange things begin happening in this bedroom, and the woman becomes aware of the fact that the ghost has moved into the house from the garage. She still has not seen it, but her husband reports sometimes seeing a strange, shadowy figure, always in one particular corner of the bedroom. It is indistinct, he says, like the movement of shadows or like a shadow melting into the wall. "It's hard to describe something you've never seen before," he says.

The ghost goes away for awhile. Things are quiet at the duplex for three months, and then, suddenly, the woman encounters the old man herself. It is not a visual experience but an incredibly visceral encounter: The ghost touches her. She feels his cold fingers in the small of her back early one morning as she is making up the bed in her bedroom in the basement. She senses that it is not a malevolent touch, but a kind of tactile greeting. "I'm back, I'm home, I'm here," it says. "Did you miss me?"

The ghost becomes more active now. It is a poltergeist, not malicious or unfriendly but mischievous, revealing a "weird" sense of humor. Objects situated in certain places in the house have mysteriously been moved to other places where they do not belong. Then they might just as mysteriously be found moved back to their original locations. One night, after the woman has just drifted off to sleep, the bed suddenly jolts, shaking her back to consciousness. The old man wants her awake with him in the dark.

He goes away again. He always goes away for three or four months at a time, but he always comes back. This time when he comes back he demands the woman's attention. He is getting bolder—he wants to have some real fun with her. A sound like a mouse scratching under the bed starts one night, but the sound becomes less random and more rhythmic—a tapping. A pattern emerges: seven taps, and then a pause. Seven taps, and then a pause. Seven taps . . . and then something small and compact, about the size of a cat (the family has no cat), jumps on the bed, shaking the mattress, banishing the last vestige of control the woman has over her fright and dismay at the antics of this unwelcome house ghost. Intermittently, the shaking continues.

It's 12:30 A.M. The bed-shaking has finally stopped. Through it all, the woman's husband has slept like one of the dead. In fact, she could not awaken him while it was happening, and he barely responds now that the incident is over. He is strangely groggy and nonresponsive, rolling over and pushing her away when she begs him to wake up. She goes upstairs. The house is dark and still as a grave. She checks on her children in their bedroom, and they are both sleeping peacefully. But she thinks about how the boys don't like to go downstairs anymore because they say they saw the ghost in the corner again and the old man's face was green and evil this time, not pale and complacent as it had been before.

The woman doesn't understand what is happening. She hasn't talked to anyone about it because she knows they would think she was crazy, and maybe she is. But if she is, then her whole family is crazy, too—right along with her. Crazy or not, she knows the old man is winning. She starts thinking about finding a new place to live.

The Haunted Duplex is a real story about the experiences of an actual family living in a south-central Kansas town. The woman who recounted these incidents spoke about them very reluctantly but insisted that these things had truly occurred, and were continuing to occur, in her home.

Unlike many of the stories and legends in this book, the Haunted Duplex is not a story that has been shared as oral folklore, enlarged and embellished by a multitude of tellers, refined and passed on through generations of storytelling. The Haunted Duplex is a very personal story, an experience shared only within a small family that wishes to protect its privacy and anonymity. This story stands out as a single account told by an intelligent, rational professional woman who is evidently dealing with something she can't explain.

This is the stuff of legend, if only of personal family legend, but historical distance has not blunted its immediacy and multiple tellings have not rendered its origins cloudy. This duplex could be in any town, in any neighborhood; perhaps you'll rent the house next. If so, one hopes the old man has moved out before you move in.

Fort Ghosts

The frontier forts in Kansas are particularly fertile grounds for legendary material. The two active forts, Fort Leavenworth (1827 to the present) and Fort Riley (1853 to the present), claim the most legends and largest population of ghosts as a result of their continuous occupation as active posts over the years by the United States Army. But Fort Scott (1842–1853), Fort Larned (1859–1878), and Fort Hays (1865–1889) remain interesting research sites for historical legends or even modern-day ghost sightings at their respective historical sites. Fort Dodge (1865–1882) serves as the Kansas Soldiers' Home, and Fort Harker (1864–1872) west of Kanopolis is preserved in the Fort Harker Guardhouse Museum, housed in the only one of its four buildings left standing. All that remains of the original Fort Wallace (1865–1882) is the old post cemetery contained within the Wallace Township cemetery.

General George Armstrong Custer, a legendary character in the history of the American West, spent time at both Fort Riley and Fort Leavenworth after the Civil War in the 1860s. Custer's ghost, evidently a well-traveled phantom, is an enduring presence at both of the Kansas forts. Most likely it shows up, in story form at least, at frontier forts in other states as well as in the Little Bighorn Valley in Montana where he began and ended his infamous last campaign.

Ghost stories at the Kansas forts are plentiful, and many hearken back to frontier times and frontier tales. Victims of cholera epidemics, the widow of a pre–Civil War army officer who kills himself in a tragic accident, a pioneer mother whose children vanish on the trail to Oregon—all these ghosts and more have become part of the legend and lore of the military forts. A female phantom in nineteenth-century dress crashes a party of twentieth-century teens, and a haunted antique teddy bear rides a rocking horse from childhoods past.

These ghosts and many more augment the military population at the Kansas forts, and their stories add to the panorama of history preserved at the forts for the last 170 years.

FORT SCOTT

The Watching Widow

Fort Scott is the second-oldest United States Army fort in Kansas, established in 1842, just fifteen years after Fort Leavenworth. Fort Scott's official function was to protect the Permanent Indian Frontier, but its troops also participated in the Mexican war, accompanied missions of exploration and scouting expeditions, and escorted settlers traveling on the Santa Fe Trail to the Far West.

The army vacated Fort Scott in 1853 when the frontier moved westward. The garrison stationed at the fort was transferred to Fort Leavenworth, and the post buildings were sold at auction in 1855, becoming the town of Fort Scott. The fort was used again briefly during the Civil War as the headquarters of the Army of the Frontier; it served as a supply base for troops of the Union army, a refugee center for displaced American Indians, and the base for the First Kansas Colored Infantry, one of the first Black regiments in the war.

Fort Scott today is a National Historic Site, managed by the National Park Service, its twenty buildings fully restored as an example of an 1842 frontier military fort from the Mexican war era. Although the fort was abandoned by the army following the Civil War, one former resident from its active days may still be in residence in the officers' quarters.

In 1845, Mrs. Burdett A. Terrett, an officer's wife stationed at Fort Scott with her husband, was at the window of what is now known as Captain Sword's quarters, a house in officers' row at the fort. Mrs. Terrett was watching her husband approach the building on horseback. He was returning from morning drill and perhaps was showing off a bit for his wife, grandly riding up in full uniform and dismounting with a flourish in front of her. As he dismounted from his horse, one of his pistols discharged. The bullet entered his chest right above his heart, and he was instantly killed. Mrs. Terrett returned east with her husband's body when it was shipped back for burial. Records indicated she suffered a nervous breakdown following her husband's death.

According to Arnold Schofield, fort historian with the National Park Service at old Fort Scott National Historic Site, this may not have been the last time Mrs. Terrett was seen at the fort. In the summer of 1981, when he was chief ranger with the National Park Service at the fort, Schofield was sought out one day by another ranger to witness an incident report being written up. A man outside, a visitor to the fort from Topeka, was insisting that a record be made of an unusual incident he had just experienced.

The man and his wife had spent the day touring the grounds and such buildings as the quartermaster's storehouse, the guardhouse, the barracks, and the hospital. They had just finished touring the buildings that made up officers' row. As they left the buildings, the man happened to glance back, noticing movement in one of the second-floor windows. The curtains were open, and the man could see a beautiful woman in period clothing looking out the window, toward the yard. The woman smiled at him and waved, almost beckoning. The man from Topeka turned to his wife and said, "Come over and see this mannequin. We must have missed that room when we went through—I don't remember seeing it. Wait, it has to be a tour guide because she's waving—why didn't we see her when we went through the house?"

He began ascending the outside stairway that leads to the second story. As he approached the window, the figure of the woman turned to the left, walked from the window inside the room, and disappeared. The man called to his wife standing below the stairs and asked her if she had seen the figure, but she only said, "What are you talking about?"

Convinced that he had seen a woman in 1840s garb, the man found a park ranger and told him what he had seen. He asked if there was a tour guide in period dress working in that building. He was informed that there was no one in that building and that female costumed interpreters were not used at that time. The man continued to insist that he had seen a small shapely woman standing at the window, smiling and beckoning to him. Certain that this vision was real, the man requested that an official report be filed so it would be on record. The building was searched with no results, and the report was filed.

"This incident is not generally known, but it is documented in fort records," said Arnold Schofield. According to Schofield, the Topekan reported that there was nothing distraught about the appearance of the woman he saw. Schofield says that there is no record of any officer's wife dying in that building nor any record of a similar tragedy that might incite any other ghost to inhabit the officers' quarters. After researching fort records, Schofield feels that the only tragedy that occurred in the vicinity was the one that Mrs. Terrett witnessed when she watched her husband fatally shoot himself in front of her.

"This was the only time, the only sighting that occurred here that we know about," said Schofield. But perhaps the Widow Terrett *has* been seen by other visitors, other visitors not as willing as the tourist from Topeka to admit that they have seen a vision at the fort, a beautiful officer's wife reliving the last happy moments in her life, smiling and beckoning to her dashing cavalry officer husband moments before his life ends in an explosion of gunfire.

FORT RILEY

Custer's Ghost

Major William A. Gribbons saw the ghost of General George Armstrong Custer standing in his living room in 1955. The ghost was leaning comfortably against the fireplace, its arm resting on the mantelpiece. The shadowy features were unmistakably Custer's, and just a "ghost" of a smile was on the white lips below a bushy mustache. The apparition of the general was looking directly across the room at a picture hanging just inside the front door: a picture of the general's last battle—Custer's Last Stand.

At the time of the sighting, Major Gribbons and his wife lived in Quarters 24-A on Sheridan Avenue at Fort Riley, the post housing at that time believed to be where then–Lieutenant Colonel Custer and his wife, Libbie, also had lived some eighty-nine years before when they were stationed at Fort Riley with the Seventh Cavalry Regiment in 1866 and 1867. The Custers, both in their mid-twenties, were in residence at the fort for only seven months. Historical records and letters Mrs. Custer wrote home to her family indicate that the young couple was very happy with their assignment to Fort Riley, was quite comfortable in their new quarters, and continued there a shared love for games, jokes, and chasing each other around the house. In fact, the Custers' high-spirited romps became so noisy at times that at first some of their neighbors suspected Custer was

beating his wife. Evidently, however, he was only beating her at table cro-
quet, followed by wild dashes up and down the stairs and games of chase
in the living room with furniture being used as temporary barricades
against one another. The Custer family dogs would also get into the spirit
of the games, adding barking to the din of general laughter and clattering
feet on the stairs.

In an interview for a newspaper article in 1955, Major and Mrs. Gribbons said Custer *did* make a lot of noise on the stairs. He was a big man,
they said, six feet tall, and even as a ghost he wouldn't just walk up the
stairs, which might be tolerable, but insisted on running up and down
them, which made quite a racket. According to the Gribbonses, the family
who occupied Quarters 24-A before them asked to be reassigned to new
quarters because they couldn't stand the unexplained noises in the house
at night, especially the clattering footsteps on the stairs.

But Custer didn't frighten Major Gribbons and his wife. They felt they
had a lot in common with the Custers, and they said they felt they had
"made friends with the ghost." Mrs. Custer, in a letter, had written about
her husband and how she looked forward to hearing "the clank of his saber on the gallery and the quick springing steps of [his] feet." Mrs. Gribbons, in a letter that she wrote home, told of how "the wind blows strongly
through the gallery" at times, accompanied by unexplained clanking and
banging sounds, and the front door creaks as if it were opening.

The Gribbonses even shared a glass of wine punch with the ghost. One
cup from a set matching their German punch bowl was left, partially full,
on the fireplace mantel overnight. In the morning, the cup was gone. The
Gribbonses speculated that "the dashing young cavalryman, Custer,
probably had had a long ride that day and was thirsty when he came
home."

Major Gribbons, then, was not overly suprised to see Custer standing
by the fireplace that evening in 1955, his arm draped over the mantel. In
fact, this must have been his customary stance for a long time since, according to Mrs. Gribbons, there was a spot on the mantelpiece where "the
paint is worn thin and almost off where an elbow would rest there, and
there is a chipped place on the tile hearth which spurs might have made."

Bill McKale, curator of the United States Cavalry Museum at Fort Riley,
questions whether Custer (or his ghost) would have imbibed a cup of
wine punch: "Historically, Custer didn't drink after he married Libbie in
1864. Of course, he could have fallen off the wagon after he went in the
grave. I don't know."

Another question about the tales of Custer's ghost in Quarters 24 arises from the problematic fact that during the 1970s, when the house underwent renovation, research into the house's history by army officials revealed that Custer's quarters in actuality had been elsewhere on the fort, in Quarters 21. Since plans had already been set in motion to preserve what had commonly been referred to for twenty-five years as Custer House as a museum to the Custer family and frontier fort life, Quarters 24 was renovated and preserved as Custer House. Tours of the house now stress that it is "representative" of what Custer's home looked like in 1866. As for the obvious question: Have there been sightings of Custer's ghost in Quarters 21? "No," asserts McKale, "nothing we know of."

Despite the fact that Custer never lived in Custer House, ghost stories and tales abound about it and the strange incidents that take place there. Quarters 24, a native limestone building, is the only remaining set of the six officers' quarters that were built in 1854 and one of only four structures at the fort from the 1850s building period. It was in continuous usage as housing quarters for 120 years until 1974, when it was designated a National Historic Site and opened to the public as a museum. Stories of ghosts and hauntings have been a part of the legendary history of Custer House and Fort Riley since at least 1855, when a devastating cholera epidemic struck the fort and claimed many lives. In fact, one of the most disturbing legends about Custer House has nothing to do with Custer at all but involves an innocent-looking child's toy: a haunted teddy bear.

The Haunted Teddy Bear

The old threadbare, one-eyed teddy bear on the antique rocking horse, part of the historic display in the children's room upstairs in Custer House, was a favorite of visitors to Custer House at Fort Riley during the 1970s and 1980s. But the teddy bear, so precious and rather pathetic on its perch on the back of the aged rocking horse as visitors filed in and out of the room, became something else entirely when the tourists weren't there, according to guides and housekeepers who worked in the house.

A cleaning woman who worked in the Custer House in the late 1970s was terrified of the bear. She insisted that when she walked up the stairs to clean in the bedrooms, the teddy bear would start rocking on the rocking horse. The first few times it happened, she went into the room to investigate and found the bear swaying forward and backward on the horse, glaring at her from its one good eye. After that, she disliked going upstairs to clean unless someone else was in the house with her, and finally she quit her job.

In 1975, a custodian noticed that the bear had fallen off the horse. He set the bear on the bed instead of the horse. When he next checked the room, the bear was back on the horse. Numerous other people reported that if the bear was ever moved from the horse to any other location in the room, the next morning the bear would always be back in its customary place on the horse. Another custodian, a master sergeant, said in a 1979 *Fort Riley Post* article that he was puzzled by the bear that kept "moving from spot to spot." He speculated that perhaps curious visitors or children had picked up the toy and put it back on the horse. The only problem with that theory, he admitted, was the fact that the upstairs rooms were cordoned off from the public. "It's unlikely that the teddy bear was moved by anyone," he said, "anyone human that is!"

Legend holds that a little girl who lived in the house died during the cholera epidemic on base in 1855. The ghost of this little girl is supposedly responsible for the movement of the teddy bear and the rocking horse. A woman employed at the house as a tour guide in the 1970s recounted the experience of another guide at Custer House for a newspaper article in 1979: "One lady who worked there said that she had heard crying upstairs one day. When she went to look, she found the teddy bear on the floor with tears in his eyes [eye?]. She picked it up and placed it on the rocking horse nearby, but it fell off. She picked it up two more times, but finally gave up when the bear refused to sit in the saddle. Later that same day, the crying stopped, so again she went upstairs and found the teddy bear back up on the rocking horse."

The one-eyed bear had definitely taken on a sinister air by the time these stories were being told. Other guides reported hearing the sounds of a baby wailing upstairs, a noise like stamping feet from the second floor, or sounds that resembled a kitten crying coming from the children's bedroom. Time and again, when the crying sounds were investigated, the teddy bear was found on the floor beside the still-moving horse.

In June 1979, two officers' wives were alone in the house following a coffee. Both women were startled by a loud moaning sound that issued from the upstairs bedroom and then slowly moved down the stairs. Terrified, both women fled the premises. One of the wives described their frightening experience to the *Manhattan Mercury* newspaper in January 1980: "The noise was coming from the upstairs bedroom. It started to move toward the staircase and then down the stairs. At one point you could actually feel something. It was that frightening. We could not only hear it, we could feel it. Almost like music, the noise began to vibrate."

Another guide was sure that a sinister or ominous entity lurked in the building: "I felt there was something in the Custer House. A presence and it was real: it was a bad feeling, kind of suffocating." On one occasion when she was in the house she became aware that "something upstairs was making a thumping noise. It came from the back bedroom. It sounded like the rocking horse. You could hear it and the noise got louder." Some guides in the house quit their jobs, refusing to remain in the house under such disturbing circumstances. Other guides refused to remain alone in the house when visitors were not present, preferring to wait on the screened-in front porch for tourists to arrive before they would reenter the house.

Finally, a private first class who worked at the house in the summer of 1978 described her experiences with the paranormal inside Custer House: "I opened the Custer House every morning early and always checked every room. Quite often when I checked the upstairs bedroom, the bed looked like someone had slept on it. The first time it happened I really felt uncomfortable and wanted to run out of there, thinking that maybe someone was still in the house. I knew that no one could have slept on the bed though because the house was locked and it hadn't been broken into. The cleaning lady always refused to go upstairs; in fact she was afraid to go anywhere in that house alone, so I know she hadn't slept on the bed. I don't really know how to explain it, but I can say that I do believe in ghosts." During the quiet summer mornings before visitors began arriving, this guide says she often chose to sit out on the front steps rather than stay inside alone. "I always felt a presence whenever I was in that house alone," she said. "And whenever I'd hear strange noises I'd turn on the radio to block it out, and hopefully scare the ghost away."

The teddy bear and the antique rocking horse are gone from the children's bedroom upstairs in the Custer House now. The sinister teddy swaying to and fro on the old painted pony was taken away some years back, and the Custer House is quieter now. A current tour guide reports she has neither seen nor heard anything unusual during her time at the house, but she knows that the old stories still circulate.

According to Bill McKale, the legends surrounding the Custer House are the most predominant on base, but other ghosts haunt Fort Riley as well, at least in legend form.

The Well-Ghost

Sometime in the 1860s, a woman living in Quarters 124 at Fort Riley drowned herself in a deep well on the fort grounds. An old story gives the reason for her self-demise as "unrequited love." Not much more is known about the woman's life or the manner of her death, but legend has her buried near her house in an open pasture that was already home to two other graves. That pasture is now someone's backyard on the post.

Some seventy years later, another woman living in Quarters 124 began hearing horrific noises at night in and around her house. She described them as being almost unbearably loud and sounding like a heavy wooden log being dragged with iron chains down a flight of stairs. The ghastly sounds continued night after night until the woman began to fear she would go insane. The hapless woman became convinced that the house and the surrounding area were haunted by the ghost of the lady who had drowned in the well. She contacted a Catholic priest, Father Carius, in Junction City and begged him to perform an exorcism on Quarters 124 and its grounds. According to several reports, the priest, supposedly portrayed as "something of an odd character" in a 1934 newspaper story describing the events, agreed to the exorcism and performed the rite at the haunted house.

The exorcism was evidently successful, at least for awhile. The ghost and its gruesome noises disappeared for several years, but legend has it that the Well-Ghost returned a few years later to plague the residents of Quarters 124 again. However, before the ghost resettled into its old quarters, it evidently shopped around in the area for awhile to see if it preferred any of the surrounding houses to its own. Incidents of a ghostly face pressed up against a window at Quarters 123, windows slamming shut, and doors locked at night found unlocked in the morning left surrounding residents definitely in a state of unease. A servant ironing late one night in the kitchen of 123 looked up and saw the ghostly visage of a woman leering in the window, her features pressed into the windowpane.

The servant heaved the iron with all her might at the face in the window. The window shattered and the image melted away; not surprisingly, the servant refused to work in the house any longer.

To the relief of the neighbors, the ghost eventually decided to return home to Quarters 124, and that is where it stayed for years while stories of the pranks of the Well-Ghost still looking for the soldier who "did her wrong" circulated around the fort. Although the effects of the exorcism were relatively short-lived at the time, nothing has been seen or heard from the Well-Ghost in recent years.

More Frontier Ghosts

Joining the Well-Ghost and the ghosts at the Custer House at Fort Riley are some other phantoms who call the fort home.

THE BUCKSKIN GHOST

One of the better known is the Buckskin Ghost, a friendly ghost dressed in rustic frontier buckskins who likes children and has even been known to join in their games. The ghost became particularly fond of the two children of a lieutenant colonel and his wife at one time in the 1960s. The lieutenant colonel commented about his children's phantom playmate, "I think you can say he's a friendly ghost. He plays with our children, and they even occasionally leave cookies and snacks out at night for their nocturnal friend." The comments made by the lieutenant colonel have been reported in a number of newspaper articles mentioning the Buckskin Ghost. This ghost in the past has been known to divide its time between Quarters 171-A and 171-B on the main post.

THE SUICIDE'S GHOST

A house in the officers' quarters caught fire and burned in the winter of 1886. This building was considered a notorious haunted house, a dwelling about which it was said in the *Junction City Union* of October 8, 1887, that "nothing but evil fortune attended anyone who was unfortunate enough to occupy it. One tragedy succeeded another within its ill-starred walls." Although a series of crimes and misfortunes was connected to the house—including murder, robbery, a partial lynching, and two suicides—only one tragedy in the building can be verified.

In 1863, S. E. Vernon, a clerk in the commissary department at the fort, committed suicide in the southwest upstairs room of the building. According to information supplied in an interview with Bill McKale, museum specialist at the United States Cavalry Museum, "the story goes that after several attempts to cure [Vernon] of a loathsome disease, the hospital steward told him he never could be cured and that he had better blow his head off." McKale's account goes on, "He took the prescription that night, making a frightful mess of himself."

The *Junction City Weekly Union* described the scene in gruesome detail in a newspaper article on October 18, 1863: "Upon going to his room, a most horrible sight met our eyes. He lay cross-wise of the bed, with a double-barrelled shot-gun leaning against the bed, by his side. Both barrels of the gun were discharged, the contents making two frightful holes through his neck, and bespattering the ceiling above him with flesh and blood. The discharge of the gun blackened his neck, and set fire to his clotheing [sic], which burned but a little, as the blood prevented. . . ."

Until the house burned down twenty-three years later, "the building . . . came to be regarded with suspicion and fear, especially as strange, unaccountable knocks and pounding were frequently heard, together with the fact that no plastering would remain upon the walls." This was according to a report in the *St. Louis Globe-Democrat* in September 1887 quoted a month later in the *Junction City Union*. The St. Louis article continued, "The plastering was applied time after time, but with the same result. The building was finally deserted, and one day mysteriously burned."

In actuality, the building never was deserted but was continuously occupied until it burned to the ground in 1886.

FORT LEAVENWORTH

The Ghost of Father Fred

Fort Leavenworth is the oldest continuously operated military post west of the Mississippi. It stands to reason that it would be home to some of the oldest continuously haunting ghosts west of the Mississippi—and it is.

Perhaps the oldest ghost legend at Fort Leavenworth, and certainly one of the most popular, is that of Father Fred. St. Ignatius Chapel currently stands at the corner of McClellan and Pope Avenues on the base, but the original St. Ignatius Chapel was built in the 1870s on the grounds of what is now a residence at 632 Thomas Avenue. The original chapel and the Catholic rectory burned to the ground in 1875. A young priest assigned to St. Ignatius at the time burned to death in the fire. After the fire, the salvageable building material that survived the fire was utilized to build a residential quarters on the site of the old chapel grounds. Some scorched bricks from the original burned chapel can be found in the firewall of the fireplace in the present dining room of the house. Etched into these bricks are several names—including the name Father Fred.

Father Fred is a part of 632 Thomas Avenue and not just in name only. The legend holds that the first tenants of the house to spot the ghost of a young priest in a hooded Jesuit robe and clerical collar walking up the stairs assumed he was the Father Fred immortalized in their fireplace. Although no records exist that identify the young priest who perished in the chapel blaze, what is assumed to be his ghost has been called Father Fred since that first sighting.

John Reichley, publicist and historian with the Fort Leavenworth Historical Society, notes in his book *The Haunted Houses of Fort Leavenworth* that, according to legend, the attic of the house is the priestly ghost's domain. He has been seen walking up and down the stairs to and from his attic room numerous times and even occasionally descends just at dinnertime, in full clerical dress, to join a resident family for dinner. Some residents have spotted him on the first rising of the stairway, in the kitchen, and also standing near the fireplace in the dining room.

Father Fred is quite sociable and has even been known to visit other residences near by, particularly if there is a good party going on. At one festive event in the fall of 1973, a Polaroid snapshot was taken of the host of the party, and as the picture developed the vague but recognizable image of a robed figure appeared eerily imprinted on the wall above and behind the subject of the photo.

The good father is not only a party-down type of guy but also a diligent tailor who has been known to borrow a sewing machine to mend his robes. In 1978, a lieutenant colonel and his wife lived in the quarters at 630 Thomas, next door to Father Fred's primary residence. They claimed they often "clearly heard" footsteps on their central staircase, but when they would investigate, no one was there. The lieutenant colonel revealed to John Reichley in a conversation that their cat and dog would at times get quite agitated at the same time and "run under the sofa to whimper and meow." One particular day, the wife noticed the sound of a sewing machine coming from the house next door, 632 Thomas, for much of the day. Believing the lady of the house to be gone that day, she was surprised to hear the sounds of someone industriously sewing for hours on end in the house. When she later saw her neighbor out in her backyard, she ran over to inquire if she had been at home that day or if she had had company who might have been there sewing. The lady from 632 assured the concerned lady from 630 that she had indeed been gone all day, and, no, she had no visitors. She also told her baffled neighbor that she wasn't concerned about the odd sounds of the sewing machine coming from her house that day. "That happens all the time," she explained to her neighbor. "It's just Father Fred trying to sew his priestly garb."

About 1980, a carpenter was sent to Quarters 632 to do some repair work in the attic. The residence was vacant at the time, and no one else was in the house with the carpenter—no one else living, that is. The carpenter got down on the floor to begin mending some damaged boards but immediately began feeling a cold sensation and then felt the hairs on the back of his neck stand up. According to an account in John Reichley's book, the carpenter was terrified to next feel "the slap of a wet towel on my right shoulder." The carpenter claims he did not hear anything, nor did he see a towel, but he did see "something wet on my shoulder." Panicked, he "turned around with the hammer in my hand, to smash whoever was there, but there was no one." Not surprisingly, the carpenter left the attic very quickly and refused to return to work there until another worker accompanied him.

Evidence existed, at one time, that someone who resided in Quarters 632 had attached multiple locks to the attic door—to try and keep Father Fred in? Legend holds that two sets of initials are carved into the wallboard of a second-story alcove in the house. An arrow is carved next to the initials and is pointing to a message scrawled on the wallboard: "I lived here with a ghost—a minister."

Legend also dictates that the ghost of Father Fred finally drove one couple to distraction and completely out of the house. A colonel and his wife who lived in 632 at one time requested to be transferred from their quarters to another house. The colonel filled out the form that was required for a transfer request. Under "reason for desiring to terminate quarters," the colonel filled in: "My wife is losing her mind because of the ghost in these quarters." The request for transfer was promptly approved.

The Ghost of Catherine Sutler:
The Lost Children

A noisy crowd of trick-or-treaters ran along Scott Avenue, kicking up dry leaves and casting ominous shadows against the manicured lawns of the officers' quarters residences of Fort Leavenworth. The bluffs of the Missouri River were a stone's throw away back beyond the houses, and a full moon intermittently cast a wan yellow light across the water as it moved in and out between ragged shreds of clouds. A small ghost, a witch, a pirate, and a princess stopped between two of the houses and huddled together to compare candy. Giggling and digging through their treat bags, they were at first oblivious of the darker shadow holding a glowing light that was approaching them from among the other shadows on the street. "Ethan? Mary?" The anxious voice interrupted their candy sampling and caused them to turn and look. A woman dressed in frontier clothing and wrapped in a black shawl was standing back a few feet from them. An old-fashioned lantern was clutched in one hand while her other hand gathered her shawl into folds in the front of her calico dress. Furrows of worry creased her pale brow, and her dark eyes moved from face to face in the group of children, examining their features carefully. "Ethan, Mary," she said again, but the hopeful look upon her face had faded into sadness, and she said the names again not as a question, but in resignation. The puzzled children watched as the woman in black melted away back into the shadows, the only visible sign of her the lantern's light, bobbing along down the street, held high in the air above her head. Like other trick-or-treaters before them, these children had met the ghost of Catherine Sutler, searching for her lost children, Ethan and Mary.

Hiram and Catherine Sutler and their two children arrived at Fort Leavenworth in the fall of 1880. They had relatives at the fort, and a short visit was to be just a brief rest for the family before they continued their journey on west to settle in Oregon Territory. A morning or so after their arrival, the children were sent out to collect firewood. Driftwood was plentiful in the river, and the children may have been enticed to try and fish some wood out of the treacherous waters of the Missouri, although they had been cautioned to stay back from the bluffs and the river.

When Ethan and Mary had not returned in a reasonable amount of time, their parents became worried. When they could not find the children, they enlisted the aid of others at the fort to help their search. The day lengthened into evening, and lanterns were lit as the increasingly frantic parents and the rest of the search party looked for Ethan and Mary along the banks of the river and throughout the fort area. The search party continued their increasingly hopeless task for three days and three nights before they gave up.

The trip to Oregon was postponed as the grieving parents continued to hope against hope that their children would return. Fall turned into winter. Hiram became resigned to the fact that the children were gone and probably dead, swept away by the waters of the Missouri or carried away by animals. But Catherine would not give up her search, becoming a familiar figure in her calico dress and black shawl, hunting for her children night and day, wandering the post at night holding her lantern above her head, crying "Ethan! Mary!" in her hopeless search for her lost children.

Catherine continued looking for her children even in the snow. Late in the winter, she contracted pneumonia and died, although the legend concludes that she actually died of a broken heart over the loss of her children. The next spring when travel was again possible, Hiram returned to Indiana. Some time later, word was sent to him in Indiana that his children had been found. The children had indeed fallen in the river and been swept downstream. They had been rescued by Fox Indians who adopted them and took them along when their encampment moved for the winter. In the spring, the Fox Indians returned to the area and brought the children back to the fort. Ethan and Mary went home to Indiana and their father, but their mother remained behind, buried at Fort Leavenworth, deprived in death of the knowledge that her children had been found.

The ghost of Catherine Sutler is one of the best-known legends of Fort Leavenworth and a story that has been told and retold for many years. The apparition of the woman in the black shawl, lantern held high above her head, is most often encountered on autumn nights around the post. She has been seen floating over the golf course and walking through the National Cemetery, her lantern light dipping behind the tombstones as she wanders through the night plaintively calling out for her lost children: "Ethan! Mary!"

The Lady in Black

The ghostly Lady in Black is the fort phantom that "started the modern legends of ghosts and haunts" at Fort Leavenworth, according to John Reichley. The couple residing at 16 Sumner Place in 1975 was startled when their six-year-old son began regaling them with historic tales of frontier Kansas—colorful stories about the exploits of the Jay-hawkers, Quantrill's raid on Lawrence, and other stories from the Civil War era and later. Curious about their son's sudden precocious talents in storytelling and historical knowledge, they questioned him to determine if he was really learning all of these things in his first-grade classroom. Oh no, he assured them—he was learning them from the "nice lady in the black dress who reads stories from her book to me after I go to bed at night."

Puzzled, the parents put their son to bed that night and waited a quarter of an hour. Tiptoeing back upstairs, they quietly approached the door to his bedroom. Although they had turned out his bedside lamp when they had tucked him in and left the room earlier, a faint light was showing from under his door. They could hear a low murmuring sound coming from inside the room. Alarmed, his father pushed open the door, and the parents hurried into the room. The first thing they noticed was the unusual chill in the room. Their son was sitting up in his bed but was comfortably covered with his covers and quilt. The next thing his parents noticed was the big wooden rocking chair next to his bed, empty, but slowly rocking as if someone had just gotten up from it hurriedly.

The boy started crying and his terrified mother rushed to his side. "Are you all right?" she asked him in a panicky voice. The boy cried harder. "No," he sniffed through his tears. "She's gone and she said if my parents ever came into the room she'd go away and never come back. And you made her go away!"

The terror-stricken parents contacted the post chaplain the next day and requested information about exorcising the ghost in their quarters. The chaplain was a Southern Baptist, but when he heard their story, he referred them to the Catholic chaplain for the base. Legend has it that a Catholic army chaplain and twelve laymen performed a rite of exorcism on the house at 16 Sumner Place. While this was going on, the story goes, the family vacated the premises and went to the Ramada Inn. Although Catholic officials in Leavenworth reportedly denied any knowledge of an exorcism taking place at any time at the fort, whatever ritual took place at the house was evidently a success, because the Lady in Black ceased to appear to the couple's son, and nothing more was seen of her in their house. However, the Lady didn't go far—she just moved next door to 18 Sumner Place. The family in Quarters 16 were relieved to be rid of their ghost, but the family across the wall in Quarters 18 wasn't so happy.

Shortly after the exorcism, the residents of 18 Sumner Place began experiencing strange apparitions and sounds. Doorknobs turned when no living hand was on the handle. Lights would turn on and off. A presence was sensed at times on the stairway, in the bedrooms, and in the kitchen. One resident of Quarters 18 recalled coming home late one evening after attending her son's soccer game. She had left the family's dirty dinner dishes out on the counter, planning on washing them up after the soccer game. They unlocked the door to their house, and the mother went straight to the kitchen to do the dishes. To her amazement, all the dishes had been scraped and were stacked neatly next to the dishwasher. This woman didn't think much of sharing her house with a ghost, but she did admit that if one had to have a ghost, "it might as well be one that does the dishes on occasion."

The Lady in Black may have felt she needed to earn her keep by doing the dishes, but her real first concern is caring for children, even to the point of resenting babysitters, grandmothers, and other alternate caretakers. One visiting grandmother to the house claimed to have been pushed out of the nursery by an unseen hand. Babysitters have told stories of turned-down beds that have been remade by an invisible being and of children who refuse a bedtime story because they preferred waiting for stories "the lady" or "Nanny" would read to them instead. Visitors and residents have reported feeling a "presence" on the stairs leading up to the bedrooms and the attic, and some have even reported growing suddenly cold as they brushed past the spirit on the stairs. Others have told of invisible tugs on the shoulder and the movement of small items around the house. Even family pets have reacted to the ghost. One family's cats were in the habit of napping on the stairway landing but would at times unaccountably leap up suddenly and look up the stairs, arching their backs and bristling. One version of the Lady in Black's legend tells of a thoughtful child who sought to reassure his parents when he heard them postponing their plans for the evening because the babysitter had canceled. He informed his parents that they needn't worry about leaving him, because the Lady in Black would take care of him!

Another family at 18 Sumner was gone from the house for a period of time in 1975 when they took an extended trip. The night that they returned, the woman of the house was awakened by a light touch on her arm and the sound of someone speaking her name. Opening her eyes, she saw an apparition of a matronly woman dressed in black standing by her bed. The vision faded away quickly, but fearing this was an omen of danger or trouble, the woman immediately roused her husband, and they hurried to check on their children and the house. Everything was discovered to be all right, and the couple decided that the Lady in Black had simply missed her family and was letting them know that she was glad to have them back.

Like Father Fred, the Lady in Black seems to primarily dwell in the third-floor attic of "her" house. Part of her legend mentions the supposed existence of an army photo of the house that clearly gives the impression of someone peering out from behind the round attic window on the outside of the house. For years, passersby have reported seeing the face or the profile of the Lady in Black as she gazes out the window at them.

John Reichley links the Lady in Black to the legend of Catherine Sutler. Perhaps Catherine's black shawl and the Lady's black dress are one and the same, and Catherine, weary at times of wandering the fort looking for her children, rests from her roaming in the attic of the house on Sumner Place. Here her thwarted maternal instincts and love for children can exhibit themselves as she watches over her adopted family and reads bedtime stories to the children.

The Ghost of Custer

One might expect the ghost of Captain David H. Buel to haunt the commanding general's quarters at One Scott Avenue. Captain Buel lived in Quarters One in 1870 when he was arsenal commander at the fort. One day as Captain Buel was returning to his house, he was shot and killed in the front yard by one of his own soldiers—a disgruntled trooper. But the ghost of Captain Buel has never made its presence known. Another officer was shot at while in the house: Brigadier General Frederick Funston returned fire from his own bedroom when another disgruntled soldier began taking potshots at him from outside the house around 1910. General Funston was not hit, though, and managed to make it out of Quarters One alive.

One might also expect the house to be haunted by the ghosts of the seventy-plus soldiers who were buried on the grounds between 1827 and 1859. The brick Victorian house was built in 1861 on the site of the old Soldiers' Cemetery after as many of the graves as could be found had been moved. Some graves were missed, though, and rumor has it that the odd human bone still turns up from time to time in the yard of the house. Oddly, although the ghosts of Civil War soldiers have supposedly been seen wandering the grounds of the current cemetery at Fort Leavenworth, no ghosts of pre–Civil War era ghosts have been noticed around Quarters One.

The only ghost reputed to roam the commanding general's quarters at One Scott Avenue is the illustrious and well-traveled ghost of George Armstrong Custer. Various stories have circulated as to the connection between Custer and these quarters. One version springs from the fact that Lieutenant Colonel Custer was court-martialed at Fort Leavenworth in 1867 for "leaving his command without authority."

Custer, based at Fort Riley, was on a campaign with the Seventh Cavalry in the summer of 1867 when an epidemic of Asiatic cholera broke out at Fort Riley. Various historical sources place him at Fort Wallace or Fort Harker in Kansas or in southwestern Nebraska when the news of the epidemic reached him. Regardless, because of his concern for the safety of his wife back at Fort Riley, Custer left his regiment under the command of a subordinate and hastened back to Fort Riley.

For this infraction, Custer was tried by court-martial at Fort Leavenworth and sentenced to suspension and "loss of rank and pay for one year." He was reinstated and rejoined the Seventh Cavalry in September 1868. Custer was then able to continue his military career up until his ill-fated last campaign at the Battle of the Little Bighorn. Perhaps his ghost stalks about in his former temporary quarters, awaiting the sentencing from his court-martial.

Another version that places Custer in the commanding general's quarters asserts that Custer stayed in Quarters One for several days before leaving for Montana and the Little Bighorn Valley in 1876. If Leavenworth was one of his stops before embarking on his last journey, then Custer's ghost has plenty of reason to linger there at One Scott Avenue, musing over the folly of his final campaign.

The Ghosts of the Rookery

The Rookery, built in 1832, is the oldest house in Kansas continuously occupied as a residence. A rook is a bird similar to a crow, and a rookery is a "haunt of gregarious birds or mammals" or "a place teeming with like individuals." The Rookery at 14 Sumner at Fort Leavenworth is literally teeming with ghosts, a haunt for some particularly gregarious phantoms.

The dominant ghost in the Rookery is particularly terrifying. Reportedly, this apparition of a young woman with long scraggly hair standing out all over her head rushes at people, screaming wildly, her long nails extended, and her white gown flying. The identity of this petrifying vision is not known, but the ferocity of her exploits suggests the possibility that she was the victim of some type of horrible violence.

One story about this ghost reveals that she was the wife of an officer stationed at the fort who lived close by the Rookery. The story claims that the woman was tortured and killed by marauding Indians during an attack on the fort one day when the cavalry was away. According to this legend, the Indians scaled a log fence around the fort and massacred the women and children. This is a vivid story, but the fact is there never was a log fence around the fort, nor was there ever an Indian attack against it. Regardless, the Rookery's most ferocious phantom has supposedly been seen by a number of the residents of the house as she purportedly flies through the house, her long bone-white gown flapping behind her.

Another ghost that has been seen in the house is in the form of an old woman who sits chattering in the corner. Some witnesses claim to have seen the specter of a young girl throwing a temper tantrum. Yet another ghost is a bushy-haired old man in a white nightshirt, a macabre insomniac who delights in awakening residents and guests in the middle of the night.

John Reichley, the fort historian, recounted in his book *The Haunted Houses of Fort Leavenworth* a series of frightening experiences that happened to an Air Force colonel and his family while they lived in the Rookery in the 1970s. Ignorant of the tales of the ghosts in their new home, this family was unprepared for their subsequent introduction to the evil tricks of the Rookery's undead residents. While the colonel's wife was carrying some boxes to the basement, she "felt a distinct push, lost her balance, and fell." Just before she hit the floor at the bottom of the stairs, she "felt hands under her that broke her fall." As she had begun falling, she had twisted around to try to see her attacker, but saw no one.

The colonel's oldest daughter was inconsolable when she discovered that her favorite toys—a collection of bright-blue Smurf figurines—were missing from their box. A search of the house did not turn up a single Smurf. Later that evening, when the little girl was taken up to bed, the family was astonished to discover two rows of Smurfs, lined up single file on the bed rails on either side of the girl's bed.

Days later, the family's youngest daughter reported to her mother that she had seen a very pale lady in an old-fashioned dress accompanied by a little girl outside in the yard where she had been playing. According to the daughter, the woman had spoken to her and said: "We are ghosts who live where you now live and it's been one hundred years since we died. We need your help to leave this place." The mother searched the neighborhood but could find no evidence of a woman or a little girl in the vicinity.

Finally, some months after these experiences, the family's older son came home from college for a visit. He had not been in the house before and did not know about the strange incidents his family had experienced since they had moved into the house. One morning shortly after his arrival, he related to his mother what he assumed was a bizarre dream he had had the night before: "As [I] lay in bed, it got quite chilly in the room, and just before [I] pulled up the covers [I] saw what appeared to be a pale woman in a long white gown flying around the room . . . as she flew around her gown hit a curtain rod and knocked it off the wall. When I woke up this morning, a curtain rod was on the floor. I have no idea how it got there." The boy's mother then told him of the rest of the family's experiences with the ghost or ghosts in the house. John Reichley, who tells this story in his book, indicates that the young man "didn't visit the fort a lot after that."

The son of another family who later lived in the Rookery also had a near run-in with the ghost in the long white dress. During a party he threw for his high school friends from Leavenworth High, two girls went out to the front porch to smoke a cigarette. Both girls—at the same instant—saw the figure of a woman in a floor-length white gown half-walking, half-floating across the porch. The girls screamed, the rest of the kids came running, and everyone looked around for the phantom. But, of course, nothing more was seen of her. Luckily for the girls, the Rookery's ferocious female phantom was in a good mood that evening.

The Face in the Fire

The family was gathered around the cheerily burning fireplace in their new quarters. The unpacking was done, the boxes put away, and the general uproar of moving had quieted as the household settled in to relax around the fire. As they sat gazing into the flames, something odd became apparent in the midst of the blaze: A three-quarters profile of what appeared to be a gaunt, middle-aged man with white hair, a white mustache, and a pointed white goatee appeared in the fire. Riveted by this strange vision, the family continued to watch the fire until it had burned down. Even more astounding, when the fire was out, the same phantasmic face was etched into the rear wall of the fireplace.

From that night on, the family was subjected to other ghostly happenings. Heavy footsteps were heard in a hallway after the back porch door banged open and slammed shut. The footsteps proceeded through the hall and up the stairs. The wife, in the house with a friend, assumed it was her husband returning home and called to him. When she received no response, she went upstairs. The bedrooms were empty. She contacted her husband by phone, and he came home to check out the strange noises but could find no evidence of an intruder.

Sometimes blasts of frigid air would wrap around one's ankles and legs while walking through the house. Unexplained crashing noises in the middle of the night, more stomping footsteps up and down the stairs, and tapping sounds from the bricks in the house all were quite distressing to the residents. At times the ghostly sounds would cease for several weeks but then resume without warning.

These events took place in the quarters at 605 McClellan in the 1970s. The family also related other instances of a ghostly presence: the repeated rattling of a baby gate installed at the top of the third-floor stairs, the sounds of a "spirited" game of pool being played on the family's pool table in the basement after the family had gone to bed, and keys on a piano being struck in a tuneless pattern while the piano cover was closed and no one was in the room.

After this family moved, no other activity was reported at 605 McClellan until the 1980s. Then a new family also encountered the Face in the Fire and its ghostly pranks but with one difference: This time the body of the flaming visage joined its face in bolder visitations upon the family. These encounters are detailed in a booklet, *Ghost Stories of Fort Leavenworth*, compiled by the Musettes group of the Fort Leavenworth Museum.

Early one morning the husband got up and went into the bathroom to shave and shower. Upon opening the door, he discovered a "tall, thin, dark-haired man standing in front of the mirror with shaving cream on his face." In his drowsy condition, the man assumed he had walked in on his son already up and shaving. Later his son denied that he had been up early that morning or that he had been in the bathroom shaving.

The daughter of the family was awakened quite early one morning by the sensation that someone was in the room with her. Opening her eyes and sitting up, she saw the figure of a "tall, thin man in an Army uniform with a hat somewhat tilted over his face." This gentleman stood in her doorway momentarily, then walked past her in front of her bed, and vanished into her closet.

Another ghostly visitation to the family echoed the experience of the earlier family some ten years before. One evening the wife was preparing dinner and expecting her husband home at any time. Suddenly she heard the unmistakable sounds of a pool cue striking pool balls and the balls rolling across a pool table. Surprised, she went down to the basement to investigate; perhaps her husband had already come home through the basement door and was playing a game of pool before dinner. As she descended the stairs into the basement, the noises stopped. She flipped on the light switch at the bottom of the stairs and looked around the room. The room was empty, the basement door shut and locked; the pool table was an empty expanse of green felt, and the pool cues were hung up, the pool balls racked.

Who is or was the Face in the Fire? The house at 605 McClellan was evidently at one time the rectory for the new St. Ignatius Chapel. Stories mention an old priest who lived in the rectory; his untimely death prevented him from receiving the last rites, the sacrament necessary for a peaceful eternal rest. Other stories tell of a priest who lived at the rectory with his sister, whose husband had died "under strange circumstances." The questions remain: If the Face in the Fire is a priest, who was the military man in an army uniform who appeared in the one daughter's room? Why does the face have white hair, but the ghostly figure surprised shaving in the bathroom has dark hair? If the ghost is the priest's sister's husband who died under strange circumstances, why are there no stories about him? Did the rectory have a pool table, and did the priests like to play? And most important, did these priests know Father Fred?

And the Rest

The preceding tales all dealt with the predominant—the most famous—ghosts at Fort Leavenworth. Incredibly, there are quite a few more stories of fort phantoms and ghostly occurrences on this army base—too many to recount in a single chapter. It is hard to overlook the

Toilet-Flushing Ghost, a ghost with a toilet-flushing fetish; the Tea Party Ghosts, who laugh, talk, and clink cups and glasses in an empty room; the Weeping Woman Ghost at Root Hall; General Sheridan's Wife's Ghost; the Harmonica-Playing Ghost, a teenage Civil War–era ghost who plays a mournful tune; or the Suicidal Cat who committed suicide to escape a ghost.

Just before each Halloween in recent years, John Reichley has hosted an extremely popular presentation, complete with slides, on the ghosts of Fort Leavenworth. This "spook show" has attracted such large crowds that it is now presented on two separate nights in a large auditorium on the base. Fort Leavenworth (like the town of Atchison, which has a Ghost Trolley, and the Reno County Museum in Hutchinson, which hosts a Ghost Town Tour) is intent on preserving its local ghosts.

School and Theater Ghosts

S chools are the perfect breeding grounds for ghosts and ghost stories. Teenagers and young adults are the most active disseminators of supernatural legends and the group most likely to go legend tripping to the site, or purported site, of a haunting. Many young people delight in telling and retelling ghost tales and horror stories that have been passed down from class to class, among sorority sisters and fraternity brothers, and among residents at college dorms.

The ghosts that haunt colleges, high schools, junior highs, and middle schools are often supposed to be the restless spirits of students or teachers who have died untimely deaths at the school or in some sort of accident elsewhere. Haunted music halls, school auditoriums and stages, gymnasiums, and hallways are all represented in this chapter, but a preponderance of university ghosts can be found in dormitories and in fraternity and sorority houses. Evidently, the ghosts congregate where living quarters are shared and stories are most likely to be passed around.

Some ghost stories overlap into two categories in this compilation, and often school ghosts are also theater ghosts and vice versa. But Paola High School's ghostly trumpeter and Kansas University's and Kansas State University's fraternity ghosts are all quirky representatives of the classification of school ghosts. Kansas University and Kansas State University, because of their large enrollment numbers and higher concentration of students living together on campus, have a wider variety of legends and ghosts. But the other universities and colleges in the state have their share of phantoms and poltergeists. High school, junior high, and middle school ghosts are harder to find, but they definitely are out there, and their legends are actively told.

Earl, the Brown Grand Theatre Ghost in Concordia, is an excellent representative of the legendary stories that often live a long life on and around the stages of historic restored theaters in the state. The magnificently restored Columbian Theatre in Wamego has a resident ghost as does the Jayhawk Theater in Topeka. The Jayhawk, the last remaining historic theater in Topeka, is just now in the early stages of the renovation/restoration process. The ghosts of the Brown Grand in Concordia and the Columbian in Wamego have both been quite helpful, in their own ways, to the restoration process at their respective theaters. One can only hope that the Jayhawk's ghost will prove to be just as civic-minded.

The stories included in this chapter are merely a sampling, the tip of the iceberg when it comes to the rich tradition of ghost legends that can be found in many schools and colleges, all of the state universities, and a number of historic theaters across the state. A comprehensive collection of Kansas school and theater legends and ghosts alone could fill an entire book.

The Oxford Middle School Ghost

Billie was killed in a school bus accident at a country intersection outside of Oxford in 1943. Billie was a popular sophomore at the high school, vivacious and involved in numerous school activities. Her particular passion was Girl Reserves, a forerunner of Kayettes, an organization for young women interested in school and community volunteerism. Billie had also been known as a fun-loving "prankster" at school, a girl who enjoyed playing harmless tricks on friends and teachers, a girl who had a sense of mischief.

When a car and the school bus collided at a wet intersection on a rainy afternoon, students and teachers, as well as the community, were stunned to learn that the vital young girl was dead. Billie was only fifteen, but she had already left an indelible impression on her school and town. The man who was driving the school bus when it met head-on with the car was so traumatized by the accident that, although exonerated of any liability or negligence, he quit his job and never drove a school bus again.

Some time after Billie's death, the school routine returned to normal, and as time went by stories of Billie faded. New classes came and went in the high school building and, with the exception of family and close friends, Billie was forgotten.

The first group to suspect that Billie didn't like being forgotten was the janitorial staff. A maintenance person, sweeping up trash and dusting down lockers on the first floor, would be surprised to hear footsteps overhead on the second floor. A quick check would be made upstairs—no one was around. Returning to his chores, the janitor would again be startled by a sound on the second floor: A heavy wooden door would squeak open and then be vigorously slammed shut. Another quick check upstairs, another fruitless search. The hallways were empty and dark, and all the classrooms were locked. Two janitors in particular insisted that the second-floor hallway was "always cold, even in the summertime." What was this cold essence, and what was producing the errant noises and interruptions of their work?

Stories began to circulate around the school that Billie, who had always loved high jinks and horseplay, was back to frolic in the halls and make sure that she wasn't forgotten at her old school. One janitor snorted in derision that "there was no such things as a ghost" and was promptly hit on the nose by a falling light fixture (previously thought to be in good repair). This was taken to be a definite sign from Billie that foolish disbelief in her ghost was going to be met with a solid response. The doubting janitor nursed his cut nose and in the future kept his skepticism to himself.

The ghost stories about Billie moved beyond the maintenance crew, through the coaching staff, and into the teachers' lounge. One coach claimed to have distinctly heard a voice in the girls' locker room when he was in the gym area after school. When he checked in the locker room, it was empty. A teacher accustomed to occasionally staying at the school until after dark, catching up on work and grading papers, described experiencing a weird feeling one evening that he was not alone. First he ignored it; then, continuing to feel uneasy, he got up from his desk and turned on all the lights in the room. When the light failed to chase the feeling away, he felt compelled to look out in the hallway and test the front doors to make sure they were indeed locked. They were. Finally, as his feelings of apprehension turned into an advanced case of the jitters, he put away his papers and pencils and left the building for home.

Not just the adults in the school were feeling spooked. Students who were in the building when it was relatively or completely deserted consistently reported the intermittent sounds of a female voice in the hallways or behind locked doors. One boy hired for summer maintenance work in the school building apprehended a "shadow" walking up the stairs and onto the landing. When he got near to this bodiless shade, it vanished from the landing. A girl leaned over in the hallway to pick up a piece of trash she had dropped on the floor. She heard a laugh and assumed it was a friend of hers behind her, laughing at her and the unflattering picture she presented from the back as she bent to retrieve her paper. She straightened up and turned around to give the friend a dirty look. The hall behind her was vacant, the corridor of lockers stretching out into the dark at the end of the hall. She squinted and peered more closely down the hall; her tentative "Hello?" was met by what she described as an awful laugh echoing up the narrow passageway flanked by empty classrooms and closed lockers.

Nearly forty years ago a new high school was built, and the old high school building became the middle school. But Billie's pranks and ghostly presence in the building have continued unabated. Legend has it that the ghost hides in a balcony projection room above the lunch room in an area that was originally the gym and auditorium. Gym equipment left out in readiness for the next day's classes has been found to be moved, or in some instances confiscated, by an unseen presence. Summer activity equipment has seemingly relocated itself from one storage locker into another. As in the past, a disembodied female voice has been heard speaking in various locations throughout the school, speaking in a tone always just below the level where words could be distinguished, but loud enough so that attempts to locate the source could be initiated. Of course, the source of the disembodied voice has never been discovered.

Phyllis Hege, librarian at the Oxford Public Library, reports that the tales of the ghost continue up to the present. At the school, "the story is talked about all the time," she says. "When pipes bang in the middle hall near the projection/spotlight room, people say it is the ghost." The librarian also reported that the floor in the area of the projection room "always stays cold."

If the prankish spirit at the Oxford Middle School building is indeed that of Billie, then she has attempted to maintain a link with her past substantive life. Traditional legend at the school holds that Billie is always present at the annual Kayette slumber party held in the middle school lunchroom. Evidently, she descends from her perch in the balcony projection room and invisibly joins the girls in their night of gossip and fun.

One year during the festivities, the Kayette girls were telling ghost stories and giggling and laughing. Their laughter was interrupted by the muffled sounds of a voice or voices emanating from a classroom down the hall from the lunchroom. Their sponsor and several of the bravest girls left the safety of the group in the lunchroom and ventured out to explore the hallway and the surrounding rooms. As they drew near one particular door, the voices stopped, and complete silence descended on the hallway. The girls huddled closer to their adult sponsor. "Come on, girls," she said, "there's nothing to be afraid of. Someone's just in here having a little fun with us." She reached out to turn the door handle of the room, but it wouldn't budge. She jiggled it and the lock rattled. No sounds came from the room now, and the lights were off and the room was dark behind the locked door. The girls and the sponsor ran back to the lunchroom, and locked *their* door for the rest of the night.

When the story of the Kayettes' nighttime fright was told around at school the next week, some adults and students scoffed at the idea that the experience was anything more than imagined sounds in a classroom during a slumber party highlighted by silliness and ghost stories. Some said it was no doubt "air in the furnace vents" or "the building's heat and plumbing pipes expanding and contracting." But there were plenty of others in the building, teachers and students alike, who were convinced that Billie was back, just playing some harmless pranks on her pals in the Kayettes, joining in the "spirit" of the evening like any other fun-loving fifteen-year-old.

The Ghostly Trumpeter of Paola High School

More than anything in the world, the young boy wanted to be first trumpet in the Paola High School band. Like the old Avis rental car slogan, the teenager could say he tried harder than his number one competitor—and he did. The boy worked and worked, practiced and practiced for hours, all to no avail. He just wasn't able to unseat the first chair and take his place as the best trumpeter in the high school band. But still he kept trying.

One night, the band had gone out to the football stadium to march and practice their routines for the half-time show of the next Friday night's football game. The boy was about to go out onto the field, trumpet in hand, when the band director called him by name. A piece of equipment had been left behind at the school. The band director knew the boy was dependable and conscientious, so he tapped him to return to the school quickly, retrieve the equipment, and get back to the stadium as soon as possible so that practice wouldn't be delayed very long.

The boy left immediately. Back at the school, he dashed into the building and hurried to the stage where band class met. Above the stage was a storage room where the band equipment was kept. A somewhat narrow, winding flight of stairs led up to the storage room. The boy sprinted up the metal stairs and grabbed the necessary equipment. He turned around and started racing down the stairs. Band shoes and a heavy band uniform do not lend agility, especially rushing down a narrow flight of steep and curved steps. The boy tripped, caught his foot, missed a step—no one ever knew for sure what actually made him fall. Regardless, he lost his balance, falling to his death at the bottom of the steps. There he lay, on the stage, just a few feet from the first chair in the trumpet section he had aspired to for so long.

Everyone in town knew the boy and his tenacity and his dogged determination to make first chair with his beloved trumpet. Not long after his death, people began to report hearing ghostly music issuing from the front door of the high school building when they would drive or walk past it. Especially on windy days, the sounds of a wailing trumpet could be heard blowing with the wind, swirling up and around the building's facade, mournfully blowing the same note, sustained, over and over. Individuals with perfect pitch have even claimed that the note heard is a B flat, the pitch that trumpet players tune to.

The legend of Paola's ghostly trumpeter has swirled around the school like the trumpeter's music for at least forty years, and possibly longer. Like many durable local legends of this type, the story has had many versions and differing plot lines over the years. In the 1970s, at least three different plots of the story coexisted and seemed to be equally acceptable as the "true" version, depending on who was telling the tale. The version recounted above apparently was the most widely told, but another story of the phantom trumpeter of Paola High popular at the same time had one very different element: the main character.

The second version of the story named the band director as the musical ghost. "When the building was new," it went, "there was a certain band director here." The well-loved director was a talented musician, teacher, and bandleader, and the trumpet was his specialty. "One day his students received word that their band director suffered a concussion." It seems the unfortunate man had sustained a blow to the head from a bad fall he had taken the night before. Some of his students went to his house to see him and pay their respects. Although he had been unconscious for some time after his accident, he had recovered consciousness and was eager to see his students and receive visitors. The director was "in a jolly mood" when his students entered the room, and some time was passed in talk of general school activities and goings-on, as well as shoptalk about band and the substitute band director who was filling in temporarily. The meeting ended with the injured band director's promising his students that he would return to school and band very soon.

The next morning, a somber announcement was made to the members of the band as soon as they had filed into the bandroom after the bell. Their beloved teacher and friend had died of complications from the concussion. He had passed away unexpectedly at home some time after the students had left his house. Among people who tell this version of the legend, "some say that this is when the ghostly trumpet began to sound" at the school. "Had he returned to school as he promised?" these people asked. Many believed so.

Still another version of this tale again appoints the student trumpeter as the lead character. This story also sends the boy off to the storage room above the stage, this time to find some misplaced band uniforms. But the winding stairs play no real role in this version: "Whatever happened, no one knows, for he was never seen again." The trumpet player disappeared, and the story speculates that the ghostly tooting heard in and around the school is the sound of the poor lost boy calling for help in the only way he can.

Outside of the central figure, the element that most noticeably changes from story to story is the item the boy is sent to find or retrieve from the storage room. Sometimes it is sheet music, sometimes a band uniform or uniforms, sometimes a lost musical instrument. Other times it is simply band equipment or just equipment.

Another changing element is found in the actual cause of death for the trumpeter, be he a student or a band director. Most common is a concussion or a blow to the head, most likely from falling down the winding stairs to the storage room. But, as evidenced above, sometimes in his incarnation as a student, the trumpeter simply gets lost in the school, in the stage area, or in the storage room, never to be seen again—only heard. However, another version purports that the ghostly trumpeter was a student who practiced so long and so hard in his quest for perfection and the first chair designation that he suffered a heart attack and died from the stress of his efforts. An extension of this story even has him keeling over in the main hall of the high school where he was blowing his horn in a marathon practice session that had lasted well into the night. Now, this story goes, anyone who drives by the school at night can hear the sounds of the tenacious trumpeter serenading himself and anyone else in the vicinity with his final solo.

Many individuals verify that what seems to be the sonorous sounding of a trumpet can be heard at certain times when one passes by the old high school. One explanation for the monotonous sounding of the B-flat tone blames the Baptist Church across the street. This theory posits that the sound is caused by "wind from the speed of the car, rebounding between the high school and the Baptist Church." Although this conjecture would seem to make about as much scientific sense as the ghost of a dead boy tooting a trumpet in the front hall, it is an honest attempt to explain what appears to be an unnatural phenomenon. The ultimate rationalization for the residual bouncing B-flat car-wind sounds is the observation that "before the church was built in the 1950s, there was no trumpet sound, but people tend to forget that fact because the stories are so good." At least one portion of the hypothesis is correct: The stories *are* so good.

The old makeup and storage room above the stage is a real room, but the steps leading up to it have long since been removed, and the doors to the room have been nailed shut. It is not commonly known that the room still exists, but it does. Perhaps it should be checked for evidence of the ghostly trumpeter. A final version of the story has the boy walled up forever behind the doors of the room, a Rip Van Winkle–like figure slumbering through eternity in the tiny room, awakening only to periodically play a mournful tune on his horn.

This variation tells the story of the same second chair trumpet player practicing his tunes ad nauseum to win the first chair prize. When everyone was sick of hearing him, he was banished up to the old makeup room above the stage where the sounds would at least be muffled. Exhausted from his nonstop tootling, the boy fell into a sound sleep. So soundly did he sleep (he must have been comatose, actually) that he did not know that the powers-that-be at the school had decided to close up the old room permanently (and evidently immediately). The doors were walled up, the stairs were removed, all while the trumpeter slept away in ignorance. Perhaps his hearing had been affected by all the blasts from his trumpet reverberating around inside that little room. Anyway, Rip Van Trumpeter continued to slumber, now suspended in mid-air above the stage, walled in with his trumpet and his snores. The end of this variant of the legend concludes that, on windy nights, "when you go past the high school's main door, you can hear him playing up there," snug in his personal practice chamber, eternally sounding his tuning note, perpetually playing his songs in his never-ending quest for perfection and first chair.

Death Takes a Holiday:
The Salina Central High Stage Ghost

Joyce was a petite, blonde beauty and one of the most popular girls at Washington High School in Salina in 1949. She was the treasurer of the Student Council, a member of the Honor Society, and the 1948 Homecoming Queen. According to a former classmate, Joyce "was always the girl every boy wished to be his girlfriend." Before graduating in the spring of 1949, she also won the part of the female lead in the all-school play, *Death Takes a Holiday*.

Joyce's character, Grazia, was a metaphor for kindness and beauty. The author of the original 1928 play, Alberto Casella, had death, personified as the character Death, take a three-day "holiday" on earth from his duties as the grim reaper. He fell in love with the winsome Grazia after "saving" her from dying in a car wreck. When Death's holiday ended, so did Grazia's life, as Death took her with him at the end of the play.

The Washington High production of *Death Takes a Holiday* was a success, partly because of Joyce's winning performance as Grazia. After graduating from Washington that spring, Joyce enrolled at Kansas University, and she left Salina for Lawrence in the fall of 1949 to begin her freshman year. In the spring of 1950, almost exactly one year after her role as the ill-fated Grazia, Joyce was killed in a head-on crash between the convertible in which she was riding and a gasoline transport truck on Kansas Highway 10 between Lawrence and Kansas City. Death was not on a holiday that day: Joyce was thrown from the car and died instantly; the other three young people in the car, all students at Kansas University, were also killed. Joyce, like Grazia, was eighteen when Death claimed her for his own.

It is hard to pinpoint exactly when the stories of a benevolent ghost haunting the high school stage began. But certainly the macabre coincidence of "life imitating art" in such a tragic fashion for Joyce was a strong impetus for the formation of the legend, as were the similarities between Joyce and the character of Grazia in terms of beauty, personality, and age. Tales began circulating of the ghostly figure of a beautiful girl, dressed in a pink dress similar to that supposedly worn by Joyce in her last performance at the school, seen wandering high above the stage in the catwalk area or glimpsed moving about the auditorium or behind the main stage curtain.

Two years after the accident, the new Salina High School building opened, replacing the old Washington High. Legend holds that the theater curtain from the stage at Washington High was moved to the new building and that the ghost moved with it. Although it seems unlikely that the old curtain was moved (the former Washington school and its auditorium were used for community theater for years after the new high school opened, curtain apparently intact), this remains a firm tenet of the legend, and so it is generally accepted as fact.

Salina High became Salina Central High School, but still the stories of the theater ghost persisted. Always helpful, the ghost was credited with whispering lines to forgetful thespians, steadying actors about to trip, and blinking lights at appropriate times. Oftentimes the stories mentioned a "face" that could be seen in the old theater curtain, the supposed visible "proof" that Joyce had come along with the old curtain to the new school.

A 1972 graduate of Salina Central recalled that the old curtain, supposedly the holdover from Washington School, was "ratty and torn." In a story entitled "The Ghost of Central" in the 1982 Salina Central yearbook, this graduate recalled details of the strange silhouette known as "the face in the curtain": "On the stageside lining there was a stain, a water spot, that resembled a face real clearly. . . . The strange thing was it was different at times, a full face once, then a profile, then three quarters." This individual also vividly recalled what she felt was an encounter a friend of hers had with the watchful ghost. The friend was on the "grid," or catwalk, high above the stage, crawling along because there was no room to walk. It was dark and dangerous in this position, since the grid was in an area above the stage lights that contained holes and openings and could prove to be treacherous to anyone moving along it. Suddenly the girl "crawled into a real distinct cold spot." Then she "felt something that felt like a hand on her shoulder holding her in place. She stopped and creeped forward to find a hole in the grid she wasn't aware of, six inches in front of her."

Obviously, the impression left by this experience is that someone (or something) physically intervened to protect the young girl who was in imminent danger of falling and seriously injuring or killing herself. Was it Joyce? This informant felt that it could have been. Regardless, she remained convinced, some ten years after her experience, that "there is some type of force in the Central auditorium." "When you're in the theater there is a general feeling of someone else being around," she said. "There is a presence of something else. But, I was never afraid, I always felt [it was] benevolent. It could be Joyce. I don't know what it is."

Over time, the stories of the protective theater ghost continued to grow and be embellished by the students at Central, and variations were passed down from class to class, particularly among the drama students. In 1977, a Kansas State University student who had recently graduated from Salina Central told her version of the story to the *Kansas State Collegian* newspaper: "It was around Christmas years back. [The drama students] were doing the play *Death Takes a Holiday* and there was a part in it where a girl was decapitated in a car accident. The girl never got to play her part and was replaced by her understudy. Before opening night she was in a car accident and decapitated just like the character in the play." Some of the details have been changed in this version (the performance at Christmas instead of spring, the girl being killed before the play rather than after, the explicit mention of decapitation), but the basic story, although embellished, remains the same. This source also asserted that the ghost of the doomed actress "returns whenever a play opens," and she indicated that "technical workers and light crews have reported seeing a white shadow" who plays pranks such as causing all of the auditorium seats to come "flopping down."

In 1982, the drama director at that time, Richard Junk, tired of all the stories and decided that restaging the infamous play, *Death Takes a Holiday,* would help bring about an end to all the rumors. "Knowing the play was never put on here [Salina Central]," he was quoted as saying in the yearbook story, "I personally don't hold much credence to the entire story. In the last two or three years the story has been blown out of proportion." One unshakable story asserted that school officials would never allow the restaging of the play because of the ghost. Junk also wanted to prove that particular rumor to be false. As he recalled for a *Salina Journal* article in 1984, he was determined to do something about it: "It was getting out of control. Every time I turned around someone was talking about it."

The play was presented in the spring of 1982 in the Central auditorium, thirty-three years after Joyce starred as Grazia in the Salina High production. No mishaps occurred, but the stories of Joyce and her ghostly presence were not laid to rest. "We had absolutely no trouble with it," Junk recalled in an interview with the *Salina Journal* in 1984, "and I thought it would end. Obviously, it didn't work." Junk also expressed his opinion that the persistence of the story among the students is due not to a belief in the ghost but to the fact that they enjoy the story—"It makes them feel special."

Several drama students were also interviewed in the 1984 newspaper article about the legendary ghost of the Central theater. One senior indicated that he *did* believe in the ghost and reiterated that "everyone in drama does." He also recounted an incident when he was alone in the theater and heard a soft voice calling his name. "I turned around," he said, "and no one was there. . . ." However, a junior thespian dispelled the idea that all members of the drama class believed in the ghost of Joyce: "It's just a good story. A lot of theaters have ghosts. . . . I'm not sure if anyone really believes in it."

Whether anyone really believes the story or not, it continues to be perpetuated by individuals who have come in contact with the legend of Salina Central's ghost. A current version collected from a Washburn University student from Salina even reveals the belief that *multiple* phantoms haunt the backstage area of the Central stage, all the ghosts of former high school actors. Students at Salina Central maintain a scrapbook that contains articles about the legend and the ghost of Joyce.

Brad McDonald is the current director of theater at Salina Central High School. He verified that the story was still very much alive in his department: "None of my students claims to have encountered anything unusual. But when anything goes wrong, or anything unusual happens, we tend to say, 'Joyce is at it again.' We tend to crack jokes about it. Eventually every year, we get to talking about her."

According to McDonald, this is how the legend has sustained itself—through oral sharing of the story with each year's new crop of drama students. Although McDonald said he knew of custodians in the building "who have claimed to experience things while working late at night in the building," he insisted that "my kids haven't experienced anything." The theater director felt that knowing the story of Joyce was an initiation ritual or bonding experience among the drama and theater students. "Maybe eventually we'll make it a requirement," he joked. "For anyone to graduate they have to recite the story of Joyce!"

Unlike the former drama director who was annoyed by the stories, Brad

McDonald seems to accept the legend as part of the theater tradition at his school. Like the former director, however, McDonald is considering a re-staging of the play that has itself played an important role in the legends of Salina high schools: "There is a possibility that I might decide to produce the *Death Takes a Holiday* play again. I always keep the schedule a secret until we annouce the next season's productions at the spring banquet—but we may restage it at some point."

Interestingly enough, the timing for another production of the play might be about right. Late in 1996, *Entertainment Weekly* revealed that Universal pictures was planning a remake of the 1934 film, *Death Takes a Holiday,* to be entitled *Meet Joe Black.* The reported star of the film, signed for $17.5 million to play the title role, is a former young thespian from Kickapoo High School in Springfield, Missouri—Brad Pitt.

George and the Night Nurse:
Kansas State University

The old Saint Mary's Hospital building at Eleventh and Fremont became a spacious new home for the Delta Sigma Phi fraternity at Kansas State in 1955, but there were two "things" remaining from the old hospital that the brothers didn't know about when they first moved in: George, the last patient to die in the hospital, and the Night Nurse, a candle-wielding angel of mercy who roams the first-floor hallways as she was accustomed to doing on the night shift.

George, an elderly gentleman, met his demise in what would have been a comedy of errors if it had not been so tragic. A group of elderly patients was being transferred from the third floor of Saint Mary's to the new hospital. While waiting his turn to be transported, George somehow managed to roll off his bed and become trapped between the wall and the bed frame. Wedged in and unable to move, George tried to call for help. But his voice, weak to begin with, was muffled by the bedclothes as well as the wall, and very soon his plaintive cries ceased altogether. An orderly sent to fetch George, finding his bed empty, assumed that another attendant had already bundled George up on a gurney and taken him down to the waiting ambulance for transport. Little did he know that George was not only bundled up but bunched up as well, right under the orderly's nose. Under poor George's nose was a wad of covers and only a very small air pocket. Sometime during the night, George's air ran out completely, his old lungs exhausted from struggling to breathe. George died before morning, suffocated in his own sheets.

George has not proven to be a very apparent ghost, at least not visually. Although never seen, he is often heard as he cries out loudly at nights, presumably calling for someone to come help him untangle himself from the side of his bed. George must manage to disengage himself from time to time, for various activities that can only be ascribed to a ghost occur at regular intervals in the hospital cum fraternity house.

Lights have gone on and off; locked doors and windows have opened and closed. Some of the men who have lived in the house claim that George gets bored at times and, from the sounds of it, uses the third-floor hallway as his own personal bowling alley. Not only was he evidently a bowler when he was alive, but George seems to have had a penchant for being Mr. Home Improvement as well. On occasion he has been known to perform helpful tasks around the house. For example, it is believed that George is responsible for the repair of some broken clocks that were at one time just "lying around the premises."

Most amazing, George's ghost appears to be an ardent Trekkie. (The more politically correct term, at least among ardent "Star Trek" fans, is actually Trekker.) One fraternity member, in an interview with the *Manhattan Mercury* in 1985, illuminated this claim: "In 1973 there was an ice storm. The electricity was off all along our street, but every day at four in the afternoon the electricity would come back on in our house and stay on until "Star Trek" was over. No other house around us had electricity. We figured that George wanted to watch the show."

As Mr. Spock would say: *fascinating.*

George's phantasmic companion in the halls of Delta Sigma Phi is a taciturn, stern-faced female nurse who is perpetually on the night shift in the corridors of the former hospital. The Night Nurse roams the hallways of the fraternity at night, making her rounds, carrying her medicine tray in one hand and a lit candle in the other. Unlike George, her ghostly cohort, the nurse has been experienced as a shadowy vision, seen walking the first-floor halls late at night or sometimes wheeling a medical cart filled with assorted supplies and medicines. The last reported sighting of the nurse dates back to the 1960s, so firsthand experience with her unearthly nighttime rounds is confined to alumni of the fraternity who lived in the house at that time.

George, on the other hand, may still be checked in at the old hospital. According to Kyle Klenke, a 1996–1997 senior studying management at Kansas State and an active member of Delta Sigma Phi, the only recent antics blamed on George all have to do with televisions sets: "The latest thing [attributed to the ghost] would be TVs turning on and off unexpectedly, or channels skipping around or being skipped over." Although George seems to have tired of creating too much commotion around the house, he still is quite active in tales that are told and retold within the fraternity. "The stories still circulate," said Klenke. "And the house still has bats that live in the attic, and in the old elevator shaft. That adds to the story."

The legend is told to rushees when they come to the house and mentioned to visitors or guests who are curious about the building and its history. Although the spirit of George is mostly evoked nowadays through practical jokes played on pledges and other naive members, the legend of George remains very vivid. According to the stories, "you can't see George, you just hear him," observed Klenke. "It's supposed to sound like thunder, or like a bowling alley on the top floor at nights."

Klenke's observation is from hearsay, not personal experience, since George hasn't done much bowling in recent years. But he evidently hasn't given up one of his favorite pastimes: television. George obviously doesn't need a remote control to change the channel or flip off the set if a program doesn't please him. Maybe the men of Delta Sigma Phi should check and see what show is playing the next time a television set abruptly flickers on spontaneously. If it is "Star Trek Voyager" or "Deep Space 9," it's bound to be George.

Virginia, the Ghost of Sigma Nu:
University of Kansas

"The world of strife shut out, the world of love shut in." This enigmatic quote is engraved in Gothic letters on a plaque set into an imposing stone fireplace in the living room of the Sigma Nu fraternity house at the University of Kansas. According to the legend passed down from pledge class to pledge class since 1922, the cremated ashes of a young girl named Virginia were walled into the fireplace behind the plaque in 1911.

Virginia died in the house in a particularly ghastly fashion. She was found hanged in the third-floor ballroom—some say from a crystal chandelier; some say from overhead pipes above the small stage. The puzzle of her death remains unsolved, although varying versions of the legend speculate that it was clearly murder or murder arranged to look like suicide.

The house was built in 1907 by Walter Stubbs, governor of Kansas from 1908 until 1912. Stubbs, a Lawrence building contractor, was reportedly a tall, powerfully built man with unruly red hair and a "big booming voice." Before becoming governor, he served as Speaker of the House in the Kansas legislature. One evening in April 1911, so the story goes, the governor left the statehouse in Topeka and returned to his lavish three-story home in Lawrence near the University of Kansas campus. There he found Virginia, an eighteen-year-old maid at the house, swinging at the end of a rope in the ballroom and quite dead.

Some variations of the legend say that Virginia was the governor's ward, not his maid. Most variants hint at a scandalous affair and a jealous wife. One version gives a graphic description of the governor's wife, huddled in the corner of the ballroom below Virginia's hanging body, gone quite "loony." Most renditions of the tale purport that poor Virginia was cremated, her ashes secretly entombed in the fireplace by the governor. The cryptic plaque is supposedly the marker that bears witness to Virginia's final place of rest.

But according to the men of Sigma Nu, even if Virginia's ashes are resting in the fireplace, her ghost has been nothing if not restless over the last seventy-five years. The governor sold his house in Lawrence to the Sigma Nu fraternity in 1922. Since that time, seventy-five pledge classes and hundreds of brothers have learned of the stories of Virginia, some of them experiencing her ghostly activities firsthand.

Often in April, the anniversary month of her death, Virginia comes out from the fireplace to wander the halls of Sigma Nu in her white gown or run up and down the stairs from the fireplace to the ballroom, and back again. On a weekend night in April 1978, two Sigma Nu brothers were studying late in their room. The house was quiet and nearly empty, as most of the residents had gone out for the evening. The quiet was broken, however, when two sets of footsteps could plainly be heard sprinting up the front stairs to the area of the third-floor bedrooms where the ballroom used to be, running down the hall, and clattering back down the rear stairs, ending in the vicinity of the living room fireplace.

Amused, the two young men assumed that several of their friends had returned from a night of partying and were engaged in a spirited game of tag. They closed their books and went out into the hall to apprehend the revelers. The footsteps ascended the front stairs again and began their race down the hall. They stopped abruptly in front of the astonished men. But instead of confronting a couple of inebriated brothers, as they had expected, the two Sigma Nus found themselves confronting . . . nothing. Empty air stood in the nonexistent shoes that had been making the ruckus.

Thoroughly unnerved, the two men began a search of the house to discover the source of the footsteps and noise. All they disturbed was the sleep of several of their snoring brothers in other rooms. During their search of the third floor, they entered the bedroom that occupied the place where legend held that Virginia's body had been suspended from the ceiling. The residents of the room were gone, and the space was empty and dark. They turned on the light and checked the room, but everything seemed secure. As the men turned to leave the room, the door handle began to rattle. Then the door started vibrating. The men left the room and closed the door. Still the door rattled and shook. As they moved away from the door in consternation, the shaking ceased, and the light behind the door flickered out. They turned and took a few steps back toward the door, and the rattling resumed.

One of the Sigma Nus caught in this ghostly game was interviewed by the *Lawrence Journal-World* in October 1982. "The closer we got to the door," he said, "the more violently it would shake. I have to admit," he continued, "we were really terrified at that point." Terrified maybe, but they were still convinced that pranking Sigma Nus had to be behind the disturbance. They approached the door once more, seized the handle, and swung the door open. Still no one. The men never solved the mystery of the running footsteps and the rattling door, but they came to believe that at least one of the pranksters that night was Virginia. The second time they entered "Virginia's room," there was "a funny feeling that came over both of us," one said. The *Journal-World* reported that "the hairs on the backs of their necks stood up . . . and they felt something like 'a heavy static electricity in the air.'"

From the 1920s on, numerous Sigma Nu brothers who have lived in the chapter house on Sigma Nu Place have reported similar experiences with the paranormal in the building. Legend and tradition within the fraternity credit the ghost of Virginia with any suspected supernatural visitations. Although additions have been made to the house in the nearly eight decades since the Sigma Nus (and Virginia) took possession of it, legend also dictates that Virginia haunts only within a certain circumscribed area of the building.

Ryan Smartt, a senior business major at the University of Kansas slated to graduate in the spring of 1997 and the 1996 president of the Sigma Nu house, explained in an interview: "According to the legend, these occurrences can only take place within the original structure. Additions have been made to the house by the fraternity, but it is not possible for encounters to take place outside what was the original house."

Smartt remembered that when he was a freshman in the house in 1993, several of the senior men had stories about the ghost and house members who had had "experiences" with her. "One guy over Christmas break was the only one in the house. While he was putting some stuff away, he heard a radio going off and on in the basement. He was on the second floor and the music or sounds were very loud. He went down to check, but there was no radio in the basement. After he checked, he heard no more sounds." "Another guy," he continued, "was in the house over the summer. He was by himself, walking down the hall on the third floor. He looked and saw the figure of a woman in a white dress walking down the stairs. He looked again and nothing was there."

Both of these occurrences were told to Smartt by seniors and would have taken place in approximately 1991 or 1992, he thinks. Smartt was in residence at the Sigma Nu house from 1993 through spring of 1997, but "since I've been here," he said, "I haven't heard of anything happening." Although Virginia's ghost doesn't seem to be currently active in the house, the story of her legend is still actively told, according to Smartt: "It's a fun little story to go along with all the other traditions."

Virginia's crypt, more commonly called the fireplace, is still readily seen just inside the side door of the fraternity house off from the carport deck. Opposite a wide, wooden stairway, the heavy stone fireplace looms over this entryway into the house. Originally double sided, with an opening on both sides, the fireplace is now walled over on the side that would open into what was formerly the dining room. That room is now called the music room. An iron bar made to hold a cooking pot in the early days originally swung from inside the fireplace into the dining room area. The bar can now only swing into the entryway. Logically, there is no reason for the old dining room side of the fireplace to be walled up.

Above the fireplace is the mysterious plaque, an artifact described by a former University of Kansas student in a Halloween 1982 *Lawrence Journal-World* article as "a major heebie-jeebie," like something "you see in Hitchcock movies." In *Psycho,* the shocker was "mother" upstairs in the bedroom in her rocker; in the Sigma Nu house, Virginia is upstairs in her room, too, but she's also downstairs in the fireplace. "The world of love" may be shut in with her there, but at least every April, Virginia escapes her ashy mausoleum in the Sigma Nu foyer to fly up the stairs to the grand ballroom and her gallows.

The Musical Ghost of McCray Hall:
Pittsburg State University

Spreading the pages of his composition around him, the fourth-year music student sighed and took another sip from a Styrofoam cup of coffee perched on the edge of a book that was serving as a paperweight. It was nearing midnight, and he was still in the third-floor practice room in McCray Hall, trying to complete a musical piece that was due the next day as an assignment for a class.

A slight motion in the corner of the small practice room attracted his attention. He turned his head and looked into the shape of a face. It seemed like a face, except there were no features. No eyes looked back at him, no ears heard the amazed "huh!" that escaped his lips. No mouth registered a friendly smile or a threatening grimace. Only the blank, featureless visage of an empty face returned the student's stunned gaze into the black void that reason told him should have been the countenance of a living being.

The student closed his eyes and shook his head slowly as if casting off cobwebs or the last remnants of a dream. He opened his eyes and reluctantly looked toward the same corner of the room again. This time the corner was completely empty of any faces or forms; the practice room now appeared to contain only the young man, his coffee, and his composition.

Convinced that he had been working way too long and too hard on this assignment, the music student went back to work and completed the composition some time after midnight. He tossed his empty coffee cup in the trash, gathered up his papers and materials, and stood up to leave the room. He glanced back over his shoulder toward the corner again and was relieved to see that nothing frightening or out of the ordinary was lurking there. He turned out the light and left the room.

Making his way through the dark building, he descended to the first floor. But as he stepped into the first-floor hallway, his nightmare began again. Suddenly the air was "thick" all around him. Too terrified to run, the student managed to keep moving through the hallway, but the presence that had surrounded him impeded his forward motion, and the young man fought to stay on his feet and continue on his path toward the front door. He finally gained the door and pushed it open, but the heavy entity that had surrounded him since he had stepped off the stairway between the first and second floors remained with him as he burst outside into the chill autumn air. The cold reinvigorated him, and he conquered the inertia that had slowed him down. He began running, and about ten feet from the building, he felt his body pull out of whatever had had him in its grasp, like an insect wriggling free from a spider's web. He sprinted to his car in the parking lot, certain that he would never again work or practice alone late at night at McCray Hall.

The music student's late-night composing was interrupted in the fall of 1993. Although he claimed to have heard a couple of stories about the building being haunted before his experience that night, the student said he had passed them off until he had his frightening face-to-nonface encounter. Stories of the ghost of McCray Hall had circulated for quite a few years prior to 1993, especially among the students and faculty of the Pittsburg State Music Department and among the custodians who cleaned the building.

An article in the Pittsburg *Morning Sun* in October 1995 reported the experiences of two custodians, one woman and one man, who reportedly "have had many encounters with the ghost." The female custodian had a work history of fourteen years with the university and related numerous occasions on which she had felt the presence of the ghost or endured its antics. Most eerie were the times when she had heard piano or organ music emanating from rooms or floors that were empty or deserted. Practice room 307 hosted the ghostly pianist several times, but when the custodian checked the room, no one was ever inside. She had also heard organ music being played on the fourth floor at a time when she was certain McCray Hall was vacant. Each time a ghostly concert had begun when she was in the building, the custodian had checked the room or floor from which the music seemed to be issuing. Each time as she approached the area, the music stopped. Often, she had passed through an "ice cold spot" when she entered a room where she had heard the ghost.

On one occasion, the custodian was entering the third-floor hallway when she caught a glimpse of what she described as a thirtyish, dark-haired man dressed in khaki pants and a plaid shirt walking into a room down the hall. Since it was after hours and all the rooms were supposedly locked, the custodian hastened to the door through which the odd figure had disappeared. She tried the door handle, and it was locked. She used her master key and opened the door. The room was empty—the man had vanished.

The male custodian, who claimed that he "almost quit as custodian because of all the unexplained happenings," had also consistently encountered "a very active presence" at McCray Hall since going to work for the university in 1989. He, too, had experienced "penetrating cold spots" and ghostly music that would cease as soon as he neared the spot where the phantom musician was playing. Lights just turned off spontaneously flipped back on. Doors to unoccupied rooms slammed. Door latches on doors to locked rooms moved. One evening the ghost demonstrated its musical versatility by expanding its repertoire of musical instruments. The custodian began hearing the distinctive sounds of kettledrums being played all over the building. He checked the downstairs locker where the drums were normally stored, and they were all in their places, silent and undisturbed. Just as suddenly as it had begun, the drumming stopped.

Another evening, the custodian had moved the chairs in room 318 at McCray so that he could sweep the floor. When he had finished sweeping, he arranged all eighty chairs in perfect rows. He left the room briefly to get a drink. When he returned, the chairs had been rearranged to accommodate an aisle down the middle of the rows of chairs. The custodian was certain that no one else had been in the room, and he had heard no sounds of chairs being moved. Nothing else in the room had been disturbed. Although he described the experience as a "losing my mind type of thing," he did admit in the interview with the *Morning Sun* that ever after he would arrange the chairs in that room with an aisle down the middle.

The male custodian also felt that he had had an encounter with a physical manifestation of the ghost. Whereas the woman custodian saw a male figure vanish into a room known as the break room, the male custodian claimed to have seen "a female form in a red dress" walk into the same break room and close the door. He followed her into the room, but when he entered, she had disappeared and the room was empty.

In view of the fact that a wide variety of supernatural events has been experienced in McCray Hall and that ghostly figures of both sexes have been seen, one might assume that more than one ghost wanders the hallways of McCray. But consistently the ghostly manifestations in the hall building have been perceived by the students and the custodians to be the work of only one ghost, albeit a shape-shifter with a large repertory of tricks and musical talents. The phantom's favorite activity, however, continues to be connected to music, particularly playing the piano. Many students have related tales of hearing the phantom of the music hall.

Dr. Gene Vollen, now retired, joined the Pittsburg State University Music Department in 1970 and served as chairman of the department from 1978 to 1995. Dr. Vollen is quite familiar with the ghostly legend of McCray Hall: "I have seen nothing firsthand, but most stories were reported to me. There was some discussion of it before I started as chair in 1978, but it became more of a common story after that time, in the late 1970s, at least to my knowledge."

According to Dr. Vollen, the ghost went through a messy phase of bringing the outdoors inside or at least a phase where it liked to antagonize the custodians in McCray Hall: "There was a period in the 1970s when little piles of dirt, or sand, would be found around, behind the doors. It was often suspected that one custodian was trying to make another one mad, but nothing was proven." However, most people who worked or attended classes in the hall attributed the odd little piles of debris to the mischievous poltergeist who haunted the building.

What does Dr. Vollen think of the stories of the ghost? "I've always kind of smiled and said, 'oh, yeah,' but I have no evidence one way or the other."

The evidence for the existence of the musically inclined ghost of McCray Hall may not be compelling enough for Dr. Vollen, but other individuals who have been treated to personal piano, organ, or kettledrum concerts certainly feel convinced of the ghost's presence in the building. And any students working late in McCray, alone in a practice room on the third floor, absorbed in their practicing or music until a tiny movement over in the corner draws their attention . . . any students who turn and peer into the faceless void that forms the outline of some phantasmic *thing* hovering over the piano will surely have evidence enough to clear out of the room quickly, making way for the McCray Hall ghost to play a tune or two.

Earl, the Brown Grand Theatre Ghost

"Four years ago I became the first, and perhaps one of only two persons, to see the ghost." With this opening sentence, Susan Sutton, president of the Brown Grand Theatre in Concordia, began an incredible accounting of personal experiences with Earl, the resident ghost of the

Brown Grand. In a June 19, 1996, letter, Susan recounted her initial encounter with Earl in the autumn of 1992: "Sitting in the house during a late-night rehearsal of a college play, a student sitting across the aisle from me suddenly glanced toward the balcony. Noticing the strange look on his face, I turned to look in the same direction. There, silhouetted in a window was a figure of a man wearing a frock coat and top hat. His hands appeared to be in the pockets of his coat. I quickly turned back to the student, who asked, 'Did you see what I saw?' I said that I had, but when we turned to look again, the figure was gone. The only possible sign of him was an open door above the balcony stairs that can only be reached by ladder. This door is kept latched, but on this fall night, it had been strangely opened."

The man in the antiquated frock coat and top hat gazing toward the stage of the theater was presumed to be Earl, the phantom of the Brown Grand. The ghost has identified itself, by means of a Ouija board, as Earl Van Dorn Brown, son and only child of Colonel Napoleon Bonaparte Brown. Colonel N. B. Brown was a wealthy Concordia banker and the builder, in 1906 and 1907, of the opulent Brown Grand Theatre.

According to published accounts, local Concordia legend has Napoleon Bonaparte Brown arriving in town in 1876 with "a suitcase full of money, a beautiful bride, and a thirst for the high interest rates of the midwest." In 1877 he established the N. B. Brown and Company bank, the first bank in Concordia, and with the implementation of a 10 percent interest rate on loans, Brown increased his personal wealth so rapidly that he liquidated his business in 1883 and retired. By the time he died in 1910 at the age of seventy-six, Colonel Brown was the richest man in the county.

In 1905, Brown determined to build a lavish new opera house in downtown Concordia, a replacement for the old theater (which had been condemned as a firetrap) and a monument to the Brown name. Providing the financial backing for the $40,000 edifice was Colonel Brown's main contribution to the erection of this imposing edifice. The colonel's son, Earl Van Dorn Brown, who had been only five years old when his family arrived in Concordia, was the chief design engineer, architect, foreman of the construction, and manager of the project. His father did not even set foot in the opera house until opening night, September 17, 1907.

The colonel was an imposing figure around Concordia, sporting "piercing blue eyes, white flowing hair, luxuriantly drooping mustache, and aristocratic mien." A native Virginian, he had a medical degree, and after settling in Concordia and opening his bank, he also obtained a law degree, going on to become a state senator in 1880. His wife, Katherine, originally from New York, was a leader in Concordia society and active in town affairs.

Earl V. D. Brown shared his father's dreams for Concordia and for the magnificent stone and brick Renaissance-style theater that would bear their name. Earl was born in Missouri in 1871 and was described as "a handsome rake, his mother's darling, and the town's problem child." After attending (and being kicked out of) several colleges, he eventually graduated from Harvard Law School. When construction began on the Brown Grand in 1906, Earl was city attorney for Concordia, but he resigned his position, in part to allow himself more time to devote to the planning and managing of the theater. Pictures of Earl verify his description as a dashing young man with piercing dark eyes, luxuriant dark hair and mustache, and movie star good looks—a turn-of-the-century Tom Selleck.

In 1901, Earl married his wife, Gertrude, in Boston. Beautiful, well-educated, and a talented musician and architect, Gertrude was a perfect match for Earl. She consulted with her husband on the plans for the Brown Grand and did much of the planning with the building's architects. Unfortunately, Earl's mother "loathed her daughter-in-law with a passion." Gertrude had beauty, charm, and sophistication—and worst of all, in Katherine's eyes, Gertrude had Earl. Gertrude confided to her housekeeper one time that "Earl had had many girl friends in Concordia, but his mother was too jealous for him to marry any of them."

The grand opening of the Brown Grand in 1907 was a spectacular, gala affair. Opera gowns, flowers, and jewels were de rigueur for the ladies, and top hats and frock coats on the gentlemen graced the elegant interior as one thousand patrons filled the plush green leather seats. Earl had a special surprise for his father on opening night: a massive drop curtain for the stage painted with a stunning copy of Vernet's *Napoleon at Austerlitz* painting, portraying Napoleon, on horseback, leading his army.

For the next three years, the fortunes of the Brown Grand echoed the fortunes of the Brown family. Opera and acting companies, musicians, lecturers, churches, educators, and philanthropic clubs kept Concordia's pride humming with activity, thanks to Earl Brown's expert management. Plays such as *Dr. Jekyll and Mr. Hyde, Parsifal, Faust,* and *Hamlet* played to packed houses; the age of live theater was at its peak. At the beginning of 1910, the Browns and the Brown Grand were at the pinnacle of their success in Concordia—by June, the tragic second act of the Brown family drama had begun.

On June 1, 1910, Colonel Napoleon Bonaparte Brown, old and ill by this time, died. The "largest funeral ever seen in Concordia" was held for him. Not quite sixteen months later, on September 30, 1911, Earl Van Dorn Brown was dead at the age of forty. Painful gallstones had compelled Earl to seek treatment at Penn Valley hospital in Kansas City. The surgery was successful, and he seemed to be recuperating well. However, peritonitis set in, and five days after surgery, with his wife, Gertrude, and mother, Katherine, by his side, he died.

If his father's funeral had been impressive, Earl's was over-the-top. Hundreds of townspeople met the special Pullman car carrying Earl's casket, and a procession accompanied the flower-draped coffin from the train station to the family home. Along Sixth Street, "the children of the grade schools stood in solid ranks with bared heads as the funeral procession passed through," and the final procession to the Brown family monument at the cemetery was "fully a mile long."

Colonel Brown had been admired and respected in town but had been described as an austere and "eccentric and selfish man." His son, however, was universally loved and revered for his generosity and kindness of spirit as well as his fun-loving nature. If the colonel and Katherine as a couple had been the head of Concordia business and society, Earl and Gertrude were the heart. The editor of the Concordia newspaper eulogized Earl: "He was 'one of our kind' in every walk of life, and he was not spoiled by his wealth. He was simply a great-hearted, neighborly man."

The fortunes of the theater fell as well after the deaths of the Brown men. The widows inherited the Brown Grand, but not wishing to take over its management themselves, they bequeathed it as a gift to the city of Concordia. By 1915, road shows were declining and so was the attendance at the theater. It became a financial burden to the city and thus was returned to the Brown family estate. Gertrude had since remarried, and her husband, Ray Green, took over the management of the theater from 1915 to 1925. But the advent of talkies and the decline of live theater resulted in the sale of the Brown Grand to the Concordia Amusement Company and its renovation into a movie house.

From 1925 until 1974 the once-proud opera palace remained a movie theater, showing the best of the silver screen to Concordians. In 1971, the year of Concordia's centennial, serious efforts toward restoration of the Brown Grand to its former glory began. With tremendous support from a small community numbering only about six thousand people, the full $500,000 needed was raised for the restoration of the Brown Grand. On

September 17, 1980, seventy-three years to the day after its initial grand opening, the fully restored theater was reopened with a restaging of the original opening night play, *The Vanderbilt Cup*. The centerpiece of the old theater, the impressive *Napoleon at Austerlitz* drop curtain, had been irreparably water damaged after a 1967 tornado, but it too was replaced (at a cost of $9,000) by a meticulously researched and executed replica. Colorful large framed playbills from the 1920s advertising some of the productions to play at the theater were used to grace the lobby areas.

The Brown Grand Theatre was no longer a faded lady, but a fully restored and beautifully renovated grande dame, revitalized to her former elegance and glory. With the return of the Brown Grand came also the return of her most ardent lover and supporter: Earl Brown.

Actually, Earl had made his presence around the theater known as far back as the 1960s, when the building was owned and managed by Jack Roney and operated as a movie house. Susie Haver, curator of the Brown Grand, recalled in an interview that the first time she ever heard about the ghost was in the late 1960s: "Mr. Roney lived on site at the theater in the dressing rooms area after he purchased it. Sometimes at night he would hear voices, somewhat like a board meeting, coming from the area of the bathroom. He would hear men talking—kind of a 'hubbub' of voices—and when he went towards the sound, it would move away." Haver also reported that sometimes when Roney drove by the theater at night, he would see lights. At times, the first employee to arrive in the mornings reported that windows were open and lights were on. Extra attention was then mandated to making sure things were locked up and turned off at nights, but lights still would be found on and windows found open the next day.

In addition to having ghostly board meetings in the 1960s, Earl seems to have been determined to get a jump start on the renovation process: Nails were discovered protruding from the walls and floors in odd locations. According to Susie Haver, employees in the 1960s and 1970s told of feeling a "presence" in the building and of being unnerved by the bizarre appearance of "barely pounded-in" nails in various places. "They would find nails driven in backstage—really long nails," she told me, "and others on the stairs and in the carpet. Two little nails were pounded in the proscenium arch, just barely pounded in. They fell out."

Susan Sutton's sighting of the apparition in the balcony was the first visual verification that Earl was attending performances once again, dressed in evening finery befitting the restored formality of his theater and its return to live theatrical performances. Illuminated by the light from the window, framed by the green velvet drapes, the ghost of Earl was sitting in (standing in) on rehearsals for a period play, *La Ronde,* a French drama being produced by the community college. On hearing of the figure observed in the balcony by Sutton and one of the students, other students went to look for the strangely dressed man or any indication of an intruder in the theater. According to Sutton, one student claimed to see "a blue glow," but, she said, "I didn't see it." The most telling piece of evidence was the unlatched lock on the little "door to nowhere," as it is called.

The "door to nowhere" is adjacent to what was originally the first projection booth in the theater. Behind the tiny paneled door is an empty space that was used for storage of materials when the theater was a movie house—film supplies, film spools, and so-called junk. The space is contained in a small area suspended above a stairway and between the walls of a staircase descending from the balcony level. The door literally "floats" between the walls overhead as one descends the staircase—the only way to reach the door, latched on the outside by an old-fashioned latch hook, is by way of a sizable ladder balanced precariously on the steps.

The night of the ghostly appearance in the balcony, the "door to nowhere," previously secured and locked, was found ajar, the latch lock unhooked. Oddly enough, projectionists in previous years had often reported feeling a "presence" coming downstairs on the east stairway from the gallery—right by the "door to nowhere."

The following summer of 1993, during production of a play, *Alto Part,* Susan Sutton, Susie Haver, and other individuals began playing around with a Ouija board that was being used as a prop in the play. According to Haver and Sutton, they used the board to try to garner information about the supposed "ghost" in the theater. The questions posed were all in fun, but quickly, according to Haver, the answers began to make "the hair on the back of our necks stand up":

Question: "Is it you Earl?"
Answer: "Of course."
Question: "Are you alone here?"
Answer: "No. Other spirits are here with me."
Question: "How many are with you?"
Answer: "Three."
Question: "Are they men?"
Answer: "No."
Question: "Are they women?"
Answer: "Yes."

Question: "Are you pleased with the restoration [of the theater]?"
Answer: "Yes, pleased with it."

Susan Sutton said that by this point the pointer on the Ouija board was "flying back and forth," mostly with yes and no responses, and spelling out short words.

Question: "Was it Earl we saw in the window?"
Answer: "Yes."
Question: "Are you doing the pranks in the building?"
Answer: "Yes."

Earl, always the ladies' man, also admitted that none of his female companions was his widow, Gertrude. In addition, he slyly described himself as the Phantom of the Opera.

During the Ouija session, Sutton said, she "got down and looked" under the board and under the table. No hands were touching the board, she insisted. The session with Earl lasted about fifteen minutes, during which time the plastic indicator on the board was active. After that, "it went cold." Haver admitted that the whole episode was rather "spooky," especially the strong feeling that it was really Earl communicating with them.

One of Susan Sutton's earliest experiences with what might be presumed to be "Earl the practical joker" was in the fall of 1986. She described what happened: "I was alone in the theater waiting for a welder to arrive and work on the construction of a *West Side Story* set. Suddenly, the lights and electricity went out on the stage. This was of particular concern as the welder needed 220 volts to run his equipment, and that was only to be found on the stage—which was totally dead. I quickly got on the phone to an electrician who arrived shortly and after a trip to the basement, had the electricity back on. On his way out, I asked what had been wrong. He informed me that someone had pulled the master switch located in the basement. Knowing full well that I was alone in the building, I asked him if it could have blown on its own. He replied, 'No,' that a person would have had to pull the large lever on the switch box."

One of the most recent expressions of Earl's playful nature occurred in the fall of 1995. Sutton related: "A three-inch piece of dowel began to spin on the floor of the stage during an evening of set building. Then, a dark shadow passed over me as I was looking down at [the dowel stick]. Try as we would, we could never get that dowel to spin with the flashing speed that we had observed. *Earl?*"

If it is Earl, then he tends to schedule his antics as the phantom of the Concordia opera house on a seasonal basis. The ghostly events that happen at the Brown Grand seem to occur most frequently in autumn, often during the fall theatrical production. Perhaps it is more than just coincidence that Earl Brown died in September and that the grand opening (and reopening) of his beloved opera house was also during that month.

Other stories about Earl are part of the legend of the ghost of the Brown Grand. An office manager was leaning up against a radiator one morning inside the theater building near the front doors. All of a sudden the interior doors burst open, then, after a pause, the outside doors flew open— as if several people had just walked out. Wind could not have caused this phenomenon: The heavy front doors are what is known as crash doors, and they have to be pushed to come open.

In addition, water fountains have been found running continuously for no apparent reason. A piano tuner once became spooked while working in the theater one evening and announced he would never return at night. Oddest of all, a very large bat makes sporadic appearances in the theater. During the run of one play, it would come out and do nightly "laps" around the auditorium and stage. It will still occasionally make a "special guest appearance" during a performance. Fortunately, audience members tend to think it is just a bird. Members of the Brown Grand Theatre board of directors know better—the bat has buzzed them during a board meeting, startling them with its acrobatics and foot-long wingspan.

Although there are now just 660 seats in the house instead of the original 1,000, both the size and grandeur of the Brown Grand Theatre are still impressive. Elegant framed photographs of the Brown family decorate a cozy reception room just inside the front doors. An austere colonel, white handlebar mustache elegantly draped nearly to his shirtfront, is displayed above the mantel of the fireplace. Katherine, coquettish yet dignified in flounces, flowers, and a ruffled parasol, ornaments the wall above the period sofa. Gertrude, serenely beautiful, is all the decoration needed on another wall to the left of the fireplace. And a clean-shaven Earl, young and handsome with the barest hint of a smile about his lips, rests on a green velvet chair at his father's right hand.

Sit in dark green velveteen seats in the auditorium and listen to the old building creak and groan. Is it the steam heat? Stand up on the stage in front of the massive Napoleon drop curtain and feel the air moving under your feet and around your shoulders while the backstage curtains ripple and move. Is it the wind? Lift your eyes and look up into the first balcony—there, on the left, in front of the window, just to the right of the box seat: that shadow. Is it Earl?

Graveyard Ghosts

W hat better place to find a ghost than in a graveyard, and Kansas is no exception to this rule.

Many folkloric sayings warn against certain activities near cemeteries or offer charms or incantations against harmful spirits that may be waiting to prey on the living who dare to violate the boundaries of the graveyard, especially at night: "Never whistle in a graveyard"; "don't open your mouth when you pass by a cemetery or your own spirit will fly out"; "graveyards are to be avoided at night when ghosts may stroll"; "cross yourself when you cross a graveyard"; "carry salt in your pocket to keep spirits at bay"; "hold your breath as you walk by a cemetery, or you'll be the next one in it"; "a silver cross or silver jewelry will keep spirits away"; "an iron rod placed on a grave will prevent a ghost from rising out of the ground."

All these cautions and charms will do you no good if you encounter one of the legendary cemetery ghosts in certain Kansas graveyards. The Albino Woman ghost of Topeka has haunted a graveyard north of town and its immediate area for generations. Demonic legends swirl around an abandoned nineteenth-century church on a hill, and the cemetery that surrounds it, in a tiny town not far from Lawrence. Emporia has a glowing tombstone, and in the 1960s, Clearwater had a blue-eyed monster, or monstrous ghost, in its cemetery.

Graveyards are favorite haunts for legend tripping by adventurous teens and others on Halloween and nights of a full moon. Many cemeteries, especially in the cities, post security guards at the gates or in the cemeteries on nights like these (especially Halloween) to prevent vandalism or unlawful trespassing.

*　　*　　*　　*　　*

The Albino Woman

Lean over a bridge spanning the Kansas River in Topeka on a moonlit night, and you will see the face of the Albino Woman in the dark water, her features rippling with the currents of the river. From a different part of the bridge you can see the pale hand of La Llorona, the Albino Woman's ghostly Hispanic sister-in-kind, rising from the waters in silent supplication. A Mexican-American youth swore he had seen this.

Look for the phantom in the "dark misty area" of a mirror at night, a young blond woman urged, her blue eyes wide. And say "Albino Woman" three times. She will appear in the mirror, and scratches will materialize all over your body.

A middle-aged man confessed that he didn't believe in the Albino Woman until he went looking for her fifteen years ago, and her albino dog bit him on the leg. He claimed he has the scar to prove it.

"She has killed," warned a sixteen-year-old African-American girl, telling in a rush of words a tale of a murderous attack on unsuspecting teens parked in a car, a tale of a car ripped open, a head ripped off. A man with a pitchfork and a one-eyed albino pit bull were accessories to the crime.

"She is harmless," insisted a seventy-two-year-old woman, explaining that the Albino Lady is a benign spirit who rises from her grave in Rochester Cemetery and walks the grounds with her little white poodle dog.

A teenage boy described the phantom: "She wears a white wedding gown, has pink eyes, kinda long white hair with black showing in it. . . . My grandfather told me about her. . . . He said she would become visible when you got close to her grave and if you found her grave, she would pull you down into the very soil she was buried in, in 1879."

The ghostly figure of a woman in white has haunted Topeka north of the Kansas River for at least three generations. The woman is known as the Albino Woman, or Albino Lady, and is reputed to be a startling apparition with pink or red eyes, a pale complexion, and waist-length white hair. She is usually dressed in flowing white robes or a white dress of some sort. She is often accompanied by a dog, a canine that has been described as everything from a poodle, to an Irish setter, to a pit bull.

The Lady wanders the area surrounding Rochester Cemetery and has been "seen" in the cemetery, on isolated roads in the vicinity, and by the banks of Soldier Creek near the cemetery. Longtime residents of North Topeka remember a true albino woman who lived and worked in Topeka in the 1930s and 1940s. Older residents in the neighborhood of Rochester

Cemetery remember a "crazy lady" with long white hair who lived in the vicinity for years. Could these two individuals have "merged" into one legendary figure many years ago? Stories of the Albino Woman seem to change to reflect the concerns of different individuals and different generations. Accounts of the Lady have become markedly more violent in recent years.

Numerous versions of this legend exist and are actively (and eagerly) told by Topekans of all ages. Representative stories created from a blending of several versions illustrate how the legend came to be, and how it has changed, over the years.

1930s

The solitary woman walking north on Kansas Avenue attracted curious stares as she made her way along the sidewalk. Downtown Topeka, south and north of the Kansas River, was a bustling business and shopping district in the 1930s, home to Crosby Brothers department store, the Santa Fe shops and offices, Saffell Cafe, and the state Capitol.

The slight figure, almost an apparition of a woman, startled passersby because of the starkness of her white complexion, her shock of white hair, and the odd pinkish cast of her pale eyes that rarely returned the gaze of those around her. She was impeccably dressed, perhaps walking home after a day of work at one of the office buildings downtown. The determined click of her sensible heels could be heard receding down the avenue, a pale figure of a woman, ordinary in her pursuits, extraordinary because of her odd and arresting appearance. She was an albino, and almost ghostlike.

1940s

Maude's sister had been dead six weeks. Maude and her sister, both spinsters, had lived together since 1939 to conserve money and to combine ration cards during World War II. After the war they had stayed together, sharing an apartment in the Gem Apartments. Maude's sister, always sickly, caught pneumonia walking home in the rain one wet March afternoon in 1948 and died rather abruptly soon after. Maude came to visit her sister's grave site two evenings a week after work was done at the Santa Fe offices where she worked as a clerk.

It was a warm evening in early May. Maude climbed the sloping dirt drive up into Rochester Cemetery and walked along the road toward her sister's grave site. Cicadas were humming in the trees around her. In the distance she could see a solitary yellow light shining from a window in the small stone house that served as the cemetery caretaker's residence and office. No one else was visiting that evening. The cemetery was deserted, the mid-spring breeze was balmy. Shadows were deepening in the woods to the right of Maude's path.

A line of old, tilting tombstones ran parallel to the woods, close to the edge of the trees. From the corner of her eye, Maude saw a white figure appear to rise up from behind the stones. Maude turned and saw the figure, a woman, move along behind the headstones. The woman turned, too, and gazed at Maude. Her eyes looked pink, perhaps from crying, and her hair was long and loose. She was dressed in white and she carried a small dog. A white poodle. The woman turned again, away from Maude, and moved into the woods. She vanished into the shadows between the trees.

1950s

"Crazy Lilly" lived alone in the old farmhouse near Rochester Road. Her parents had died years before, and Lilly had inherited the house and acreage that her grandfather had built and cultivated at the turn of the century. Lilly's neighbors and former grade school classmates at Rochester School described her as "odd" and "reclusive," a "harmless eccentric." She had married late in life after many years of being alone, but her husband had died soon after the marriage, and he was buried nearby, just down the road in Rochester Cemetery, near the rest of her family.

Neighbors living close to the cemetery became accustomed to seeing a thin, wraithlike figure with long grayish-white hair traveling Rochester Road between Lilly's house and the cemetery at night, a figure that would disappear up the graveled entrance road into the graveyard. This same specter startled and frightened more conventional visitors to the cemetery who might be making a visitation at the same time as Lilly.

Toward the end of her life, Lilly took to wandering the woods around the cemetery, bent on pursuits only she was aware of, a "wild woman" and legendary figure in the area. A homeowner who lived next to the cemetery tells of coming upon Lilly unexpectedly in the woods behind his house, a wild-eyed and forgotten-looking creature, wiry gray hair tangled about her shoulders, clothes in disarray. His first instinct was to run from the frightening witchlike woman, but he spoke to her instead, and received the information that she was looking for her pet squirrel. Lilly was always wandering around, looking for one thing or another. Lilly eventually died and was buried beside her husband in Rochester Cemetery.

1960s

The two teenage couples had just left the Cloverleaf Drive-In at the corner of Rochester Road and Highway 24. Franco Zeffirelli's *Romeo and Juliet* had drawn large crowds to its first Friday night showing, but how much of the movie most of the teenage audience had actually watched was questionable. It was just after midnight. The four friends in the old blue Hudson, a bomb of a car even in 1968, all went to high school together in Topeka.

The boys wanted to drive a mile or so down the gravel road beyond the drive-in to the old cemetery where other kids claimed to have seen the ghostly white figure of a woman floating in the woods and around the tombstones. They had friends who swore her ghastly white face had materialized beside their car windows or insisted they had seen her red eyes shining in the dark of the cemetery road. The Albino Woman, as she was called, was rumored to be buried (but restless) somewhere in the cemetery. The heavy old car ground through the gravel on the road as they drove up the slight incline into the cemetery grounds and pulled to a stop along the dark entrance road that was known locally as a lovers' lane.

The couple in the backseat, laughing nervously, looked around out the windows. The wind picked up, and trees and bushes in the cemetery began to move back and forth. In the front seat, Rhonda watched as her boyfriend, Steve, ratcheted the broken chrome handle that (sometimes) opened the car door, and got out. He said he was going to look around a bit. No one else made a move to get out of the car. Rhonda leaned her head against the cracked upholstery behind her, feeling the humid wind blowing across the front seat through her lowered window.

Suddenly, a blank white hairless head thrust itself into Rhonda's window, moaning hideously. Rhonda threw herself across the seat against the other door, pitching backward away from the horrible apparition. The girl in the back began screaming. Her date fell over against her laughing. The "apparition" unwrapped his white T-shirt from around his head and caught his breath from laughing. Rhonda, back on her side of the seat, was furious. "Don't you ever, *ever,* do that again, Steve!" she yelled. "Now take me home and shut up about the stupid Albino Woman." A low moan came from behind the car. "I said *stop it,* Steve," she said. But Steve was still standing beside her window, his shirt back on, *his* eyes now widened in fright. The moaning became a keening sound that was picked up by the wind and sent over and through the car.

In the distance, blue lights seemed to move and dance from the direction of an old stone house at the other end of the cemetery. Deserted for years, the old house reputedly was the ghostly home of the Albino Woman, from which she peered out through the windows and watched over her cemetery. Steve's eyes met Rhonda's. "Steve," she whispered. In slow motion, the teenager made his way around the front of the car and slid into the driver's seat next to Rhonda. He turned the key in the ignition, but the engine barely turned over. He tried again, and the engine nearly rasped to life, but died again. The four sat frozen in the car as the blue lights seemed to dance closer and closer through the woods. Suddenly the pale form of a woman clothed in a white robe blowing in the breeze moved out of the woods and approached their car. Red orbits glowed in the middle of her face, and the keening sound they had heard before issued from a black hole in the white of her face, below the glowing coals that were her eyes. Her long colorless hair, glowing like her face, blew straight out from her head. The figure melted down momentarily into the gravel of the road and then, maliciously, began pelting the car with rocks. Pings and thuds were heard as the rocks hit their mark. The figure moved closer. The keening sounds from its mouth took on the shape of an otherworldly tune, and as the driver of the car desperately attempted to revive the stalled engine, the ghostly Albino Woman laughed and sang her macabre song.

Tiring of her game, the phantom flowed backward into the woods. Unexpectedly, the car engine caught, and the Hudson lurched forward through the gravel and dirt, spinning its tires and shimmying off the road for an instant, narrowly missing a tombstone. Behind the cloud of dust left on the cemetery road, the Albino Woman wafted through the trees, back toward the century-old stone house, laughing and singing to herself. Somewhere in the distance, a dog howled.

1970s

What follows is the verbatim text of an interview with Michelle, age thirty-two, a homemaker and mother of two who grew up in the area around Rochester Cemetery.

> My friends and I were told that the Albino Lady lived [by] . . . Wilder Road and Rochester. It was kind of wooded there—we were told that's where she lived. We would walk Rochester Road back and forth to school, to Rochester School. On the opposite side, on the west side of Rochester, there was like a creek, some kind of sewer-thing. It was wooded there, and you could go down in there. I was in fourth or fifth grade when this happened [about 1974].

We were told she lived there. When you would go by, you could hear like a "see-saw" going, but it was like nobody was on it. It was just "clack" then "clack," but it was just going up and down with nobody on it. That was supposed to be her back in those woods.

We had heard these stories of her. One day in the afternoon we were walking home. We had heard those noises quite a bit. It was 3:00, or something like that. Me and a friend of mine, and my brother was with us too, stopped at the little creek thing, went down in the trees, to go wading or something. When we came back up, she was standing there, right on Rochester Road.

The rest of the story moves quickly.

She was not real tall, just medium height. She had long hair, but it was like rough, wiry gray with white in it. It was really ugly. It was long and straight, with a part down the middle. It came to the middle of her back. There was a pink rim around her eyes, kind of a dark red, like makeup or something, and her eyes were pink. I remember those suckers.

All she did was kind of smile at us, and she laughed. It wasn't a traditional witch laugh, like a cackle, but we were sure she was out to kill us. And we just ran. We looked back once. I remember looking back, and she was just looking after us. We ran home. We usually ran past that point after that when we went to and from school. We never saw her again.

She was a real person. I don't know where she went, down in the woods maybe. She was evil-looking.

1980s AND 1990s

The boy was seventeen, his girlfriend sixteen. They had hung out at the mall earlier with friends, then gone to the late show at the mall cinema.

Driving home in North Topeka, it was just past midnight. The lights of the Goodyear Tire and Rubber plant flashed by them on the left as they drove east on U.S. Highway 24. Turning left onto Rochester Road, the boy slowed the car as he drove over the bridge crossing Soldier Creek. The moonlight on the creek below them made strange shimmerings and wavering white figures on the water. Ahead, he made a left and drove past the towering stone archway that marked the entrance into Rochester Cemetery. Just beyond the cemetery, the road curved to the right. The boy had heard stories from his mother of how the Albino Woman, a ghostly woman dressed in white, haunted Soldier Creek and the entire area, flying over the trees past the cemetery. He thought of these stories now, and he suppressed a shudder.

When he approached the next intersection, he slowed down once again. It was still a little early; neither of them had to be home before 1:00 A.M. The girl suggested they park for awhile and talk, maybe over on the road between the woods a block away. It was secluded and dark there and beautiful in a creepy sort of way, particularly when there was a full moon, as there was on that night.

They drove into the intersection, and then turned left, pulling off the road onto the shoulder, by the trees. The roads were deserted in all four directions, as far as they could see. Night creatures were murmuring and stirring in the leaves on and above the ground, but the couple did not hear any sounds outside the car. At least not at first. The convertible top of the sporty small car was up, as were the windows. It was August, and an unbearably hot night. Inside the car, the engine was running, the air-conditioning was on, and the body of the car was vibrating with the low bass tones emanating from the compact disc player.

Outside the car, something moved rapidly through the trees, snuffling and scratching. The girl looked up at the first ripping sounds on top of the car. Strips of the moonlit sky showed through the jagged tears that were appearing above her head. She turned and looked in astonishment at the boy just before she was engulfed in what seemed to be white gauzy fabric, white swirls of sheer material. Lifted effortlessly out of the top of the car, the girl's body seemed to hover above the slashed roof of the car for an instant, then was flung, headless, onto the soft shoulder of the roadway. A gaunt and fearsome white animal, a spectral pit bull missing one eye, was already dragging his ghastly trophy away through the woods, luminescent jaws clamped onto blond hair reddened by blood. His ghostly mistress followed.

Through the woods and over the old railroad tracks, across fields and down to the banks of Soldier Creek, the Lady wandered that night. Her white form floated along the course of the creek, the old creek named in honor of the soldiers who camped along its banks during the early days of Bleeding Kansas territorial history. Her ghostly shape moved through the shallows of the water, trailing streamers of white and ribbons of blood; her gory companion padded silently behind, sniffing the night air.

The preceding stories illustrate the unusual complexity of the legend cycle that comprises the fifty-year history of the Albino Woman. For whatever reasons, this durable legend-figure has remained constant over this period of time, the stories about her changing to keep current with the times. With each new generation of Topekans, there are always grandparents, parents, siblings, teachers, or peers who relate the story and pass it on to a new crop of listeners. The stories are most popular at Halloween time and among teenagers at the various city high schools.

Early versions of the story usually perceive the Albino Woman to be a benign figure, a real person who was an outcast from society who may have frightened children with her strange pale features, white hair, and pink eyes.

In the 1970s and early 1980s, the Lady is more scary, definitely a ghost, and a wanderer. She was frightening, possibly evil, but not usually violent.

In the late 1980s and now the 1990s, many teenagers relating the story of the Albino Woman describe her as a more malevolent spirit, frightening in her appearance and her actions, accompanied by pit bulls (albino, one-eyed, three-legged, or headless) or hellhounds and occasionally by a man with a pitchfork.

Like the widespread Hispanic legend of La Llorona, which shares many elements with some versions of the Albino Woman legend (as well as with the Theorosa figure in another Kansas legend—see the Theorosa's Bridge story in this book), the Lady is often searching for her children or for any-one else's children. And in some 1990s versions of the story, the Lady is not only capable of killing children but of eating them as well. This fear-some ghost also attacks young couples parked in cars in the area she haunts. One particularly graphic rendition, retold above, has a horren-dously bloodthirsty apparition pulling a victim out of the top of a car and ripping her head off. No such horrible crime was ever reported in the To-peka newspapers, so one assumes that this is just an unusually appalling version of the Albino Woman's legend originally told by someone with an impressive imagination.

The first written account of the Albino Woman legend seems to have appeared in the Washburn University (Topeka) student newspaper, the *Washburn Review.* A student columnist in the early 1970s did a story on the Albino Woman, complete with not-too-convincing spirit photogra-phy (spooky black-and-white photos of a coed in a white robe kneeling by a tombstone) and interviews with individuals who had "seen" the Lady. He renamed the cemetery Rockingham and used made-up names for his informants, including a cemetery caretaker called Mr. Sanderson (the caretaker of Rochester Cemetery at that time was a woman). In a later col-umn near Halloween in 1971, he admitted that his column on the legend was primarily a "spoof," part real legendary material and part invention on his part. He mentioned that he had been "found out" by a class of junior high students in town who had researched the names of the people and places mentioned in his article and found them all to be false.

Over one hundred versions of the Albino Woman legend collected over a three-year period reveal fascinating patterns and prove that the Lady herself is an ever-changing, shape-shifting creature, one who performs many functions within the community that nurtures her legend. Studying the stories may provide an understanding of the function of legend for teenagers and preteens, the segment of the local population that tells the tale most often. The changing elements of the narrative seem to mirror social changes in the culture of Topeka (perhaps American culture in general) and reflect concerns, fears, and attempts to contend with a society that is as shape shifting and unsettling as this apparition. Certainly the elements of initiation rites, dating rituals, dating fears (à la the Hook urban legend; see the Hamburger Man story in this book), and parental warnings against potentially dangerous social activities (parking in secluded spots, visiting graveyards at midnight, and so on) are all part of the Albino Woman's ghostly garb.

The Albino Woman legend is quite a bit like the infamous Lady herself: flying through the generations; constantly being re-created out of each individual teller and listener's fears, sense of evil, and sense of mischief; and wandering the cultural landscape of Topeka as well as the physical landscape of cemetery, creek, woods, roads, and river that she calls home.

The Blue-Eyed Monster of Clearwater Cemetery

The "thing" moved among the gravestones in Clearwater Cemetery, its phosphorescent blue eyes glowing in the dark. Two different sets of witnesses claimed to have seen the six-foot-tall monster with its mesmerizing eyes prowling the cemetery in mid-May 1965.

At 9:30 P.M. Saturday night, several teenagers called the Clearwater police to report the strange apparition, asserting that the monster had come within five feet of them. The teens described the creature to a detective: "They said it was hunkered down behind a barrel, and suddenly raised up, and started toward them. It had its left arm across its chest, and with its right hand motioned for them to come toward it." The witnesses decided that it might not be in their best interest to respond to the monster's beckoning hand. Instead, one boy had the bright idea to curse the creature in response. The monster took offense at being called names, and in reaction "its eyes changed from round to diamond-shaped and turned bright amber," according to the boy who cursed at it. The detective reported that when the creature's eyes changed shape and color, "that's when they turned and ran."

Sunday night a group of both teenagers and adults visited the cemetery to see if the first sighting was a hoax. At 8:30 they, too, called the authorities and reported sighting the ghostly monster. Both groups described its tall frame and dark aspect, but its most chilling feature was its glowing blue orbs. From a report in the Wichita *Beacon:* "The body is shrouded in darkness, they say, but the eyes hold a ghostly hypnotic effect. It moves among the gravestones, silently and stealthily, then disappears."

With assistance from the Sedgwick County sheriff's office and Sheriff Vern Miller, a stakeout was set up at the cemetery by the Clearwater Police Department. Following the second reported sighting of the "monster," police staked out the area until 1:30 A.M., watching the cemetery through binoculars. But the police didn't see the "thing." They did, however, see tracks in the hard sand in the vicinity of the cemetery. The "strange" tracks were roughly two inches in diameter, round, and spaced about six feet apart. A sheriff's detective, Eddie Miller, described them as looking like impressions that a pogo stick or pair of stilts might have made.

The next night, the police and a sheriff's officer were back out at the scene, hoping the creature would show up again on the third night. Hiding by the side of the road, police were hopeful to catch a glimpse of the ghost monster and his blue eyes, but no such luck. The monster didn't show.

The newspaper report emphasized that the creature "doesn't seem to be trying to communicate with anyone, but it isn't trying to hide, either. It just appears and moves and glows among the gravestones."

No further sightings were reported, so evidently the monster took his baby blues and moved on to another area. Perhaps it was getting too crowded with police and sightseers for his taste. Two days later, in a *Wichita Eagle* article, the Clearwater chief of police speculated that the Clearwater Ghost was a mixture of deer and imagination. For lack of a better explanation, it was concluded that the strange tracks found in the cemetery were deer tracks, and the chief said that he later "saw a deer." But did it have blue eyes?

* * * * *

The Demonic Church

In the title cut from their 1992 release *Stull,* the rock group Urge Overkill sings about a tiny country graveyard that can be found on a county road about ten miles west of Lawrence. On the cover of the compact disc, the crumbling remains of a nineteenth-century stone church make a foreboding presence overlooking the cemetery, and a prominent tombstone bearing the chiseled name Stull is in the foreground.

The church, the graveyard, and the tombstone are all part of the tiny, almost-a-ghost-town hamlet of Stull. Since the auto shop and bait shop recently closed, Stull claims only a few houses, two churches, and no more than twenty residents. Unfortunately, Stull also must claim a particularly fiendish and bothersome legend that has attached itself to the deteriorating old church that rises above the surrounding area from the top of Emmanuel Hill in the middle of town. For years, tales of demons, witches, werewolves, apparitions, and supernatural happenings have swirled around a community that is most unhappy with its image as a haunted site and the location of one of the "seven gates of hell."

Although legend indicates that devilish revelry and strange occurrences have been a part of Stull's history for more than one hundred years, published accounts of the strange stories of Stull did not appear until the 1970s. Perhaps it is more than coincidental that this time period corresponded with a wave of public interest in stories of demonic possession and satanic activities that followed the publication of William Peter Blatty's bestselling book, *The Exorcist,* in 1971 and the 1973 release of the screen adaptation of the same novel, the blockbuster movie *The Exorcist,* which starred Linda Blair as a young girl possessed by the devil.

This author recalls no elements of demonism attributed to the Stull Cemetery in the late 1960s, when Stull was deemed a suitable spot for a picnic lunch while driving the local route between Topeka and Lawrence. An ancient spreading pine tree in the cemetery was the primary point of interest then. A small tombstone appeared to be embedded in the roots of the massive tree. As the tree had grown and the base of the trunk had spread, the tombstone had been split in two, leaving half of the marker on each side of the tree. Curiously, the stone marked the final resting place of two individuals, Bettie and Frankie Thomas, both of whom died in 1879. Then, as now, the tree was considered one of the oldest and largest pine trees in the area, if not the state, the trunk measuring nearly fifteen feet in circumference. Sitting in the shade of the tree, one could look up the hill to the old abandoned church. The prevailing wisdom among Topeka teenagers in 1966 or so was that the church had burned and had been vacated. The site was seen to be spooky but not demonic.

In November 1974, an article appeared in the University of Kansas student newspaper, the *University Daily Kansan,* entitled "Legend of Devil Haunts Tiny Town." The article began: "Far removed from the horrible story of 'The Exorcist' or the bizarre black masses recently discovered in Los Angeles, and tucked away on a rough county road between Topeka and Lawrence is the tiny town of Stull." The piece recounted several episodes of different individuals' supposed experiences with the occult and the supernatural in the cemetery. "According to legend," stated the article, "this graveyard is one of the two places on earth where the devil appears in person twice a year." The article declared that Stull was "haunted by legends of diabolical, supernatural happenings" and asserted that the legend had been "told and retold, although it has probably never been recorded." The newspaper piece indicated that "some people say they heard it from grandparents and great-grandparents" as well as "friends" who had passed the stories on.

A freshman at the University of Kansas from Bonner Springs revealed to the newspaper that her grandmother had told her of the devil's yearly visit to Stull and drove with her past the cemetery when she was ten or eleven years old. She said they saw a house that was glowing red and seemed to be on fire in Stull, but when they passed it, the house appeared normal. The young woman told the paper that for years after her visit to Stull, she was terrified of trick-or-treaters in devil suits.

A University of Kansas junior was also interviewed for the article and related his experiences in the Stull Cemetery one night. Accompanied by two fraternity brothers, he was walking across the graveyard when he heard a noise behind him and a hand grabbed his arm. "I'll never forget how cold the fingers felt," he told the newspaper. Assuming it was one of his companions, he turned around, but the other men were a considerable distance behind him, and the graveyard was empty of any other living beings. Another source told of students who had gone "devil-hunting" in Stull and had all suffered three- to four-hour "memory lapses" and lost all recollection of what they had seen there. Stories of witches and witches' covens were also mentioned in the piece.

Several residents of the town of Stull interviewed for the article claimed never to have heard of the stories. The pastor of the Stull church at that time indicated he "thought it was possible that the legend might have been an invention of KU students." Robert Smith, then associate professor of anthropology at KU and teacher of folklore classes, agreed with the minister when contacted for his opinion by the *University Daily Kansan* for a March 20, 1978, article. On the day of the spring equinox, the student newspaper reported that "the devil allegedly materializes in Stull Cemetery on Halloween night and during the spring equinox." Smith opined that the legend of Stull Cemetery was a creation of KU students.

On March 20, 1978, approximately 150 people, the majority of them University of Kansas students, convened in Stull Cemetery to await the arrival of the devil. The word had been passed around that the spirits of those buried in the graveyard who had died violent deaths would return to haunt their killers and dance with the devil. But, as an article in the *University Daily Kansan* on March 22, 1978, noted, "the only spirits that showed up at Stull Cemetery Monday night, during the equinox, were in beer cans and liquor bottles."

Alcohol flowed freely that night of the equinox, and so did the stories. A number of tales about the cemetery that are still being passed around in the 1990s can be traced back to that time. Two men told of being frightened when a strong wind began blowing in the Stull graveyard. They returned to their car only to find it moved to the other side of the highway and turned facing the opposite direction. Another man also experienced the strange wind but while inside the old church. He claimed to have been blown to the floor and unable to move. Numerous individuals asserted that the devil had been appearing in Stull Cemetery since the 1850s (regardless of the fact that the church was not built until 1867, and the cemetery was not platted until 1869). Some people even insisted that the original name of the town had been Skull and that the town's official name was simply a corruption of that. (In actuality, the town was simply called Deer Creek Community until 1899, when the last name of the first [and only] postmaster, Sylvester Stull, was adopted as the name of the town. The post office closed in 1903, but the name was retained.)

By 1980, the main story line of the legend had grown more fanciful. An article in the *Kansas City Times* in November 1980 outlined the story of Stull: "For reasons known only to the devil himself, legend says he chose the tumbleweed hamlet of Stull, Kansas, to make one of his two appearances on Earth every Halloween. The other visit, which occurs simultaneously at the witching hour, is someplace on a desolate plain of India.

From those sites, the legend goes, the devil gathers all the people who died violent deaths for a midnight prance across the Earth."

The article went on to reveal more details: "One mainstream account puts the story's beginnings in the 1850s, when a stable hand allegedly stabbed the mayor to death in the cemetery's old stone barn. Years later the barn was converted to a church, which in turn was gutted by fire. A decaying wooden crucifix that still hangs from one wall is thought to sometimes turn upside down when passers-by step inside the building at midnight. . . ."

That account makes for a fascinating story, but again the historical facts get in the way. The original Deer Creek settlement consisted of only six families in 1857, hardly enough people to warrant a mayor. In fact, the tiny unincorporated town has *never* had a mayor. The 1867 stone church, the first public building constructed in the small German community, did not have a barn, and contrary to popular belief, the church never burned.

Imaginative details were added to the legend throughout the 1980s:

"The cemetery . . . is the devil's walking place, when he appears on the last night of Winter or the first night of Spring, to visit a witch supposedly buried there." (An old tombstone bearing the name of Wittich can be found in relative close proximity to the church.)

"The devil only walks in two places . . . at the Stull Cemetery in Douglas County and at another cemetery, also named Stull, also in a town named Stull, in England. His reasons were to visit witches who supposedly were buried in either of the two places."

"A child [is] buried in the Stull, Douglas County Cemetery; legends say the parents were a witch and the Devil!"

"The skeleton of the old church in the cemetery glow[s] red, as if it were on fire. Moments later, it appear[s] normal."

"The rural cemetery at Stull, Kansas, is legendarily possessed by demonic werewolves, vampires, and other Satanic proxies that materialize at the Spring and Fall equinoxes."

"A photo was obtained of a werewolf-like boy standing in a cemetery tree. He appears to be holding out a mask."

"[It is] a place that is rumored to be one of the seven gateways to hell. "

Jill Maycumber, a 1991 graduate of the University of Kansas, remembered excursions to Stull in 1989 and 1990 when she was a student: "We always heard it was a 'gateway to hell' type of thing. We went there several different times. We would always take bottles and throw them against the wall. We had heard that they would not break, and of course, there were some bottles that did not break. I don't know if maybe we just didn't throw them hard enough. It was such an eerie place."

Curt Oglesby, a Topeka resident, recalled stories of the "burned out" church from grade school in Topeka in the early 1980s. In an interview, he said that he had heard that when the church burned, the congregation built a new church across the road and abandoned it. He also heard in grade school that the old church was haunted "because all the souls in the cemetery would meet in the church. They would all still 'go to church' together in the old church building." He described the stories at that time as being "not really scary—kind of cool." But by the late 1980s, when he was attending Topeka High School, the stories had picked up the demonic aspects that became so prevalent in the tales of Stull Cemetery. By the time he graduated in 1988, he was quite familiar with accounts of the legend featuring the old church building as a gateway to the netherworld.

The old church was indeed abandoned by its congregation, but not because of a fire. The old building simply grew too small to meet the demands of an expanding congregation and was boarded up and left in 1922 when the new church building across the road (still in use) was completed.

By 1989, crowds at Stull on Halloween nights had grown so large that the Douglas County Sheriff's Department had to station deputies outside the cemetery to discourage "ghostbusters and ghoul seekers" and to hand out tickets for criminal trespass to anyone caught in the graveyard. Estimates of up to five hundred were made for the number of curiosity seekers who had shown up at the cemetery the previous Halloween. Vandalism had become a major concern, as the throngs of people had toppled and broken numerous gravestones.

Over time, a number of local residents went from mere bemusement at the odd attention their small community was attracting, to concern about the periodic trespassing on private cemetery grounds and anger at vandalism and property damage occurring in the small rural cemetery where many of their loved ones were buried. In a 1989 *Kansas City Times* newspaper article, one cemetery board member expressed frustration at the situation: "It gets a little irritating to think people can't have more respect for the dead than that, to tear their headstones up and graves. In my estimation, it's getting pretty low." A local debunked the legendary stories that drew the crowds: "The rumor around here is that [the cemetery] is haunted. I've been here 50 years and I haven't seen any ghosts yet." Another local resident was just plain angry in an interview with a *Topeka*

Capital-Journal reporter on Halloween night, 1989. She said she wanted to see the rumors of witch covens and Satan's stomping grounds stopped: "I've got relatives buried up there, and it's just sickening to see beer cans up on the graves and stones turned over."

The *Kansas City Times* article datelined Halloween 1989 also related an incredibly detailed and descriptive rendition of the legend:

> According to the legend, the people who settled in Stull practiced witchcraft and at least one witch was said to have been hanged from a tree in the graveyard. To repent of their sorcery, the settlers built a church in 1867. They abandoned it in the early 1900s to build a new church downhill.
>
> A church in an abandoned graveyard was the perfect place for the devil to appear and, according to legend, he appeared in Stull every Halloween and received his followers at the old church. The walls of the drafty church even bled during Lucifer's visits.
>
> The myth has grown over the years, embellished by the fact that the name of the town—Stull—used to be "skull" and referred to the devil, the town's ZIP code begins with "666"—the numbers symbolizing the devil, and the date inscribed over the door was removed, indicating that the church was possessed.

Continued trespassing and vandalism at the Stull Cemetery have necessitated the recent installation of a chain-link security fence around the cemetery grounds. Sheriff's officers still patrol the area at Halloween. The patrols and the fence have diminished the number of unauthorized interlopers in the area, but the stories of the haunted cemetery and the demonic church refuse to die out. Students at the University of Kansas remain the most active disseminators of the legend, but many individuals who grew up in the Lawrence, Lecompton, Tecumseh, and Topeka areas are well aware of the stories of Stull and are familiar with any number of the various versions. Knowledge of this infamous legend has not only grown beyond the region but also beyond the state, as evidenced by inclusion of the story in the publications *Haunted Places: The National Directory* and *Ghost Trackers Newsletter* and by Stull's featured role as the cover shot and title song for the 1992 Urge Overkill musical release.

An obvious question comes to mind when contemplating the dismay and destruction this particular legend has brought to a small but proud community, a number of whom are the descendants of the resilient and quite religious German families who were the original settlers of Stull. Why has the old stone church been allowed to stand vacant for seventy-five years, crumbling and deteriorating at the apex of Emmanuel Hill? During 1996, the last remnants of the roof blew off. Now completely open to the elements, the interior walls are covered with graffiti (much of it obscene or demonic in nature), and the dirt floor is littered with fallen timbers, shards of glass, cigarette butts, and beer cans. Until recently the stone walls remained apparently solid, but now a large crack is visible on one side. (A local resident speculates that lightning may have struck the church—an ominous pronouncement sure to add further colorful elements to the legend.) In December 1996, the stark outline of the decrepit and definitely creepy remains of the church building posed an incongruous contrast to the sight of two women placing bouquets of silk flowers and red-and-green–decorated Christmas wreaths at the gravesites of loved ones buried near the church.

Why not just tear the old building down (the probability that it will fall down of its own accord in the next ten years would seem to be high anyway)? That would rid the town not only of an eerie landmark but also of the source of the troublesome legend as well. One of the women decorating graves for Christmas seemed saddened by the question when it was asked of her. She was with her daughter and said that her parents, grandparents, and husband were buried in the cemetery. Her grandfather and great-grandfather had helped build the new church across the road. Regarding the old church, "I would hate to see it torn down," she said. "It's a sentimental thing." But she did remark that the legend centered in the old church did cause problems and "when gravestones are destroyed, it is sad. A lot of the deceased people don't have any family around to repair them."

Another resident who lives near the cemetery, a descendant of one of the town's founders, indicated that there had been "some talk of trying to restore" the old church building at one time. He said that some interest had been shown in it by a state historical group, but he admitted that "nothing has been done at this point, and I'm not sure anything will be done." When asked if he thought the legend incited vandalism at the cemetery, he responded that he hadn't really thought of that, but it could be. So, why has the church, last used for church services in 1922, been left to literally rot and become creepier with each passing year? "I can't really say," he said. Why not pull down what's left of the church and do away with the source of the legend? "I don't really know," he said.

Perhaps the real answer does lie in sentimentality and strong community ties to the structure that was the church of their childhood or the church of their parents, grandparents, and great-grandparents. Perhaps restoration is still a possibility before the old Stull church falls in upon itself, demolishing a decaying monument to the nineteenth-century settlers who established Deer Creek Community in Kanwaka Township and put down permanent roots by Emmanuel Hill. But until the macabre old church is obliterated by means of restoration, demolition, or nature's own destruction, the legends that have tormented the town of Stull are going to continue to be devilishly hard to put to rest.

The Caretaker Ghosts

The old abandoned cemetery sat high on a grassy hill north and east of Seneca. Its ground had been unbroken for years, and the nineteenth-century graves contained in it were unkempt and overgrown. Windblown prairie grasses vied with weeds and wildflowers for dominance of the small patch of land. Two small and twisted trees were the only other living things residing on the hill. The strange trees were not native to Kansas, and local legend declared that their seed had been brought in to the territory from "some other regions." By whatever means they had arrived there, and from whatever remote regions the seed had been carried, the sister trees served as sentinels on the cemetery hill, guarding the long-forgotten souls who were sleeping under their branches.

At dusk, cracked and tilting tombstones were silhouetted against the setting sun at the top of the hill. At night, the tiny graveyard was as dark as any place on earth could be, unless the moon was shining. In the moonlight, small shadows flickered in the breeze, insects hummed from deep within the grasses and weeds, and night birds called from the arms of the trees.

Around 1909, the locals around this rural area began to notice a light up on the hill. Each night close to midnight, a bright, white unwavering light would appear between the trees and remain until sometime after midnight. The light did not move or change in color or intensity. It materialized all at once, quite suddenly becoming visible, and remained fixed at the hill's very summit. It was described as being "very bright." After a period of time, the light would simply vanish, quickly diminishing to a pinpoint, then extinguishing itself like a blown-out match.

Most people in the area were afraid to investigate the light. A generally accepted explanation for the strange glow was that the ghosts of the dead buried in the old cemetery were caring for their own neglected graves and that the otherworldly light was either a fusion of the combined luminosity from several ghosts or a ghostly lantern hung between the trees to light the area in which the ghosts were working. Regardless, most mortals living in the vicinity declined to climb the hillock at midnight to find out firsthand.

Miss Alma taught school in the old Flag School House that was located not far from the hill. Miss Alma boarded with a family in the area, and she had witnessed the phenomenon of the ghost light several times. Convinced that a natural explanation existed for the unnatural light, she determined to climb the hill and wait for the light to appear some night.

She enlisted the daughter of her host family to serve as her companion in this quest, and the two women slipped out of the house unnoticed late one evening after dark. By the time they reached the hill, the moon was high in the sky and shadows surrounded the base of the hillock. The women quickly ascended the slope and reached the top. Nothing stirred but a slight wind running through the grass and the branches of the gnarled trees.

A large flat limestone rock sat on the ground between the two trees. Since the light seemed always to be positioned between the trees, Miss Alma and her friend decided that a seat on the rock would ensure a meeting with the source, if indeed it happened to make an appearance. The two women made themselves comfortable on the rock and began to wait. They talked and laughed, strangely not feeling afraid or threatened although sitting in the middle of a desolate cemetery waiting for a ghostly light or presence to reveal itself to them. Miss Alma looked around at the tombstones and old graves illuminated in the bright moonlight and remarked to her friend, "If ghosts are tending this cemetery, they aren't doing a very good job of it." Immediately around the two women, hand-carved headstones and gray rock footstones were partially hidden among the overgrowth of weeds and grass.

Midnight came and went, and no light, outside of moonlight, appeared. Satisfied that nothing was going to happen that night, the women rose from their rock and proceeded to make their way back through the graves to descend the hill. "Wait, let's go down the other way," said Miss Alma's young companion. "Let's see the other side of the hill on our way down."

They turned around and walked back through the weedy grave sites. As they approached the far side of the cemetery, beyond the trees where the darkness seemed to rise up from below the crest of the hill, they noticed a change in the texture of the ground beneath their feet. Weeds were no longer brushing their ankles and scratching against their skirts. Their feet were no longer shuffling and crunching through dried grasses and thistles. Looking down, they discerned that in this part of the old grave-yard, the grass was neatly trimmed and the grave sites were clearly visible, marked by gravestones that were upright, not crooked, and free from debris.

Astonished, the two women looked at one another and then glanced behind themselves to the two little trees. Darkness had settled in between the trees and over the rock. Miss Alma and her companion hurried down the far side of the hill and returned home as quickly as they could. Numer-ous times as they made their way back, they turned and looked at the hill and searched for the signs of a light, but they saw nothing.

No light appeared that night or for several nights after. But with the sanctity of their silent place restored, eventually the caretaker ghosts re-turned. Hanging their lantern between the trees, they resumed their work at the old graveyard, clearing the weeds and trimming the grass, and righting the stones marking the final resting place of their long-ago friends and families.

The Glowing Tombstone

Arthur Cooper died a gruesome death attempting to jump a train from Kansas City back home to Emporia in February 1872. The *Emporia Gazette* described his death in graphic detail, reporting that the twenty-five-year-old was "crushed by the wheels [and] the body was hor-ribly mangled. It was severed in the middle [and] his head was mashed."

Arthur was buried 125 years ago in an Emporia cemetery beneath a highly polished stone marker—reputedly the Glowing Tombstone. For at least thirty years, this luminous stone has been one of the most persistent ghostly legends in the Emporia area. At night, viewed from just the right location a short distance away, Arthur's marker appears to radiate with a greenish glow. Different theories propose that reflected light from a street-light is radiating from the polished stone or that car headlights passing by the cemetery illuminate the flat surface of the marker and irradiate it with an eerie gleam.

Legend also suggests that lights from a nearby church may be responsi-ble for the tombstone's inner light. In fact, the cemetery records note that

Arthur's monument is "polished" and "catches gas light from Church parking lot and bounces off as an eerie glow." However, one problem with this theory is the fact that the church in question stands behind the marker, and any lights from the church area would reflect on the unpolished side of the stone, not on the front, the side known to glow.

Some confusion has existed in the past as to exactly which tombstone in the cemetery is the one that glows. Some individuals from Emporia who attended high school in the late 1960s recall stories of the Glowing Grave, but the story then concerned a marker for a young child cut in the shape and form of a little boy. This tombstone had flecks or grains of glass or some other reflective material embedded in the actual stone, and these polished bits supposedly caught illumination from any nearby or passing light source. Newspaper reports from the 1960s tell of vandalism at the cemetery and the defacement of a small stone monument, carved in the shape of a young boy. The monument had been erected in 1897 in a tribute to La Roy, a three-year-old boy. At one point, the stone was even stolen as a prank and damaged further before it was returned to the cemetery.

Another version of the glowing tombstone tale states that the luminous marker actually belongs to the grave site of Preston Plumb, a wealthy newspaperman and one of the founders of Emporia. Plumb was the only Kansas senator to hail from Emporia, serving in the U.S. Senate from 1877 to 1891. Plumb Hall at Emporia State University is named for him.

Dr. James Hoy, author, professor of English at Emporia State, and recognized authority on folklore of the Flint Hills and Kansas, has heard a story about Preston Plumb and the large granite boulder that rests on top of his grave: "Preston Plumb went on the train to Colorado with his mistress. His wife got on the same train and followed him out to Colorado Springs. Mrs. Plumb spied her husband and his mistress 'dallying' on a granite boulder. She contacted a contractor to move the boulder back to Emporia, and put it in their front yard. When the senator returned home, he saw the boulder and knew he had been 'caught.' Some time later, when Preston Plumb died, Mrs. Plumb had the boulder put on his grave. Legend decrees that she then said, 'That should keep the son of a !#*?! down!' " Actually, according to Dr. Hoy, the granite boulder came from Vermont and was placed on Plumb's grave several years after his death as a tribute by some of his friends.

Whichever tombstone is glowing in the local cemetery, the legend remains centered in the graveyard, and the stories add luminosity to the folklore of Emporia.

Ghosts on the Range

"Ghosts, ghosts on the range, Where the ghouls and the revenants play" will never catch on as the state song, but sometimes, while researching literally hundreds of ghost stories and legends across the state, it seemed like an appropriate alternative!

The ghosts in this chapter are not all literally on the range, but they tend to be associated with the wide-open spaces, rural areas, and outlying areas or attached to specific landscape features such as bridges, hollows, hills, roads, ponds, and rivers.

On the range such disconcerting sights as headless ghosts, drowned ghosts, fiery ghosts, or barefoot ghosts might greet you. You might catch a glimpse of a phantom cowboy riding on his ghost horse out by St. Jacob's Well south of Dodge City. Or you might hear the plaintive voice of the ghost of Theorosa calling for the baby she threw off a bridge north of Wichita. Or most horrible of all, you might run into the Hamburger Man in the sand hills north of Hutchinson where he hides among the hillocks behind low trees and scrub brush waiting to snag someone with the hook on his one hand and slice them up with the knife in his other.

Ghosts out in the open tend to be more free ranging and less likely to stay in one place (unlike, for instance, house ghosts or fort ghosts). An abundance of phantoms in Kansas roam in the panorama of the hills or on the prairies—echoing the settling habits of their live progenitors who moved to Kansas to inhabit the plains. Legends in Kansas are often landscape linked, inextricably part of the features that define the midwestern terrain. Their campestral territory is defined and populated by imaginative people who were drawn to the freedom and space of the open prairies. The tales and stories spun by these people reflect this same imagination in their depiction of the ghosts who "live" side by side with them and are equally "at home on the range."

The Ghost of the Cimarron

One might expect to find a legend or two in Satanta, Kansas. Even the name of this small Haskell County town of just over one thousand residents suggests the possibility of a demon or at least a devilish ghost. But Satanta has nothing to do with the prince of darkness. Rather, the town in far southwest Kansas was named for Chief Satanta of the Kiowas, a Native American tribe found in that part of Kansas until the mid-1800s.

West of Satanta runs the sand and gravel streambed of the Cimarron River. The Cimarron is dry the better part of each year, carrying water only during times of heavy precipitation, even though it is the major river in southwestern Kansas. But in the fall of 1915, the Cimarron was running with water—enough water to drown in or to be murdered in.

Nellie Byers died in or by the river one Friday night right before Halloween in 1915. Her body was found in the river the next morning, barefoot. Nellie, a schoolteacher, was crossing the shallow river to get from the schoolhouse on one side to the farmhouse on the other side, where the family she boarded with lived. She never made it home alive, and legend over the last eighty-plus years has her still trying to make that crossing, carrying a lantern. The ghostly light is said to dance across the prairie outside of Satanta in the vicinity of the old schoolhouse, a spook light that is extinguished as soon as it reaches the river. Many people in the area claim to have seen the light, and many people tell the story of poor Nellie and what happened to her that night.

One who recalled the story clearly was Katie Bryant, formerly a resident of rural Satanta. Although she herself has since passed away, Katie recalled the details surrounding the legend for a newspaper article in 1980. Katie was about ten years old the year Nellie Byers died. In Katie's words, "A schoolteacher taught at the country school and had to walk across the Cimarron River to the place where she was boarding. She was late coming home [one] night because they were going to have a Halloween program at the schoolhouse. She had her shoes off for crossing the river—there was water in it all summer then—and here came this herd of cattle down the riverbed. Some prominent citizens from Moscow [Kansas] and Ulysses were stealing the cattle, and their tracks couldn't be traced if they went down the river. Nellie recognized them, but she had no idea they were rustling cattle; they wouldn't have had to kill her."

Nellie's body was found in the Cimarron the next day, and she was taken home and buried. But Katie verified that shortly thereafter people living in and traveling through the area began seeing a mysterious light at night, bobbing and dipping, moving just above the ground in the vicinity of the river. Katie saw it, too. "I did see this light," she said. "When I was young, a bunch of us kids went on horseback to see the light that went from the schoolhouse to the river. It was only a few feet off the ground, as if it were someone carrying a lantern light."

The legend grew that the ghost of Nellie Byers was repeating her tramp, night after night, from the schoolhouse to the river, carrying a lantern to light her way in one hand, her shoes and stockings in the other.

But Nellie's ghost is not the only mysterious element in this legend. How and why Nellie died is as unclear now as it was eighty years ago. Nellie's brother, Ora Byers of Ulysses, was in his early nineties when he was interviewed about the case in 1980. Byers said his sister's intended destination that evening was not the house where she boarded but the house of some friends. She had planned a shopping trip into Satanta the next day with her friends. Nellie's brother verified that she was barefoot in order to ford the river and was evidently carrying her shoes and stockings when calamity struck. She was found dead the next morning, her mutilated body in the river.

The immediate suspect was not a cattle rustler, but an old bachelor by the name of Archie Sweet. Sweet lived by the river and would have, or should have, heard Nellie's screams or any kind of commotion. According to Byers, the old man claimed he was rabbit hunting at the time of the crime. He admitted that he had seen Nellie that evening, but she was alive when he left her. The general consensus was that Sweet was the murderer. He was convicted and sent to the penitentiary at Lansing. Although he continually professed his innocence and desire to get out of jail in order to find the true killers, he died in prison and was never officially exonerated.

The next scenario in this muddled chain of events finds an unnamed man in Moscow, perhaps one of the rumored cattle rustlers, confessing on his deathbed to his doctor his role in the nefarious deed. Detectives who were called in originally to help solve the murder also played a part in the legend. Nellie's brother, Ora, referred to the detectives as "crooked" and claimed they simply "came in to make money on it, but they weren't really detectives." Ora also believed the deathbed confession story was just that—another story. That cattle rustlers killed his sister, running the cattle over her prostrate body in the riverbed was just an unproven conjecture as far as Ora was concerned, perhaps originating with the shady detectives.

The only certain fact in the whole tangled story is that Nellie Byers died under suspicious circumstances in 1915. As often happens in a legend of this type, perhaps over time three separate incidents—Nellie Byers's murder, a cattle rustling involving local people, and a strange light spotted near the river—became entwined together in people's minds and were elaborated upon and reborn as the legend of the Ghost of the Cimarron.

The Hamburger Man

The ramshackle lean-to, ominous in the deepening shadows of early evening, sagged into the side of a brush-covered mound out in the sand hills north of Hutchinson. The remnant of a filthy red sheet flapped like a tongue in the low opening that served as the door to the grime-encrusted shack.

A young couple rounded the side of the hillock and stopped in front of the decrepit structure. Earlier in the afternoon they had parked their car in the visitor's parking lot of the Sandhills State Park and taken one of the hiking trails through the sandy terrain. Dinner had been sandwiches and soft drinks from their knapsacks as they sat among the prairie grasses on a low knoll off trail and deep in the sand hills. As late afternoon had moved toward dusk, the couple had packed up the remains of their meal and headed back in what they thought was the right direction. In the fading light, they had missed their path and had wandered into an area not crossed by the hiking trails. Although anxious to find the trail and get back to their car, the couple was surprised to come upon the rude shelter built into the hill and distracted by its curious appearance. If they had been from Hutchinson, or grown up there, they probably would have known what it was they had stumbled upon. And they would have known to run, not stop and stare.

The weathered wood structure they had accidentally found provided a shelter of sorts for one of the most frightening legendary figures in the state—the infamous Hamburger Man. As the unwitting couple moved closer to the shack, perhaps to steal a peek behind the ratty sheet, they failed to see a flash of light from the bushes just beyond the hill—the reflection of a dying ray of sunlight glinting off curved steel.

A sudden gust of wind blew into the shack and sucked the rag of a door inward with a snapping sound. The couple jumped back from the door and looked at each other in fright. "Let's get out of here," one said to the other, and they walked quickly away from the hovel, moving west toward what remained of the sun on the horizon. Shortly they regained the trail, and before long they were back in their car and driving away from the sand hills and the dirty old shack hidden in the dunes and trees. And the monstrous man or ghost hidden in its shadows.

Legend claims that the Hamburger Man roams the sand hills under cover of night, searching for unsuspecting hikers, tourists, or romantic teens parked in cars on the remote sandy roads in the vicinity of his homely shanty. Stories of the Hamburger Man have been around for many years—going back at least to the 1950s. Individuals who grew up in Hutchinson twenty, thirty, even forty years ago remember cautionary tales of this monstrous man and what he would do to his prey if he caught it.

The Hamburger Man most commonly is believed to have earned his descriptive name because of his horribly disfigured face. Many versions of the tale mention some kind of unnamed unfortunate accident that mutilated and scarred his face, rendering it frightening and disgusting to look upon. Shunned by society and scorned as a monstrous creature, the Hamburger Man fled to the sand hills and built his pathetic abode to live out the rest of his life in isolation in his desolate surroundings. For those individuals foolhardy enough to be out after dark in the area or, worse, crazy enough to look for him or his house, their fate, suggest the stories, might be worse than death. The Hamburger Man's weapon of choice is usually an ax, sometimes a large curved knife. If he catches you, he'll "chop you up for hamburger meat," according to several versions of the legend.

Hamburger Hill is either a favorite parking spot for teenagers near where the Hamburger Man is known to roam, or it is the site of his shack in the sand hills. Take your pick—depending on the version of the legend you hear. One account says that "what he does to the young folks he catches there [at Hamburger Hill] is too horrible to put into words." This account also mentions dastardly deeds done to livestock and small children.

Drawing elements from a common urban legend retold throughout the United States, some versions of the Hamburger Man legend place a steel or silver hook on one of the Hamburger Man's hands, making him a fearsome version of the Hookman legend come to life in the sand hills. Hookman stories told all over the country usually involve teenagers parked in a remote location or local lovers' lane who hear an announcement over the radio that an escaped killer and/or lunatic with a hook for a hand is on the loose in the area. The girl speedily rolls up the car window while the boy steps on the accelerator and takes off in a cloud of dust. When they arrive home a short time later, they discover a disembodied hook hanging from the rolled-up car window, indicating that the "hookman" was about to get his hook in them when they hit the gas and took off!

Candy Miller is a local Hutchinson resident who grew up in town and graduated from Hutchinson High School in the mid-1960s. She said that it was common knowledge during her high school days that after dark "you couldn't go out to the sand hills and park with your date because the Hamburger Man would get you both and chop you up for hamburger. We all laughed, but it was always in the back of our minds."

Candy said that she first heard the legend from her father, who graduated from Hutchinson High in the early 1930s. Her mother also "kind of remembered" details of the legend and definitely remembered Candy's father telling the story to her daughter. "I think [the legend] started in the 1930s and 1940s," Candy asserted. "The sand hills weren't green like they are now. Even back in the 1950s and 1960s they were sandy and desolate—there was very little vegetation, and no trees. Kids would tell the story—it was passed down from generation to generation. I had two older brothers; I also heard it from one of their friends. They would say, 'Don't go out and park—the Hamburger Man will get you.'"

Candy's description of the Hamburger Man is a product of her imagination, not personal observation: "When you heard the story, you would imagine what he looked like. I don't remember anyone describing him; I just used my imagination. I think he would have looked like Jason from the [*Friday the 13th*] horror movies." "He had a shack-type thing in the sand hills," Candy continued. "It was so desolate. It was a lean-to type shack. There were a lot of them out there. The sand hills have become more 'treed'; it's not the same now. It was very eerie back then: There was very little light and sand roads."

Some individuals who tell the story of the Hamburger Man describe it as a Vietnam War–era story. The tellers of this version of the tale preface the usual story of the horribly deformed monster-ghost lurking in the sand hills with the information that the Hamburger Man is actually a deranged Vietnam veteran who was burned by napalm or wounded in a way that defaced his features. When these informants speak of the Hamburger Man from Hamburger Hill, they are making a dual reference to the Hamburger Man's hideout in Hutchinson's sand hills and the battle of Hamburger Hill, a major ten-day assault by the U.S. forces on a hill in South Vietnam that produced many dead and wounded casualties.

John Stratton, a 1971 graduate of Hutchinson High, also has specific memories of stories not only of the Hamburger Man and Hamburger Hill but also of the Hamburger People. Although Stratton's version does not invoke the Vietnam War as the prelude to the story, it does introduce a new element into the legend. Stratton related that young people in Hutchinson in the 1960s and 1970s would often travel to the northern edge of town, into the sand hills. "It was a good place to go with your girlfriend or boyfriend to park—there were no homes up there then; the only light would be from an occasional barnyard light." "It was a spooky place up there," said John. "Kids were always coming to school and telling stories about how 'something happened to somebody out at Hamburger Hill' the night before, or the weekend before."

Not only did John and his friends stay on the lookout for the Hamburger Man when they were up in the sand hills, but they were also watching out for a *group* of Hamburger People! John related that the Hamburger People reputedly were all burned in an accident or were part of a family all born deformed. "Their skin," said John, "was somehow scarred, or disfigured." As a group, the Hamburger People withdrew north of town to isolate themselves from the rest of the townspeople and their cruel stares and comments. According to John's rendition of the tale, the Hamburger People's main occupation seems to have been terrorizing the young people who went up into the sand hills to park or hang out.

Valerie Hemphill, a 1981 graduate of Burrton High School (located just east of Hutchinson), heard the legend in the early 1980s: "What I heard was there was a house in the country, and people said that the Hamburger Man lived there in that empty house. People said that he had a terrible face."

An older informant who would have grown up in Hutchinson in the 1930s and 1940s indicated that she had not heard the stories of the Hamburger Man but remembered an incident from sometime in the 1940s or 1950s that involved a house fire that killed most of the members of a family in town. As she recalled, one member of the family, a son, survived the fire but was badly burned and scarred. He remained in town for awhile but later "moved up north," and eventually died. This event might have spawned the horrible stories of a "hamburger man" and "hamburger people," giving rise to the tales of the ghost of a mangled or disfigured man or the living embodiment of a maimed hookman, living in the sand hills north of Hutchinson. But the legend of the Hamburger Man seems to predate the story of the fire. Perhaps there is a link to "Hamburger Gene," a real-life individual who sold "Hot Hamburgers—5 Cents" from a meat wagon (festooned with knives and carving implements) in downtown Hutchinson from around 1907 until his death in 1931.

Regardless, the Hamburger Man, whether in a group or alone, seems to have it all from a horror story standpoint: a desolate and spooky area in which to hang out, a ghastly facial disfigurement, an ax, a big knife, a hook for a hand, and a really bad attitude. Although he is commonly perceived as being more ghastly than ghostly, it seems safe to place this monstrous man in or on the fringes of the ghost category. Besides, one doesn't dare ignore him. Certainly, if he is a ghost, he is a monstrous ghost. And by all accounts, still quite active.

Theorosa's Bridge

Valley Center, population three thousand, is a small town just north of Wichita. On a country road about three miles north of Valley Center, a nondescript concrete bridge spans scenic Jester Creek where the water cuts under the road and meanders through a dense, lush line of trees zigzagging through a patchwork of fields and farms.

The bridge is officially known as the 109th Street Bridge, but around Valley Center and Wichita for at least thirty years it has been known more commonly by the name Theorosa's Bridge. A variety of stories circulating through the years tells the tale of Theorosa. The oldest setting for the story is the Kansas plains in the late 1800s when white settlers were traveling through the Jester Creek area. According to the story, a pioneer wagon train was attacked by Indians in the area, and a settler's baby, Theorosa, was stolen and carried away by the raiders. Theorosa's mother, grief-stricken, fled the wagon train to find her child. Legend has it that she roams Jester Creek yet, searching for her baby, her mournful cry heard from the bridge at night: "Theorosa, Theorosa. . . ."

Another variation of this turn-of-the-century tale has an Indian woman, Theorosa, as its central figure. This Theorosa has an illegitimate child, the result of an affair with a white settler. To hide her shame, she drowns the baby in Jester Creek and then, overcome with guilt and grief, drowns herself as well. An alternate version tells a story of murder; it places Theorosa on the banks of the creek, babe in arms, where she is stabbed by her vengeful Indian husband. Wounded, she accidentally drops the baby into the creek, where it is carried away by the rushing waters. Theorosa herself dies two "moons" and a day later, and her spirit returns to the place of her murder to eternally search the creek for her baby. Tellers of this tale report that the sounds of a baby crying can sometimes be heard, late at night, from the bridge and in the vicinity of that part of the creek.

More contemporary versions of the story identify Theorosa as a local farm wife who threw her illegitimate child from the bridge into the creek. She then drowned herself, or in some versions she returned to her farmhouse where she shot herself. Some tellers caution that if someone now stands on the bridge and repeats over and over, "Theorosa, Theorosa, I am your baby, I am your child," the ghost of Theorosa will come rushing up from the creek bed and try to throw the foolhardy individual off the bridge into the water below.

The original old wooden and iron trestle bridge that spanned the creek in that spot for generations burned in 1974, was rebuilt, and then burned again in 1976. For fifteen years, what remained of the bridge was closed off, and the road was barricaded. The husk of the bridge was overgrown with weeds and undergrowth at both ends, and the area was littered with trash from thrill-seeking party goers. The burned-out bridge became a popular site for beer parties and "woodsies" in the 1970s and 1980s, attracting young people from as far away as Hays and Wellington as well as teens and curiosity seekers from Wichita and Valley Center. A new modern concrete bridge was constructed in 1991, and the road was reopened.

The first published accounts of the legend, in the *Ark Valley News* and the *Wichita Sun,* date back to the early 1970s. Articles in the *Wichita Sun* referred to the legend, as did a full-page story ("The Legend Lives On") with pictures in the 1974 Valley Center High School yearbook, *The Hornet.* One neighbor who lives in the vicinity of the bridge, a resident of the area for thirty years, personally believes that the legend is a fabrication of teenagers from Wichita in the early 1970s—a time, she thinks, when Wichita had a curfew for teenagers and late-night party goers were forced out of Wichita to look for other party sites. The bridge became a popular gathering site for teens and others, and the legend became a fixture around the area. However, other local residents report hearing the legend in the 1960s and possibly before.

White ghostly shapes, the figure of a woman, feelings of unease, pockets of cold air on the bridge, white lights, cars stalling on the bridge, rain falling in the surrounding area while the bridge remains dry, unexplained footprints in the dew, mournful calls for "Theorosa" in the wind, the faint sounds of a baby crying under the bridge—all have been reported at various times by tellers of the tale. Stories of Theorosa's Bridge from years back weave a legend that is often fraught with sadness and searching, but certain variants of the tale mix more frightening elements of terror and the supernatural into the fabric of the legend. One such story, adapted from a student paper for a Kansas State University folklore class in 1974, might be aptly titled "Terror at Theorosa's Bridge."

Tuesday night, June 15, 1971, was a warm early-summer evening. A bright full moon was riding streaks of dark clouds high in the sky. Sometime after midnight it began to shower intermittently, turning the dusty dirt and gravel roads outside of Valley Center into muddy tracks with soft shoulders. The rusted iron framework of the old trestle bridge spanning Jester Creek at 109th Street creaked in the sporadic gusts of wind, its skeletal form appearing dark and ominous as it loomed over the warped boards of its wooden driving surface. A deep rumbling sound arose as a car drove slowly over the boards to the middle of the bridge and stopped.

The rain showers had died down, but the wind continued, leaving the trees surrounding the bridge and sheltering the creek moving in continuous nervous agitation. Water was standing in puddles in the road leading to the bridge, but, oddly, the wooden planks on the floor of the bridge were dry.

Two teenage boys got out of the car and leaned against it, looking out over the side of the bridge toward the south part of the creek. Inside the car were several of their friends, girls and boys. They had come out to the bridge to look around, half-seriously hoping to experience some of the "incidents" others of their friends had reported happening when they had gone out to the old bridge in search of "Theorosa's ghost."

One boy regaled the other teens with what he had heard of the legend: "So the background of the bridge is that a woman sometime within the last forty or fifty years had killed her two kids and cut their bodies up and threw them in the creek and then shot herself in the head, because her husband had left her. Her body was found under the bridge some weeks later. The police department was notified of body parts that were found in the water and then they followed the stream until they found the kids' bodies, or what was left of them. Since then, three people have disappeared around here and nobody has ever found them."

Following the instructions of other friends who had made the pilgrimage out to Theorosa's Bridge, after the recitation of the legend, the boys leaned over the edge of the bridge and called out over the water, "Theorosa, Theorosa, come to me!" Then they jumped into the car, and backed it off the bridge about fifty feet.

Their friends in the car were laughing and making jokes, looking around out the windows expectantly. Nothing was happening and one girl in the car suggested they leave. At that moment, someone said, "Look!" and pointed out the window toward an empty field adjacent to the car. Something was moving about 100 yards out. It was barely visible behind a hedge row but continued moving until it reached a ten-foot break in the hedge. It passed through the opening in the hedge and then all the occupants of the car could see it.

What appeared to be a pulsating grayish-white mass with arms and the shape of a head was moving toward the car across the field. A fence separated the field from the roadway and as the form met this wooden obstruction it raised its "arms" above its head and passed right through the fence. Everyone in the car was frozen with fear. When this pulsing entity approached to within five feet of the car, suddenly someone in the back seat screamed, "Let's get out of here!" The sound prodded the others into action as windows were rolled up and doors were locked. One boy in the front began shrieking continuously and this sound seemed to discourage the ghoul. It began to fade backwards the same way it had come, back through the fence and back into the field.

As the ghastly gray thing receded back behind the tree line and into the creek, the sounds of a car moving at high speed down a muddy country backroad faded into the distance. The trees beyond the bridge moved restlessly and the iron trestle cried and moaned in the wind.

The above rendition of a lengthy and vivid 1970s-era version of Theorosa's legend is representative of some stories told then about the bridge and its ghost. Other versions of the legend feature a "figure in white" rather than the ghoulish ghost described above.

Another incidence of a sighting occurred in the early 1970s at Theorosa's Bridge, and this time the ghost, described as having a pale misty appearance, was a white cloudlike apparition that moved along the road before vanishing.

As frightening as the legend of Theorosa was in the 1970s and 1980s, the stories that are currently circulating make the old tales seem tame. The tradition of sharing stories about the ghost of Theorosa and her baby has continued, especially among the young people at Valley Center High School. Even though the old bridge is no more, the legend has survived the burning of the bridge and is well known in an astonishing variety of versions. In May 1996, several of Nancy Hopkins's English classes at Valley Center High produced nearly *thirty* depictions of Theorosa and her ill-fated baby or children. Here are some samples:

"If you go down there at night and walk down by the water and say, 'Theorosa, I have your baby' three times there will be a ghost that comes screaming and running at you. You get so scared and run or else, if you are brave, you might just close your eyes. But I'm never brave enough to stay out there, I always run."

"One of my friends said that his aunt went there to party one night and said, 'Theorosa, I have your baby,' and something jumped on her and scratched down her back. The next morning she looked in the mirror and she had nail scratches down her back. Now I've been there before two or three times and one time we said, 'Theorosa, we have your baby,' and the water got really fast so we left because we got too scared."

"I was told by my mother and grandparents about the Theorosa bridge. They said they remember when it was on the news about a woman that cut up her baby and threw the pieces over the bridge. She was then cursed to stay at the site to find every piece of her baby. My grandfather and his sons went out to the bridge and started calling her name and saying they had her baby, and then they said they saw a white shadow coming toward them, so they started running to the car and when they got to the car and got in, she jumped on the car and started banging on the window shield and shaking the car. It then stopped and they left."

"Well, I heard that if you go out to the bridge on Halloween at 12:00 A.M. and keep your car on and someone says, 'Theorosa, Theorosa, Theorosa, bring forth you or your baby's head,' she's supposed to rise on the right side, she's dressed in a white dress, she locks all the doors and turns off your engine, and then she possesses someone in the car who kills everybody including themselves, then she returns to the bridge. The story is told like this: Theorosa went down to the river and was going to kill her baby to protect it from the Indians. She was supposed to shoot it or cut its head off, but instead she drowned it and the Indians saw her and killed her, so now she haunts the bridge."

Theorosa is an unusually active ghost, and besides haunting, wandering, searching, moaning, screaming, running, attacking, scratching, banging on windows and shaking cars, and generally frightening a large number of people half to death, she also has been known to ride horseback for sport. One story has it that a farmer in the area who used to pasture horses near the bridge found one of his horses dead one morning— a horse that had seemed in perfect health the day before. One explanation offered for the inexplicable demise of the horse was that Theorosa's ghost had taken the horse out for a ride and ridden it to death.

The Valley Center Police Department has made numerous calls out to the Theorosa's Bridge area over the last twenty-five years to control partying as well as some individuals whose imaginations were in overdrive. Police indicate that activity near the old bridge site is nearly nonexistent these days. Although the stories of the ghost remain active and alive, the site itself as an attraction pretty much died in the fire that consumed Theorosa's Bridge.

A Ghostly Sisyphus

In Greek mythology, King Sisyphus was the cleverest of men, always wreaking havoc of some sort among the gods and other mortals on earth. After Sisyphus died, Hades, the god of the underworld, wanted to keep order in his nether realm and preferred to keep Sisyphus busy so he wouldn't have spare time on his hands to dream up disruptive schemes. So Hades devised a scheme of his own to occupy Sisyphus. He set Sisyphus to the task of pushing an enormous boulder up a hill. But every time he had nearly reached the top of the hill, the boulder would slip away from him and roll back down to the bottom of the hill. Poor Sisyphus was condemned to repeat this task over and over for eternity, a job that effectively kept his attention fixed and kept him out of trouble.

Junction City has a ghostly Sisyphus of its own in its local ghost lore. Stories from the turn of the century relate the tale of Moose, a hunchback Pottawatomie and his beloved Lura, the chief's daughter. Moose and Lura were supposedly part of a band of Pottawatomie who were encamped near the Junction City area in the 1860s. The site of the camp was a mound a few miles west of the city and close to the Smoky Hill River, now known as Indian Hill. The base of the hill came to be known as Deadman's Hollow. The physically deformed young brave, with his "moose-like shoulders," was madly in love with the beautiful Lura, but she was repelled by his deformity and refused to return his affection.

One day a white trader, a charlatan dispensing quack remedies and liquor, came into the camp. Handsome and dashing in appearance, the trader caught the eye of the lovely Lura and became Moose's rival for her attention. The desperate Moose sought the trader's advice for a remedy or charm to straighten his spine and boost his physical appeal. The trader, seeing an opportunity to get rid of Moose for awhile, sent Moose to the top of the nearby hill with a special incantation designed to make him whole and comely. The gullible brave was to chant the spell or prayer that evening until he was cured.

That evening Moose was perched on the hill, chanting, happily contemplating his rosy future with Lura. The trader and Lura, meanwhile, had arranged a tryst at the base of the hill overlooking the hollow. An 1890 *Junction City Republican* chronicle of the event reported: "Looking down in the moonlight, he (Moose) saw the trader and his divinity in lover-like proximity." The newspaper story continued with the account of Moose's revenge: "Angered, maddened, desperate, he pondered on his course of revenge. Seeing a large, nearly round boulder on the edge of the hill, he pried it loose and sent it on its mission of destruction. Bounding, leaping down the declivity it rushed and swept the two lovers into the hollow. Their bodies were found long afterward."

Horrified at what he had done, Moose barricaded himself atop the hill. The next day found him incoherently babbling the incantation the trader had taught him and pitching stones at anyone who tried to approach him. Lura's father, the chief, ordered his tribesmen to stop the assault, but Moose's madness lent him fury, and he continually drove off his friends with a terrible onslaught of rocks. He was finally brought down in a volley of arrows and buried on the top of the hill.

The saga of Moose, Lura, and the trader supposedly came to its tragic end in the mid-1860s, but the ghost of the doomed Moose didn't make his weirdly Sisyphus-like appearance until a quarter of a century later, when his resting place at the top of Indian Hill was disturbed. The *Junction City Republican* on January 23, 1890, repeated the original legend and then reported on recent "supernatural appearances which have there been manifested" in the vicinity of Indian Hill and Deadman's Hollow:

> A few weeks ago it was decided to cut a wagon road over the hill. To do this the crown of the eminence was torn away. Almost the first earth moved contained an Indian skeleton, with a crooked and misshapen trunk. The skull, on being loosened by the plow, rolled over the brow of the hill and following the path of the fatal boulder, bounded and leaped until it found a resting place amid the sunflowers and cattails that line the hollow at the base.
>
> Since then Dead Man's Hollow and Indian Hill have become terrors to all wanderers. Several witnesses tell of the strange sights that have been seen there. The wagon road is almost useless after dark as few will drive over the hill on that account. The apparition is described by one who

claims to have seen it as a bent figure rolling with difficulty a stone up a hill. With weird shrieks and groans he toils with his terrible load, but at last is compelled to stop when far from the top. Then the stone breaks away and rolls back to the hollow, but that is not all. The ghost's head follows it! Tumbling and leaping until it, too, stops in the weeds the body fades away only to appear again at the base of the hill, rolling up the stone, to repeat the whole ghastly spectacle. The other parties of the tragedy having, perhaps, no sin to expiate, seem to rest in peace, but the hunchback ghost on many a dark and stormy night may be seen at its terrible task, while the prairie breeze brushing the grasses bears its painful moanings to the traveler's ears.

Even the formal, somewhat stilted, language of one hundred years ago cannot blunt the imagery of the shrieking and groaning hunchbacked phantom straining to push his terrible rocky burden up the hill, only to have it break loose and roll back down the hill with the ghost's ghastly head following, "leaping and tumbling," close behind.

Although the macabre scenario of Moose chasing his head down the hill hasn't been reported in the Junction City area for generations, this Kansas version of a Greek tragedy is so vivid and compelling as an imaginative ghost legend that it truly deserves to be resurrected.

Kate Coffee and Her Ghouls

Kate Coffee is the female Paul Bunyan, in terms of size, of Kansas ghosts. Described in life as a very large woman—an amazon, in fact—her legend in central and western Kansas begins in 1869 when Kate Burns married Mike Coffee at Hays City. Together the Coffees ran a saloon in Hays until they moved to Rush County southeast of Rush Center in 1872. Their stone house in Rush County sat just south of the old Fort Hays–Fort Larned trail where it crossed Walnut Creek. The Coffees quickly set up for business in their new location, putting a saloon in their house to service thirsty travelers on the fort trail. Court records of the time establish accusations leveled against Mike Coffee for serving liquor in the county without a proper license. The Coffees' house also served the area as a post office. The name chosen for their location and post office was Economy.

Life in Economy did not last long for Kate Coffee. An article in the *To-*

peka Daily Commonwealth in June 1872 reported on the abrupt end of Mrs. Coffee: "Quite a tragedy occurred on Walnut crossing, between [Larned] and Hays, a few days ago, resulting in the death of Mrs. Kate Coffey [sic], formerly of Hays. A young man living on the creek, above Mrs. Coffey's, went to the house, it seems, to inquire for mail, and while there an altercation took place between them and during the fracas the young man stabbed Mrs. C. in the left side in the region of the heart. Medical attention was procured from Fort Larned, but little could be done for her; she lingered about thirty-six hours in great pain when death put an end to her intense suffering. . . ." The alleged murderer, John Barker, was captured three days later and brought before the judge within the week. In his deposition, Kate's husband Mike swore that "on the 22nd day of June, 1872, in the county of Rush, State of Kansas, one John J. Barker did willfully, feloniously, and with malice aforethought stab one Catherine Coffee with a butcher knife thereby causing the death of said Catherine Coffee."

Barker was adjudged guilty at his preliminary trial and sent to the Saline County jail "to await the action of the District Court at the next term," according to records. In the meantime, Mike Coffee himself was brought to trial for illegally selling "intoxicating liquors." John Barker, still awaiting trial for the murder of Kate Coffee, was subpoenaed as a witness for the state in the trial of Mike Coffee! Coffee, however, was found not guilty. The ultimate disposition of Barker's case is unknown, according to an article in the *Hays Daily News* in 1972. According to that article, Kate Coffee's final resting place is on the banks of Walnut Creek near the old Fort Hays–Fort Larned trail. But legend throughout Rush County has it that Kate might not be resting easy.

Additional elements of Kate's legend indicate that maybe she was providing more than just bar service to soldiers and travelers who wanted a little companionship with their intoxicating liquors when they stopped off at the Coffee house/saloon. The tawdry side of her legend suggests that Kate was killed by a soldier who was murderously furious with her for introducing him to a venereal disease. Kate Coffee obviously had a reputation for wild living and the earthier aspects of frontier living in Kansas. This reputation seems to have spawned some of the weirder tales of Kate's ghostly revelry along Walnut Creek and in the general area of the stone ranch house she shared with her husband and evidently some customers.

An alliterative quote from a reporter in the Hays City *Sentinel* of July 27,

1878, illustrates the power of Kate's legend even 120 years ago: "We talked to an old farmer the other day who stoutly asserted that 'in the full of the moon' on gusty nights, Kate Coffee and her fantastic host of ghouls hold high carnival on the banks of the beauteous Walnut. He says he has heard their weird, wild songs of ribaldry and watched their goblin gambols on the green."

Kate Coffee, larger than life in life and also in death, is still gamboling (mostly sans goblins) around the area more than a century later. Her ghost has been spotted in recent years on Highway 96 south of Hays and north of Larned, where the highway parallels Walnut Creek and runs through Rush Center, near her old homesite. She is evidently drawn to travelers and "trails," even now, especially in the vicinity of her old "gamboling grounds."

Carolyn Thompson of McCracken was a contributor to *Rush County Kansas . . . A Century in Story and Pictures,* a book published in 1976 and compiled by members of the Rush County Historical Society Book Committee. The Rush County book detailed the legend of Kate Coffee and her ghost, drawing upon information gleaned from newspaper articles and other written sources, such as the articles mentioned in this story.

Carolyn feels that, although Kate Coffee's legend is no longer widely known in the area, unexplainable happenings along Highway 96 in recent years are still attributed to Kate's ghost. She related an occurrence that happened to her parents about 1986: "Ten years ago my folks were driving to Great Bend from here [McCracken]. My brother was with them. They experienced something down there on Highway 96 that startled them. They were driving at night. They were through Alexander and heading east along where Walnut Creek runs by the highway. They saw something come up to the side of them, to the side of the car, while they were driving. It was a bright, white light. It startled them. Later, after the Rush County book had come out and they had read about the legend, my mother said to me, 'I think we saw the ghost of Kate Coffee!'"

Carolyn said that she has had other people as well tell her of coming through the hills east of Timken, a small town on Highway 96 and seeing fireballs as they drove through the hills. "There is a stretch of pasture land along there and a series of seven or eight hills. That's where the fireballs would be seen." She added, "People would not necessarily connect this fireball with Kate Coffee, but it is in the same general vicinity."

Whether she is recognized or not in her chosen ghost form of woman, ghoul, or fireball, it seems apparent that Kate Coffee is still around, nowadays usually running through the hills, leaping across Walnut Creek, or hurtling onto Highway 96.

The Legends of Witches Hollow

A truncated body runs haphazardly in and out of the trees lining Witches Hollow. Weaving and stumbling, the headless torso is an incongruous sight on the quiet country road just south of Girard. This nightmare scene plays itself out night after night within the confines of the legends of Witches Hollow. The headless body runs through the hollow. Its severed head, a look of supreme surprise on its face, is seen suspended from one of the arched trees lining the road. As the head twists and groans in the wind, the blackening shadows cast by the tunnel of trees over the road melt together until the road through Witches Hollow becomes as dark and obscure as a mine shaft.

Witches Hollow is pretty much gone now, itself a victim to modern progress and a local recreation area. Many of the trees are gone, and the area has lost its spooky aura. But memories of the legends and stories that lived along that stretch of country road outside of Girard persist.

Captain John Gagliardo, deputy with the Crawford County sheriff's office, has lived in Crawford County all of his life and has been with the sheriff's department since 1976. "I had not heard of the legend until I came to the sheriff's office, but I lived in another part of the county," he said. But Captain Gagliardo became familiar with the stories of Witches Hollow when he began patrolling the area around the hollow. "It's a county road, and it was seldom used back then. Trees had grown over the top of the road and formed a tunnel. It extended less than a half mile, but more than a quarter mile. It was real dark—you couldn't see through the trees." He continued, "At initiation time for schools, they would drop kids off and make them walk home. The wind would make goofy noises. With the trees grown together over the middle of the road and the wind whipping through—the combination of darkness and wind would make it seem haunted."

Captain Gagliardo estimated that the peak time period for the active telling of the legend and participation in legend tripping to the site was from the 1960s through all of the 1970s. "The kids would gather around out there," he said. "It was not really a trouble-type spot. It was always popular around Halloween." As far as Captain Gagliardo knew, the place was always known as Witches Hollow, but where that name came from, he did not know.

A report in the *Pittsburg Morning Sun* in 1979 quoted a resident from Brazilton, just northeast of Girard, who recalled "the hollow's reputation" from the early 1960s and gave a clue as to the genesis of the legendary site's name: "We used to go out there. Supposedly a witch wandered the road, looking for someone." Even in 1979, the area had lost some of its "spooky atmosphere" due to trimming of the trees, according to the Brazilton resident. He explained: "It used to be a lot worse then. The road was completely covered with trees and you couldn't see much."

Jim Sellars, since deceased, was the Crawford County sheriff in 1979. He recalled for the same *Pittsburg Morning Sun* article that in his student days in the early 1960s, he and his friends from school "used to go to Witches Hollow for parties and weenie roasts." In addition to the witch, Sellars remembered that "part of the legend attached to Witches Hollow was that a headless person was running around over there. There was an old tree on the left that the headless person was supposed to have hung from." Sellars also related that stories of human sacrifice and satanic cults had attached themselves to the site at one time. A counselor at Pittsburg High School had heard rumors during the same time period that people had been "found dead at Witches Hollow."

Activity had already subsided out around Witches Hollow by the late 1970s, and the legend has mostly become a shared memory for individuals who grew up and went to school around Girard twenty to thirty-some years ago. Captain Gagliardo reported that the road through Witches Hollow is no longer desolate or secluded: "Now it is used quite a bit—there is a recreational area there now. The trees on one side have mostly been taken out."

With most of the menacing overgrown trees gone, the malevolence of Witches Hollow exists only in the past. But it is easy to conjure up the vivid imagery that frightened at least two generations of Crawford Countians and imagine a terrified teenager dumped off at midnight in the middle of a deserted county road by pranksters sometime in the 1960s, left to run a gauntlet of witches, satanists, and headless horrors through the inky tree-enclosed cavern that was Witches Hollow.

*　　*　　*　　*　　*

The Holmes Ghost Light

Mrs. Holmes finished packing her trunk and took a last look around her "soddy," the sod home she and her husband had built west of Colby in Thomas County. It was spare and primitive, but its tarpaper roof, sod walls, and dirt floors covered with rag carpets all made for a house that was surprisingly snug and secure from the elements.

Mrs. Holmes was leaving on a trip to eastern Kansas to visit her family. She would miss her house and the plains of northwest Kansas, but most of all she would miss her husband, Gilbert, who had arranged for her to travel back to her family home to see her aged parents. "Now you take care of yourself, Gilbert, and take care of my house, too," she told him before she left. Travel was slow and tedious at the turn of the century, and Mrs. Holmes had a long journey ahead of her. She kissed Mr. Holmes before she stepped out of the sod house door, not knowing it was to be their final good-bye. Gilbert would be dead before she saw her sod house again.

Several days later, Gilbert Holmes also left the sod house to drive some mules over to Arnold Grout's farm. The Grouts owned a neighboring farmstead and were expecting Gilbert and his mules. Gilbert mounted his horse and began herding the animals. Somehow the lead rope tied to one of the mules became entangled around one of Gilbert's legs. He struggled to free himself, but as he leaned over his saddle to try and disentangle his leg, he was pulled from his horse and fell heavily to the ground. The snared mule, now frightened, began running and plunging against the rope. Gilbert, hog-tied in the animal's lead rope, was helpless as he was dragged along behind the mule for three or four miles.

Arnold Grout and his daughter, Lisetta, on horseback, were awaiting Gilbert and his mules, prepared to assist in driving the animals the rest of the way to their farm. They were unprepared, however, for the gruesome sight that galloped past them in a cloud of dust. After their initial shock, the pair spurred their horses into pursuit of the crazed mule and its terrible burden. When they finally stopped the mule and jumped down to assist Gilbert, they realized that their neighbor, though still alive, would not survive his injuries long. The unfortunate man had been dragged the entire distance on his back, over rough and rocky ground, and the torturous trip had abraded most of the flesh from his back, exposing portions of his internal organs. The father and daughter gingerly transported Gilbert back to their farm where they tried to alleviate his terrible suffering as best they could. But their efforts were mostly unsuccessful, as Gilbert Holmes slipped into unconsciousness and died before the night was over.

Word of her husband's death was sent to Mrs. Holmes, but interment of the body could not wait until she was able to get transportation back to western Kansas. The Grout family made funeral arrangements for Gilbert, and his body was buried in the Fairview Cemetery, just north of Brewster in Thomas County. As soon as she could, Mrs. Holmes returned to pay her respects at her husband's grave site and to collect their belongings from her beloved sod house. She then went back to eastern Kansas to live with her family and left the sturdy little sod house abandoned on the western Kansas high plains.

Not long after the death of Gilbert Holmes, two local men were riding to a "literary" at the old sod schoolhouse in the district. The route to the schoolhouse went past the Holmeses' deserted soddy. It was a windy evening, and the riders stopped and dismounted by the sod house so as to use the structure as a windbreak while lighting their pipes. With their heads bent low over their pipes and their backs to the sod walls, the men did not immediately notice the eerie glow that began radiating from inside the windows of the house. One man, his pipe lit, casually turned around to glance at the house. What he saw caused him to grab his partner's arm and forcibly turn him around to face the house.

"Gawd. Do you see what I see." It was a statement more than a question. The first man knew from the look on his companion's face that he, too, saw the bright white light emanating from the interior of the sod house. Transfixed, the two men watched as the ghostly light penetrated through the sod wall and appeared outside the house in the form of a ray-like beacon. The light moved away from the soddy, traveling toward the southwest.

Practically light-headed with fear, the men hesitated before deciding to follow the incandescent beam. But curiosity overcame their trepidation, and they remounted their horses and followed the light. The beacon led them on a circuitous but steady route to the Fairview Cemetery, where it entered the graveyard, hovered in place over a grave, and then vanished. The men hung back outside the cemetery for a few minutes, but when the light did not reappear, they cautiously made their way to the grave site into which the light had seemed to disappear. The name on the marker was Gilbert Holmes.

These men may have been the first to experience the Holmes Ghost Light, as it came to be called, but they were not the last. Numerous other witnesses in the Brewster area west of Colby claimed to have watched as this luminous spook light traversed the fatal final journey of Gilbert Holmes, beginning at his soddy, tracing the path where he was dragged to death by his mule, and finally extinguishing itself at his grave.

One longtime resident of the area, since deceased, related her 1905 "encounter with the unknown" to Mike Baughn, the undersheriff of Thomas County and past president of the Thomas County Historical Society. Baughn visited Mary O'Brian Bundy in the late 1980s at her home north of Brewster, where she recalled her experience, as a girl of nine, with the Holmes Ghost Light. Baughn detailed Mary Bundy's encounter in an article he wrote for the Thomas County Historical Society *Prairie Winds* newsletter in 1990: "She was riding her horse to gather the milk cows one evening when she and her horse were suddenly enveloped in a brilliant light. The frightened horse threw Mary over its head to the ground, then the light moved on, taking its path to the southwest. Mary, afoot as the frightened horse would not permit her to remount, finished driving the cattle home. Upon her arrival, she explained what had happened, and was told that it was nothing to worry about, it was just the Holmes Ghost Light. Although frightened at the time, Mary lost her fear of the bright white light, and observed it several times after her unique experience."

According to the legend, Gilbert Holmes's wife returned one more time to northwest Kansas. About 1907 or 1908, Mrs. Holmes oversaw the disinterment and removal of her husband's body from Fairview Cemetery. She then had the remains transported back to eastern Kansas and presumably buried there. "Since that time," Mike Baughn related in his article, "the Holmes Ghost Light has not been seen."

Sheriff Baughn, in a recent interview, reported that he personally searched the old Fairview–Prairie Gem Cemetery on County Road BB for any evidence of Gilbert Holmes's grave site. He could not find the Holmes name in the cemetery and believes that Holmes's wife very possibly could have had his body disinterred and moved.

All the elderly informants Sheriff Baughn talked to a few years back about their observations of the Holmes Ghost Light are now deceased. Ninety years have passed since anyone has reported seeing the unearthly beacon moving over the countryside or hovering over the old cemetery. One must assume that the ghost of Gilbert Holmes, manifested in an illusory beam of light, no longer is compelled to trace a lonely path from an abandoned soddy to an isolated graveyard. He was reunited with his wife and, restless no more, is most likely buried beside her, hundreds of miles from their sod house on the western plains.

St. Jacob's Well: The Cowboy Ghost and His Ghost Horse

J. W. "Daddy" Walters awoke at 1:00 A.M. on a hot summer's night in Clark County, Kansas, in the 1890s. It was stifling in his little frame shack, and the torpid air lay about him on his bed like an oppressive blanket. Daddy sat up stiffly and reached for his pipe and tobacco, both in their customary places on his bedside table. Thinking the front stoop might offer a bit of breeze and a welcome respite from the stagnant atmosphere inside his house, the old settler stuck his pipe in his mouth and shuffled to the front door and on outside. He sat down on the stoop and absentmindedly began tamping tobacco into the bowl of his pipe. But before he could light up, his attention was diverted by a tall dark motionless form in the distance, silhouetted against the moonlit sky.

What Daddy saw that night was a horse and rider poised at the top of the ridge surrounding St. Jacob's Well. The natural spring-fed well, actually a deep pool of water about thirty yards across, was a popular watering hole for cowboys and their horses in the Big Basin area just west and a little north of Ashland. But, as Daddy said, "It wuz purty late fer a man to be a-ridin' around in these parts at thet time." As Daddy watched, the silent shapes of the man and his mount began to move and soon disappeared below the rim of the ridge surrounding the well.

Daddy struck a match and lit his pipe. With deep satisfaction, he drew the first draught of smoke into his lungs, but he expelled it with a cough when what he heard on the hot summer wind caused him to suddenly catch his breath. "I heered the most blood-curdlingest sound ever made on this here earth," he recalled many years later. "It nigh froze me stiff, though I knowed right away it wuz the sound made by a dying horse. . . . Jest after the horse let out thet devil'sh sound I heered the faint shriek o' the man—sort a' despairin' like, then everything was still as death."

It took a minute for Daddy to regain his composure and for his knees to quit "a-knockin' agin each other," but he soon mustered the presence of mind to collect his "old nag" from the stable and ride the short distance from his shack to the edge of the well. But the settler was too late to help the hapless horse and rider or even to catch a glimpse of their demise. "When I looked over the rim o' thet pond o' Satan, thar warn't a dad-blasted ripple on th' whole thing and nary a sign o' man or beast." The cowboy and his horse were gone, sucked down into the depths of St. Jacob's Well.

According to the story told by Daddy Walters, exhaustive attempts the next day by the settler and several other local men to search the pool and drag its depths for any sign of the drowned pair were fruitless. Daddy contended that it was during this search of the well that it was first discovered that the pool was bottomless: "Thet wuz th' first anybody around these parts suspected it. We let out the-Lord-knows-how-many thousand feet o' rope and touched nary a sign of bottom, horse or man."

Old Daddy Walters continued to tell the story of the ill-fated cowboy and his horse for many years after the drowning occurred. "Nobody will ever know who thet man wuz or how it happened, but I can still hear the ghosts o' them two a-shriekin' yet on a moonlight night. Yes sir!" By the time Daddy recounted the tale for a reporter from the Dodge City *Globe* in October 1924, the legend of the ghost cowboy and his ghost horse was well known in the area, along with many other stories about the supposed bottomless "mystery pool of the west." Seventy-some years later, legend still dictates that a visitor to St. Jacob's Well on a moonlit night can hear the "blood-curdlingest" sound of the screams of a cowboy and his horse rising from the depths of the well and echoing out over the canyons and valleys of the Big Basin.

A weatherbeaten, barn-red hanging sign stands like a lone sentinel among the rock-strewn rolling hills and plateaus of the Big Basin area thirty-six miles south of Dodge City. It reads: WELCOME TO ST. JACOB'S WELL Then cometh he to a city of Samaria near the parcel of ground that Jacob gave to his son Joseph, now Jacob's well was there. John 4: 5,6.

St. Jacob's Well is part of the Big Basin Prairie Reserve, an 1,818-acre refuge acquired, with the assistance of the Nature Conservancy, by the Kansas Fish and Game Commission in 1974. The Big Basin Prairie Reserve is registered as a national landmark of the Department of Heritage Conservation and Restoration Service of the U.S. Department of the Interior. Access to the reserve is by way of a graveled road leading off Highway

160 west of Ashland. An easily missed historical marker located on the east side of the highway points the way to a primitive gravel path that winds and bumps its way around hills and up ridges until it leads to the well, about a mile off the highway. The area is leased by Thunder of the Plains Buffalo Ranch, and wild bison roam the hills of the preserve. The casual visitor must watch for bison when exiting his or her car to enjoy the sweeping vistas of the basin or before hiking down from the top of the ridge to the secluded circle of trees and brush that surrounds and protects St. Jacob's Well.

The well is actually located in the floor of the Little Basin, a mile-wide geological sinkhole, part of a series of depressions in Clark County. The Big Basin, a twelve-mile-wide depression, is located just adjacent to the Little Basin and St. Jacob's Well. The large sinkhole that is the Big Basin was most likely formed when salt and gypsum beds hundreds of feet below the surface of the ground dissolved, allowing the ground to sink. The Little Basin developed in the same fashion. St. Jacob's Well is a sinkhole, too, possibly shaped by eroded rock falling into an underground river or spring. The actual depth of the well today is only about eighteen feet, although it could have been much deeper a century ago, given changes in the geologic structure of the area over time.

The biblical Jacob's Well was considered to be bottomless or of great depth. Contrary to Daddy Walters's story, the St. Jacob's Well in Clark County was thought to be bottomless even before Daddy and his friends dredged its depths for the drowned cowboy and his horse. According to legends of the well, government surveyors in the 1880s lowered chains into the murky depths of the pool and supposedly could not strike a bottom. Settlers in the area in the nineteenth century believed that St. Jacob's Well was the crater of an extinct volcano and estimated it to be at least two hundred feet deep, if not indeed bottomless. An attempt to find the bottom was cause for a party thrown by a rancher who owned the land in the 1890s. Ranchhands, cowboys, and local men tied together all their ropes and lariats and weighted them. Several men then got on a raft and lowered the weighted rope near the center of the well but could not find the bottom of the natural well. Another rancher some time later claimed to hit bottom at thirty-eight feet, but his neighbors believed he had probably just hit a ledge. Even in recent times, local legend has continued to perpetuate the belief that the well is bottomless or that an underground spring or stream carries any ropes or measuring devices lowered into it for miles.

The well has always been a source of freshwater and has never been known to go dry, even during droughts. Nomadic Native Americans, no doubt the first to discover the well on their journeys across the plains, reputedly constructed a huge stone marker that stood atop a hill just south of the pool. That original marker, a seven-foot-tall pile of rocks marking this permanent site of potable water, was destroyed by twentieth-century vandals, but a replica was erected by the Clark County Historical Society, the rocks cemented together for permanence. Today this Living Water Marker (the name also taken from scripture: John 4:11) still points the way to St. Jacob's Well as the original did one hundred years ago for Native Americans, settlers, travelers on the overland trails, and drovers moving cattle along the cattle trails nearby.

In "the early days," St. Jacob's Well was a popular recreation spot for picnicking and Sunday afternoon jaunts. An 1896 photograph shows seven well-dressed couples (long, ruffled dresses for the ladies and bowler hats, jackets, and cravats for the gentlemen) lounging among the trees and rocks that line the slopes leading into the well. A favorite pastime of picnickers was rolling or kicking these large rocks and boulders into the well. Over time, tons of rock no doubt ended up in the well, perhaps one explanation for the increasing shallowness of the water.

Probably as a result of the reports of the well's vast depths, sightings of blind fish, fish without eyes, fish with feet, and other aquatic abnormalities have been described in the past by local residents and visitors to the pond. Although no evidence of blind or footed fish in the well exists, brightly colored lizards do scuttle around the rocks and wooden planks that make up the crude stairs that lead down to the pool's level nowadays, and perhaps these creatures, darting around the rim of the well, were mistaken for walking fish evolved from the primitive depths of St. Jacob's Well.

Local folklore also holds that a murdered man lies in the depths of the mysterious well. In 1889, a posse searched for John Jordan, an Irishman reported missing in the vicinity of the sinkhole. The only evidence linked to the man's fate was the discovery of a large number of peanuts and peanut hulls scattered on the ground on the south side of the rim of St. Jacob's Well. Speculation in the area held that someone murdered the man, hauled the body to the well in a peanut wagon, and dumped the body out of the wagon and over the rim, consequently spilling the telltale peanuts and shells. A suspect in the case, a man who had had business dealings with Jordan, was friendly with a peanut farmer and was known to often use his wagon. But no one could be found who was particularly eager to dive into the "bottomless pit" and search for the missing man, so with no body, the investigation was halted and, one hundred years later, the case remains unsolved.

For years, scuttlebutt in the Big Basin area has speculated that more than one dead body has been consigned to the depths of the well. Stories even tell of a diver who plunged into the sinkhole to explore it sometime before 1950. The diver, presumably caught under a ledge or swept away by the underground river, never resurfaced and is presumed to have joined the drowned cowboy and his horse, the murdered man from the peanut wagon, and who knows how many other unfortunates, in the bowels of the murky, unfathomable well.

Another ghost story—a haunted house story—also lingers about the area. Years ago, a house stood on a hill near St. Jacob's Well, on the north rim of the Big Basin. It was long considered to be inhabited by a ghost. Henry Ford, a lifelong resident of the Ashland area, remembers seeing the haunted house over sixty years ago: "My father, Lon Ford, was the sheriff of Clark County back in 1931 and 1932—Depression days. I was just a child. We would drive out there [near St. Jacob's Well] and sit on the hill. It was supposed to be an empty house, but a light would flash on and off in one of the windows. I wonder now if it was just an old window in the house swinging back and forth, reflecting the moon—if that's what made the light. But kids would go out there to see the haunted house and the lights in the window."

Henry Ford's father grew up just south of the well, and Henry said his dad, too, tried to find the bottom of the well at one time. "He rolled a roll of binder twine down in it, but he never hit bottom." Henry said that he has heard reports of fish with four legs being found in the well, but he thinks they might just be salamanders. He also has heard tell of dye being put in the well a few years ago, and the dye showed up in the Cimarron River.

The experimentalist writer Ronald Johnson spent twenty years working on his epic poem, *ARK*, recently published to extensive critical praise. Johnson currently lives in Topeka, but he grew up in Ashland and indicated in a *Topeka Capital-Journal* article in June 1996 that his epic "was designed with a Western Kansas setting in mind." Johnson's setting? "There's a place—a magic place, really—near Ashland, called St. Jacob's Well, which is a bottomless well. It's kind of in a box valley. . . . And I kind of imagined *ARK* as a structure, standing there."

St. Jacob's Well is a magical place and a ghostly place as well. Blind fish with feet, a phantom cowboy riding his ghostly steed across the face of the moon, a haunted house on a hill, a skeletal diver, a dead man wrapped with rope and weights and shedding peanut shells sinking into the funnel-shaped pond, and the ARK of a poet's imagination framing the dark enigmatic waters within its curved hull—all these elements contribute to the magic and mystique of St. Jacob's Well, the "mystery pool of the west."

Ghostly Oddities

Most ghosts are boring. They are repetitive and unimaginative. Patterns of the same ghostly elements, or motifs, show up in legend after legend, story after story. That is why, generally, it is easy to categorize ghost stories and arrange them chapter by chapter, as in this book. Ghosts are usually the spirits of humans, not animals, and they commonly engage in fairly ritualized ghostly behavior.

Unexplained footsteps, doors and windows being opened and closed, cold spots and drafts, strange vocal sounds, rapping sounds, electrical disturbances, odd odors, and peculiar "feelings" often signal that a ghost has taken up residence in a house or building.

Ghosts out in the open recurrently attach themselves to a landscape feature such as a bridge, a body of water, a hill, a tree, or a road. These ghosts tend to manifest themselves as a spook light or will-o'-the-wisp or appear as an apparition walking around in the open air. Wailing, moaning, screaming, and laughing are sounds that are associated with outdoor ghosts, most likely because these sounds are loud enough to be heard outside, as opposed to the indoor sounds of tappings, footsteps, whisperings, and murmurings.

Few ghosts are actually seen as apparitions. Most commonly announce themselves through sounds, smells, and feelings; poltergeists are recognized by their destructive and/or prankish behavior.

With the general rules established, it becomes necessary to create a place for the ghosts that break the rules—the ghosts that display odd and difficult-to-categorize or unusual behavior (or form).

The ghosts in this chapter are unusual for some reason. The Mystic Cow Lights and Phantom Cat stories deal with entities that appear either to *be* ghostly animals or to engage in paranormal activity connected to animals in some way. The Angel seen over Greensburg is a completely different kind of spirit, and the ballad-loving Singing Ghost near Pleasanton is an intriguing anomaly. The ghosts that inhabit the Haunted Mattress and the Haunted Hayloft exhibit predictable ghostly behavior, but their chosen haunts can be viewed as a bit unusual.

This chapter is an introduction to just a few of Kansas's more eccentric ghosts, a fascinating bunch of phantoms from a state with a long tradition of proud eccentricity and individuality that even its ghosts can share.

Mystic Cow Lights

"In March of 1931 western Kansas had enjoyed a good spring rain for two days; then the temperature dropped below zero, and a terrible blizzard raged for two days. Many cattle drifted before the storm, and when it was over several hundred were found piled against each other because they had been stopped by a stout fence." So begins a vivid remembrance of a strange and disturbing phenomenon that persisted throughout the summer of 1931 in northwestern Kansas, near the town of Wallace. The informant recalled the events of the spring and summer of 1931 during an interview in 1963 and indicated that it was a true story, told to her by the family on whose ranch the cattle had perished.

Following the blizzard, the massive task of disposing of the hundreds of dead cows began. The cow corpses, bunched in mounds along the fence, heads and bodies turned every which way, were frozen in death in the positions in which they had frozen in the snowstorm. The bodies had to be removed and buried for sanitary reasons, and as quickly as possible. Crews from the county hauled the carcasses to the creek area nearby and dumped them in a large cut or ditch dug for the purpose. After the dead cattle were dropped in the ditch, dirt was bulldozed over them.

The cows were underground, but aboveground strange things were happening. "All that summer spooky lights were seen in the area," asserted the informant. Sometimes the lights were seen to run along the ground, moving just above the earth and in a group. Like a herd? Other times the luminous phenomena "seemed to rise up into the air sharply."

According to the account, many people who lived in the area and witnessed the ghostly lights were "really disturbed by the sight, and there was much speculation as to the cause." The official explanation was that the decaying cow carcasses were buried under only a thin layer of soil, and the decomposing bodies were giving off a gas, resulting in the phenomenon of phosphorescent lights. The nighttime breezes were interpreted as the cause of the seeming spook lights running along the ground and flying up into the air. The breezes, it was explained, most likely carried the gases, and thus the phosphorescent lights, in whichever wayward direction they happened to be blowing. Inexplicably, however, the lights were only seen on quiet evenings, evenings when the wind was not blowing, and the breezes, if present at all, were gentle and mild. The spectacle of the mystic cow lights continued to be seen as long as the bodies were decaying and continued throughout the entire summer of 1931.

Odd as this episode would seem to be, it was not the first instance of ghostly lights emanating from cows or of what some people might interpret as bovine ghosts. Nine years before the phosphorescent cow corpse lights were encountered in Wallace County, Morton County in southwest Kansas had a "moonshine mystery" that was connected to cows.

The *Dodge City Daily Globe* reported in November 1922 that "whether it's a spook, or a midnight mirage, or mere imagination, anyhow there's something down there, at a certain rural schoolhouse yard, a few miles from Elkhart, that has the entire community stirred." What had the community stirred was an apparition that reportedly looked like "a reflection of a big full moon, about the size of a windmill wheel, of a dull red color, shining particularly bright on a dark night." This reddish specter was dubbed the "moonshine mystery" by the locals, and there were "any number of people who have seen it."

Miss Geneva Shuff was an out-of-county girl who was kept in the dark about the Morton County mystery when she applied for a teaching job at the rural school outside of Elkhart. The Dodge City paper reports that the local school board "feared she would not accept the place if she knew about it." According to the paper, other teachers had given up the position when they found out about the mysterious light down by the schoolhouse.

But Miss Shuff was a stalwart Reno County girl and not easily spooked. She kept her position as schoolmarm even after finding out her schoolyard was haunted. She even wrote a letter to her brother, Harold Shuff of Sylvia, suggesting that he come to Morton County and camp out by the schoolhouse and help her solve the mystery. "I just discovered last week that the schoolhouse is haunted," she wrote to him. "I didn't know anything about it until I stayed up there to work one night, until dark drove me home. It's haunted by a 'ghost-light.' Nearly everybody in the county has seen it at some time or another." "I'm not afraid of it," she continued, "but I wish you would come down here, camp out, and try to discover the cause of the light." Miss Shuff indicated in her letter that she herself had not yet seen the mysterious light, but she was anxious to do so. Accounts from her students and neighbors had made her very curious.

She writes: "Mr. Crawley's—the people I board with, and who live in plain sight of the schoolhouse less than a half mile away—have seen it a couple of times. It's just a great red light, round and about the size of our windmill wheel. It's never in the schoolhouse but is out in the yard or around the house close—across the road or elsewhere. Mr. Crawley's saw it one night about midnight as they were coming home from Wilburton. They thought at first that their car lights were making a reflection as they turned the car around, but still the light was there—across the road east of the schoolhouse. They came on home and it disappeared. Then Clarence—the oldest boy—came behind them on horseback. They saw it there and said it began to roll or rather hop along until it went over behind the schoolhouse and then out to the barn and disappeared. It was just a great big red light. The other boy was afraid to go home by himself because he would have to go past the schoolhouse."

Another tale of the spook light was recounted to her brother in Miss Shuff's letter. This story occurred some time before the schoolteacher's arrival, when the "old schoolhouse" was still on the site plagued by the ghostly light. A program was in progress in the school building when suddenly the light appeared and "raised right up and went over the schoolhouse and lit on the other side." According to the story, a number of boys attending the program ran outside, jumped on their horses, and began to chase the light. What began as a chase with the boys in pursuit of the light reversed itself after the light had rolled about a quarter of a mile in front of the boys. "When they stopped it stopped and when they turned to come back it turned and chased them," Miss Shuff told her brother. With the light now in pursuit of them, the hunters became the hunted as the startled boys fled from their glowing quarry. They rode on for awhile before deciding to turn the tables again on this bright, calculating luminosity. When the boys turned to once more give chase, the light rolled away again. "They chased it for over an hour," declared Miss Shuff, "and finally it disappeared."

Miss Shuff also had heard an older tale of a town that formerly stood on the site of the haunted schoolyard. This town was a "boomday prairie town" that had long ago gone bust and disappeared from the Kansas map. Legend told of a well—the town well—that was dug just southeast of what was now the schoolhouse. The well, two hundred feet deep, had produced water for some time, but eventually was abandoned. (Now for the cow tie-in.) The story went that in the late 1880s there had been a cattle epidemic and many cows had died. Lacking a better disposal site for the infected animals, the townspeople threw them in the old well. The story continued that "a fellow killed a man and threw him in with the cattle." Later, the well was filled in, leaving a permanent sunken place in the ground where the outline of the old well could still be seen. The oldest versions of the spook light story attributed the ghostly lights to the ghost of the murdered man buried with the dead cows.

Miss Shuff ended her letter to her brother with a repetition of her entreaty to be her partner in detecting the source of the mystery: "Won't you come out and camp with me down there sometime and uncover the cause of the light? They all tell me I'll see it before the winter is over. I hope so. I would surely like to see it."

No follow-up report indicates whether or not the intrepid Miss Shuff ever saw the spook light or if her brother came to Elkhart to help her solve the mystery. However, the Dodge City paper had evidently done some investigating of its own and had turned to an expert for a rational explanation of the strange and mysterious lights reputed to haunt the schoolyard. This authority was J. H. Mullison, superintendent of the United Water, Gas and Electric Company in Hutchinson, identified as an "expert in things electrical and scientific."

Mr. Mullison suggested that, in his opinion, "gases from decomposed carcasses of many cattle filling a deep well may be the explanation for the Morton County midnight moonshine spook." He went on to explain: "Gases from decomposing matter, either animal or vegetable, will under certain conditions cause a flickering light above the ground, rather along the surface of the ground. This is what is known as the 'ignis fatuus.' Sometimes it is known as the 'will o' the wisp' or the 'jack o' lantern.' It is very likely that this is what the people see near that schoolhouse. Imagination does the rest."

If ignis fatuus (literally, "foolish fire" or "fool's fire") arising from rotting cow carcasses is to blame for the mysterious spook lights in the Elkhart area, then one must wonder just how long it took those cow corpses to decompose. The cows were supposedly dumped in the old well sometime in the 1880s; superintendent Mullison rendered his decision on the source of the lights in 1922. Were the cows still emitting phosphorescent gases from the well in the schoolyard forty years later? Unlikely.

Spook lights, ghost lights, corpse lights, or ignis fatuus—whatever they are called, the moonshine mystery lights of Morton County may or may not have been of bovine derivation. (Maybe the "big red light" bounding along the ground in front of the schoolhouse boys on horseback was just a big red Hereford cow—a ghost cow—haunting the area of its two-hundred-foot-deep grave and reluctant to be rounded up and herded anywhere again!) Regardless, the similarities between the explanations for the mystic lights sighted in Wallace County in 1931 and the moonshine mystery lights of Morton County from the 1880s through the 1920s are remarkable. Who knew cows could be so spooky or so gaseous?

The Phantom Cat

Black cats are powerful symbols in folklore and legend. They are associated with the devil and with witches, and in parts of western Europe and the United States they are seen as omens of bad luck, sickness, and death. Black cats are bad luck, especially if they cross your path, but it is even worse luck to kill a cat, according to European and African folklore. In vampire lore, a cat that jumps over a corpse has the power to turn that corpse into a bloodsucker. Cats can suck the breath from sleeping children, and some legends portray cats as corpse eaters.

Although stories of hellhounds and demonic wolves abound, it is the cat that is the most sinister creature in the animal world in terms of ghostly anomalies and monstrous creatures. Cats are nocturnal and thus are aligned with the powers of darkness, evil, and the dead. Black cats are the most sinister of their breed, and a terrifying vision when perceived as an apparition or a ghost cat.

The Irish artist Tom McAssey captured on canvas his horrific vision of a ghostly black cat, a legendary beast that has a two-hundred-year history of being sighted in the Dower House, Killakee, Ireland. The Black Cat of Killakee, as it is known, appeared to McAssey in 1968 as he was painting in the gallery of the Dower House. McAssey described his encounter with the fearsome phantom cat in an interview in the *Dublin Evening Herald* in December 1968: "I slammed the heavy door. Halfway across the gallery I looked back. The door was open again and a monstrous black cat crouched in the hall, its red-flecked amber eyes fixed on me." McAssey's painting of his horrific vision is now displayed in the Killakee House restaurant.

Of course, the most famous black cat in literary history is Pluto, the protagonist, of sorts, in Edgar Allan Poe's short story "The Black Cat," first published in the *Saturday Evening Post* in 1843. Pluto becomes an undeserved target of his master's violent alcoholic fits of rage, and when the cat reacts in self-defense, the narrator of Poe's tale cuts one of his pet's eyes out and then hangs the cat. Subsequently, the cat's doppelgänger, or double— a one-eyed black cat—is found by the narrator at a tavern and is taken home with him.

He later attempts to kill this cat with an axe, but his horrified wife tries to stay his hand. Infuriated, the narrator plunges the axe into his wife's head and walls her body up in the basement. Unwittingly, he has walled the live cat up with the very dead corpse, and when the police come around to search his house, in his cockiness he raps the very wall concealing his crime to demonstrate the solid construction of his house. In answer to his rap, the Arch-Fiend walled within reveals the evidence of his master's horrific crime with a tremendous caterwauling, "a wailing shriek, half of horror and half of triumph, such as might have arisen only out of hell, conjointly from the throats of the damned in their agony and of the demons that exult in the damnation." As the wall is torn away by the police, the black cat is revealed to them, and to the murderer, standing on the head of the corpse, "with red extended mouth and solitary eye of fire." A more terrifying vision can hardly be imagined.

A resident of Ashland, Kansas, has seen his own, somewhat less fearsome, version of the Killakee Black Cat and Poe's Pluto. "About thirty years ago I first saw the ghost cat," said Bill Brooks. "It was black and was full grown." Brooks's phantom cat made its premiere appearance in the dining room of the Brooks home in Ashland in the early 1960s. Mrs. Brooks and a friend were chatting in the dining room, and Mr. Brooks was in an adjoining room, "half-listening to their conversation." Out of the corner of his eye, Brooks distinctly saw a black cat walk across the dining room and disappear under the dining room table. The family did not have a black cat. Mr. Brooks said he "jumped up and asked my wife where she had gotten the cat. She denied any knowledge of a cat. I looked under the table: no cat. It had disappeared like a puff of smoke. Since I was the only one that saw it, my wife thought I was just imagining the cat."

Various cats and dogs had been a part of the Brooks family before, but they had never owned an animal that resembled the one Mr. Brooks claimed to have seen intermittently throughout the next three decades. The cat's appearances never lasted very long, according to Brooks, often just "a walk across the room" and then it would vanish.

Sometimes, though, the ghost cat would be in the mood for more than just a stroll. Mr. Brooks explained: "Several times at night I would feel a cat jump up on my bed at night and lay behind my legs the way animals like to do. I could feel the weight and feel the feet as it walked across the bed. The first couple of times I felt it, I didn't have a cat, and I thought it strange that a stray cat would enter my house, climb the stairs to my bedroom, and make itself at home. I would reach down and find nothing. Even turning on the lights would not show anything on my bed but me."

Mr. Brooks's wife has never shared this eerie vision with her husband, but Brooks does have one other witness: "I saw it in 1993—I was sitting in my easy chair watching the evening news. My real cat at the time was lying in my lap. Suddenly, out of the fireplace walked the Ghost Cat. It strode across the room and faded into the divan on the other side of the room. I could see my cat watching this. It moved its head to follow the intruder across the room, then turned around and looked at me as if to say, 'What are you going to do about it?' Then I knew I hadn't been just seeing things. The only thing wrong, I couldn't get my cat to back my story."

Mr. Brooks has not experienced a change in his luck or fortunes, despite the numerous instances of this phantom black cat's having crossed his path. In fact, he does not fear his phantom feline or its announced visitations and said that he was actually "looking forward to its next visit." He indicated that he had never seen the cat outside of his house but inside the house he had been aware of a feeling of being watched at times, even when his ghostly pet was nowhere to be seen.

After a three-year absence, the Ghost Cat of Ashland returned to the Brooks house in the fall of 1996. The Brookses' current cat is a gray cat. Mr. Brooks was in his living room when he saw a cat's form walk across the room. "Is the cat inside?" Mr. Brooks asked his wife. "No," she replied, "I just put the cat out." Looking around, he again caught sight of the ghostly black cat just before it melted into the woodwork.

So far, said Mr. Brooks, the cat has not harmed anyone. Unlike the legendary Black Cat of Killakee or the literary black cat of Poe's gruesome story, the Phantom Black Cat of Ashland appears to be a benign specter, perhaps one that lived out its ninth and final life in the house and now is consigned to its tenth life as a ghost cat within the walls of its previous home.

* * * * *

Angel over Greensburg

The world's largest hand-dug well (the Big Well) is in Greensburg, Kansas, as is the world's largest pallasite meteorite (Space Wanderer). The meteorite, found on a farm east of Greensburg, is displayed in the Celestial Museum located next to the Big Well. However, the meteorite may not have been the only celestial visitor to the Greensburg area, if one accepts the proof offered by a mysterious photograph, a picture that seems to clearly depict the form of an angel hovering in the clouds over the town of Greensburg.

W. A. Sinklier was a local photographer in 1916. Early on the morning of Sunday, November 12, Sinklier had gone to his photography gallery to work on some rush-order prints that he needed to complete. Shortly before 7:00 A.M. he arrived at the gallery and began unlocking the door. It was a cold, cloudy morning. A light snow was falling, and a hard, gusty wind was blowing from the north, heralding the advent of winter. As he turned the key in the lock, something prompted him to look up, and when he did, he saw something remarkable.

An enormous black cloud was hanging low over the southwest portion of town, and standing out in sharp contrast against the black of the cloud was a startling vision: An object or figure in human shape appeared to be stooping forward and moving slowly downward and north against the wind. The form "looked like frost in the sunlight," even though the sky was overcast, and no sun was shining.

Sinklier quickly threw open the door to his studio and ran inside, grabbing his camera. He rapidly set up his tripod and camera out on the sidewalk in front of the building and made an exposure of the form in the cloud. After taking his camera inside, he returned to the front of the building to look at the apparition again, but it had disappeared.

When the photographer's picture was developed, it manifested the figure of what appears to be a bright angel emerging from the clouds over Greensburg. The corpus of the figure is hazy but distinct, and a face in profile is discernible. The angel seems to be holding the ends of its own wings, which are folded up from behind and under its arms, the feathery tips on a level with its face. The apparition is leaning forward and looking between its wings, down to a small cluster of houses and buildings (including two windmills) below the clouds. The heavy line of black clouds ends abruptly right above the rooftops, and a slice of bright sky shows between the edge of the clouds and the tops of the darkened structures. A sort of luminosity radiates out upward and forward from the head and chest area of the angel-figure, diffusing into the clouds. This phenomenon looks similar to the 1990s New Age aural photography that purports to illuminate an individual's personal aura, a phenomenon that is said to radiate around a person's body like heat waves.

In 1916, interest and belief in spiritualism, spirit photography, and spirit guides were popular in the United States and Great Britain. Spiritualism was a movement arising in the mid-nineteenth century that embraced the idea that after death, the soul, contained in a duplicate of the physical body, passed over into the spirit world. Spiritualists believed that communication with members of the spirit world was possible through certain individuals, called mediums, who had the ability to channel messages between the worlds of the living and the dead.

One of the tenets of spiritualism was a belief in spirit photography, supposed "proof" of spiritualism's version of life after death. Certain photographers claimed to be able to take photographs of living individuals that, when developed, revealed the images of a dead person or persons next to or floating around the figure of the live subject of the photo. Not surprisingly, some of the images of the extras appearing in the photographs turned out to be superimposed photos of people who were still very much alive. The existence of spirit guides or spirit helpers was another belief of spiritualism. Spirit guides were believed to be ghosts, spirits, or oftentimes angels that served as go-betweens with the spirit world and provided guidance and assistance to their assigned human.

Within the context of spiritualism, an angel hovering in the clouds above a town would not necessarily be an uncommon event, especially if the angel appeared over a house where the body of a recently deceased individual was laid out. The angel would be interpreted as the spirit guide who had arrived to guide the dead person's soul over into the spirit world. In rare instances, it was believed, the angel might be visible to a person or persons who were near the dying or dead individual.

Sinklier, the Greensburg photographer, converted his fantastic photograph into a postcard and distributed and sold copies widely throughout the area. A reproduction of the famous postcard is printed in the book *Reflections of Kansas: 1990–1930, a Prairie Postcard Album,* as well as a statement by Sinklier relating to the picture that was written on the back of the original postcard: "This photo was taken November 12, 1916, at 7 o'clock A.M. by me. The cloud and object was visible only about two minutes. The corpse of a lady lay in a residence near the church as the vision appeared

"The Angel at Greensburg." (Reprinted by courtesy of Frank Wood and Scott Daymond from *Reflections of Kansas: A Prairie Postcard Album, 1900–1930*. Wichita: Daywood Publishing Company, 1988.)

over the church building." After reading Sinklier's statement, one can assume that the "vision" of the angel in the picture was to be interpreted as a spirit guide for the recently deceased "corpse of a lady" who was laid out in a house near the church. This picture no doubt would have been circulated to boost sales for the photographer and to encourage faith in a system of beliefs that, unfortunately, often resorted to obviously faked and fraudulent photos to prove its claims.

At first glance, the Angel over Greensburg is an arresting image. On close inspection, it begins to look less celestial and more in the realm of the terrestrial.

The Haunted Mattress

A young couple living in an apartment on East 14th Street in Wichita in March 1940 had a case of the worst kind of insomnia to cure. Three months earlier they had bought a new mattress from Crooks Furniture Company at 2nd and Main in downtown Wichita. Three sleepless months later, they returned the mattress to the store complaining that it was haunted. Mr. and Mrs. Lucas told the manager that their ghostly bedmate pecked, tapped, scratched, and rocked the bed all night long, understandably causing them distress, insomnia, and bleary eyes each morning after it had enjoyed another nightlong revel in their bed.

Their friendly furniture store (whose motto evidently was The Customer Is Always Right) cheerfully gave them a new replacement mattress (ghost free this time). The store owner displayed the haunted mattress in his show window on Main Street, exhibiting his knack for enterprise as well as his famous mattress. Needless to say, the ghost-possessed mattress display in the front window attracted many curious Wichitans and perhaps some new customers.

The sleep-deprived couple was pleased to discover that their noisy spook had opted to stay with the original mattress, and they returned to peaceful wedded and bedded bliss with their new phantom-free bed. "We haven't heard a sound since the mattress left," they said happily. Employees of the furniture store were not so pleased to discover that the ghost enjoyed performing in the front window, including a new repertoire of noises for its new habitat, adding hammering sounds along with scratching and tapping.

Detectives at the Wichita Police Department had plans to rip the mattress apart and inspect it once the furniture store was done displaying it, but news reports about the story from 1940 on don't mention if this was ever done. They also don't mention whatever became of the mattress or its ghost. The last news flash was from Detective Van Welden of the police department in response to a newspaper reporter's questions. According to a news story in the April 3, 1940, *Wichita Eagle*, "Van Weldon has been too busy with other police matters to get into the mattress, he reports, but will later."

The Haunted Hayloft

Farmer Sullivan lived with his wife and two sons on the family farm outside of Axtell, west of Marysville. Sullivan worked hard in his milo fields, and his two boys helped out as much as they could. Farmer Sullivan was respected by his family and neighbors but was known to have a violent temper when he was crossed. During the fall and spring when his sons were attending school, Sullivan often hired extra help to assist him with the planting, plowing, harvesting, and other general farm chores. This particular fall he had hired a boy who had recently shown up in the area looking for work. The teenager claimed to have no family, no money, and no place to stay. The Sullivans put the young man up at their place and gave him his room and board and a small salary in exchange for work as a hired hand around the farm.

One night farmer Sullivan and the hired boy were pitching hay down at the barn until well after dark. Mrs. Sullivan had supper ready on the table for five, as the boy took his meal with the rest of the family. The Sullivan sons were working on their homework before the fireplace. Sullivan and the boy did not arrive at the house at the scheduled supper time, so Mrs. Sullivan asked one of her sons to run down to the barn and remind the two working there that their meal was getting cold. Before he could get up to do his mother's bidding, his father threw open the door and came into the farmhouse alone.

"Where's the boy?" asked Mrs. Sullivan. "Still pitching hay?"

"No." Mr. Sullivan was thoughtful for a moment before he repeated again, "No."

"Where is he?" his wife queried.

"The boy's run away," farmer Sullivan answered curtly.

The hired boy was never seen again on the Sullivan place or in the Axtell area. Neighbors, having seen examples of Sullivan's unreasonable temper before, deduced that the boy had not run away but had probably been killed by the farmer in a fit of rage. No evidence of such a deed was discovered, but the neighbors gossiped among themselves just the same.

Shortly after the disappearance of the boy, farmer Sullivan took sick. Formerly strong and fit and hardened by his years of farm labor, Sullivan inexplicably declined, growing weaker and paler by the day, suffering in his bed and sinking deeper into lethargy and finally stupor.

Corresponding exactly with the day that farmer Sullivan fell ill, a mysterious occurrence was witnessed by the neighbors and the rest of the Sullivan family. A blinding white light was seen to appear, shining from the hayloft in the Sullivans' barn. The light would hover in the loft, then move out of the loft and start up the path toward the house, and then disappear. Each progressive night the light would approach a little bit closer to the house. This ghostly light appeared every night at 11:00 P.M. and continued its journey nightly for several weeks.

One night the Sullivan sons arrived home just as the strange unearthly light was on the path. The light immediately reversed itself and moved back to the barn, into the structure, and up to the hayloft where it promptly disappeared. Inside the house, it was obvious that farmer Sullivan was dying. After several weeks of suffering, he finally lapsed into a coma and died. The night of his death, at the exact time of his death, the ghost light from the barn finally traversed the length of the pathway and made it to the house. That night was the last time the light was seen.

Although farmer Sullivan was never proved a murderer, neighbors and other people in the area firmly believed that the spook light seen in the hayloft and between the barn and the house was the ghost of the hired boy, bent on revenge in a horrible fashion, the harbinger and agent of farmer Sullivan's death.

The Singing Ghost

Bonnie McKane was born with the century and lived with her family in a farming community south of Pleasanton near the Osage River. Bonnie's family was poor, barely able to eke out a living from their hardscrabble farm in the hills. When she was a little girl, Bonnie had a secret place and a favorite pastime. When she was done with her chores, she would slip away to the creek that ran a little ways off the road that crossed in front of their farm. At a certain spot on the creek a special tree, Bonnie's tree, grew right by the side of the water. The tree leaned over the creek at an angle nearly horizontal to the water. Bonnie's favorite pastime was to climb up in her special tree, sit on a limb, and sing ballads.

Bonnie had a lovely voice and was a very pretty little girl with beautiful long flowing hair. Sometimes farmers laboring late in neighboring fields would hear her high clear voice carried on the wind from the vicinity of the creek, singing songs of lost lovers and ill-fated romances:

> Awake, arise, you drowsy sleeper!
> Awake, arise; it's near about day.
> Awake, arise; go ask your father
> If you're my bride to be.
> And if you're not, come back and tell me;
> It's the very last time I'll bother thee.
>
> I cannot go and ask my father,
> For he is on his bed of rest
> And in his hand he holds a weapon
> To kill the one I love the best.

When Bonnie was sixteen or seventeen years old, her father hired an intinerant laborer to help him with the work on the farm. The laborer was a handsome young man, and after a while, Bonnie fell in love with him. When her father found out that the two had been courting, he fired the young man. But Bonnie's love simply got a job with a neighboring farmer who lived a few miles away, and the couple continued to see each other on the sly.

Soon, however, some neighbors reported to her father that they had seen Bonnie, late at night, where she was not supposed to be. After her father thought she was safe in bed, tucked between the sheets in her little room, Bonnie would sneak out of the house and run across the fields and the road in her snowy white nightgown, her slippers on her feet, her long honey-blond hair streaming behind her. The neighbors told her father they had seen her, in her nightgown, down by the creek, talking to her lover. The young couple would lean against the tree, Bonnie's special tree, and gaze deeply into one another's eyes as they planned their future together.

Bonnie's father was enraged. The tattling neighbors had much to regret as the angry man grabbed his shotgun and ran out of the farmhouse. Soon after a shot was heard throughout the neighborhood: Bonnie's father had killed her suitor.

The following night, Bonnie disappeared. She didn't appear for breakfast; she wasn't in her room. A couple was found who had seen her, running in her nightgown, her hair flowing out behind her as ran along the road and down to the creek. When the creek was searched for signs of her, the only thing found was a pair of white slippers at the base of a tree that grew out horizontally over the waters of the creek. No other trace of her was ever found.

But Bonnie *was* seen again. Some time after she disappeared, people in the vicinity began to report hearing sounds coming from the area of the big tree down by the creek, sounds of a woman's voice singing songs that drifted on the night air. Later—even ten years later—it was reported many times over that on moonlit nights, Bonnie's ghost could be seen in her white nightgown, sitting in her tree, singing ballads in her high clear voice:

> So bury me both wide and deep,
> Place a marble stone at my head and feet,
> And on my breast place a snow-white dove
> To show to the world that I died for love.

The Most Haunted Town in Kansas: Atchison

A tchison appreciates its ghosts. Atchison *cultivates* its ghost stories. This historic and beautiful Kansas town along the banks of the Missouri River abounds in legends of all kinds—ghost legends in particular. Nestled among rolling hills and river bluffs, Atchison has a unique sense of history, demonstrated in its commitment to preservation of its historic landmarks, original brick streets, magnificent nineteenth-century mansions . . . and a truly impressive collection of ghosts!

Although other Kansas towns—Emporia, Hutchinson, and Leavenworth, to name a few—have reasons (and phantoms) to lay claim to the title of Most Haunted, Atchison scored additional points for its innovative yearly salute to its least visible residents. Since 1995, true ghost aficionados have been able to book a ticket on the Haunted Atchison Trolley Tour. For several days and nights just prior to Halloween, participants board this "ghost trolley" at the restored 1880s Santa Fe Depot that serves as the city's visitor center as well as home to the Atchison County Historical Museum. A fully narrated ride past homes associated with unique stories of ghosts and goblins, plus a side trip into Jackson Park to Molly's Hollow, translates into a super excursion into the supernatural. As the ghost trolley rumbles into the night, up and down the undulating brick streets, past a Victorian mansion studded with winged gargoyles or a brooding bungalow with a single light illuminated in a haunted attic, riders are regaled with a little bit of history, some local lore, and a lot of great ghost stories.

Lewis and Clark began their expeditions in what is now Atchison in 1804, and the town itself was founded in 1854. The Atchison, Topeka and

Santa Fe Railroad was born in Atchison, as was famed aviatrix Amelia Earhart. In 1958, after two flash floods in two weeks drastically damaged the town, Atchison earned the nickname of "the town that refused to die" by successfully reclaiming and refurbishing itself.

Atchison's healthy ghost population also refuses to die (or die out), primarily because the town has recognized the value in preserving not only its architectural heritage but also its cultural heritage embodied in oral legend traditions, storytelling, and a singular repository of Kansas folklore.

ATCHISON'S HAUNTED HOUSES

The Ghost of Sallie the Man-Hater

A turn-of-the-century house near the bluffs of the Missouri River on the northeast edge of the city is home to Atchison's most famous (or infamous) ghost. Sallie has been featured on the the television series *Sightings* several times and can be found (and "seen") on the *Sightings* web page on the Internet.

The house Sallie haunts was originally the residence of an Atchison physician. The doctor lived with his family in the upstairs of the house and used the first floor as his office, surgery room, and examination rooms. As the story goes, Sallie was a young girl about six years old who was brought into the doctor's office one day suffering from a grave illness. At this point, the story line splits into two conflicting versions of what type of illness afflicted the child.

One version indicates that Sallie's distraught mother rushed into the doctor's office one morning with her child, moaning in pain, in her arms. The little girl had been up all night with a stomachache that toward morning had suddenly become severe. Ascertaining that the child suffered from acute appendicitis, the doctor quickly moved her into his surgical room and began preparing to operate on her to remove the inflamed appendix. The pale child was crying and clutching her abdomen. Her already frightened eyes became panic-stricken as she saw the doctor laying out a shining line of scalpels and other surgical instruments. With her tormented mother standing helpless beside her, Sallie struggled as the doctor held her down on the surgical table while applying an anesthetic mask soaked in ether to her face. Sallie's struggles slowed, but she was not yet fully under the effects of the ether when the doctor picked up a scalpel and began to cut. Sallie screamed weakly and opened her eyes as the doctor made the incision, but the doctor would not stop his surgery for fear her appendix would burst. Before she closed her eyes for the last time, little Sallie gazed at her tormentor, the doctor, with fear and loathing, and then she went limp. The surgery was to no avail: The child's appendix had burst, and she died a short time later on the doctor's table.

An alternate version has little Sallie, around 1905 or 1906, brought to see the doctor for a lung disorder. A mild respiratory problem had worsened, and she was having trouble breathing. When she was brought to see the doctor, he was negligent and overlooked the seriousness of her condition. Shortly after, the child died from pneumonia. The doctor moved from the house not long after her death.

Stories about Sallie's presence in the doctor's former house began in 1993 when the residence was rented to a young family. Shortly after their arrival at the house, they began noticing strange phenomena: The family dog would bark and growl seemingly for no reason, particularly in the vicinity of the baby's room on the second floor; the television set would turn off spontaneously; one light in a room would suddenly dim; pictures on the wall would be found hanging upside down. In one bizarre incident, the family returned from an evening out to find all the stuffed toys in the nursery placed, face out, in a ring in the middle of the floor.

After a time, Sallie's pranks took a vicious turn. Reportedly, several small fires broke out in the house. Most terrifying, a series of vicious attacks began that targeted only the young husband. The first attack occurred as he entered the room on the first floor that had been the surgery room. A sudden premonition struck him, and he experienced a feeling of cold moving up and into his arm. He looked down at his arm, and a series of scratches materialized there. Later attacks supposedly left him with long raised scratches on his back, his chest, and his abdomen. Sometimes the scratches would be so severe they would bleed. Always before the entity would attack the husband, he would experience a sudden dropping of the temperature in the room or an area of coldness that would migrate to his body. He would know he was about to encounter the spirit of Sallie and her vengeful nails.

The ghost of Sallie never attacked the wife or the baby in the family, only the man. The logical connection drawn in the accounts of this frightening man-hating spirit is that Sallie perceived the husband to be an embodiment of the male doctor who let her die. Particularly if the surgical version of her demise is used, it becomes obvious that Sallie was trying to elicit "an eye for an eye" in her attacks with her sharp nails on the abdomen and stomach of her victim.

Stories of the haunting of this family in the old doctor's house included details of two visual sightings of the ghost by the husband. One night just a hand materialized over his side of the bed, moving toward his face. Another time, he claimed to have seen the figure of a little girl standing in the kitchen.

Strange anomalous photographs taken by the couple seem to indicate streaks, shapes, and shadows in the pictures that are difficult to explain. Opinions on whether these are truly otherworldly photos of Sallie in spirit form or explainable film or photographic defects superimposed on the pictures depend on who is analyzing the photos. Photos taken of the husband's back and chest showing the scratches are more disturbing, but there could be logical explanations for those as well.

The *Sightings* crew, filming at the house at the time, supposedly witnessed an attack on the husband complete with spontaneous bleeding scratches. Specialists in the fields of psychic phenomena, the paranormal, parapsychology, and spirit photography were utilized by the television program to investigate the startling occurrences at the Atchison house. A psychic was brought in as well, and he divined that a child named Sallie died in the house—in fact, he claimed to see her face in an upstairs window as he first approached the house.

The family lived in their haunted house for about a year; then, faced with the increasing ferocity of Sallie's attacks against the man of the house, they moved out. Oddly, the man continued to develop welts and scratches after they left the house, but the episodes became infrequent. Another family has rented the house, and, so far, Sallie has left them alone.

The Haunted Villa: The Ghost in the Tower

Unlike the ghost of Sallie who shows up in pictures and in person, the camera-happy ghost of the Haunted Villa can be seen only in photographs. The ghost might be that of the original owner, an Irish immigrant and harness maker who built the house in 1890. Then again, it might be that of another former resident of the house, an elderly woman who sold the house to the current occupants. A positive identification of the ghost is difficult to make because it refuses to reveal itself beyond presenting a dim, amorphous figure in otherwise innocuous photos. This shadowy form has appeared in pictures that the residents have taken of the exterior as well as the interior of the house and at different times of the year.

The Villa is a massive house of gables, balconies, and chimney tops, capped by a lantern tower at its top. The lantern tower has windows, but there is no source of illumination in the tower as it has no electricity running to it. A picture of the house, including the lantern tower, was taken one evening. After the photo was developed, close inspection revealed a "human" figure silhouetted in one of the windows of the tower. The interior of the room behind the form was bright, as if illuminated by a light.

The ghost of the Villa has also appeared in the family Christmas pictures. A large decorated Christmas tree was displayed in a second-floor bay window facing the street. Photographs of the tree were taken from inside the house as well as from the street outside. In these pictures, the ghost was seen standing between the Christmas tree and the window.

Besides showing up for family photos, the Villa ghost likes to make its presence known from time to time by raising a little ruckus. When it is active, the ghost makes noises and slams doors shut throughout the night. The doors in the house are heavy pocket doors that require a certain amount of force to close. They would not be stirred by a breeze or a gust of wind short of a tornado.

Footsteps have also been heard running up and down the back staircase. If someone shouts, "Who's there?" the clattering footsteps stop for a moment, and then they "run away." Perhaps the ghost is hurrying up to the lantern tower to pose for another picture!

The Tea-Making Ghost with a Toothache

Two hours outside of Atchison, Mrs. Brediger remarked to her husband that she just couldn't wait to get home so she could have a good hot cup of tea. Mrs. Brediger loved her tea, and they had been in the car the better part of the day, returning home from a vacation. She had already missed her morning tea, and now it was time for her afternoon "spot o' tea." Mr. Brediger smiled and assured her it wouldn't be much longer until they were back home on Kearney Street, and she could get her teapot whistling on the stove and fix herself up a big cup of Earl Grey. Mrs. Brediger sighed, settled back into the headrest, and closed her eyes. She could smell the tea brewing now.

A hundred miles or so later, they pulled into their driveway. They parked the car, removed their luggage, unlocked the front door, and went into the house. The first thing Mrs. Brediger noticed when she walked in the door was the musty, shut-up smell houses always have when one returns from a trip of more than a day's duration. The second thing she noticed was the sound of the teakettle whistling merrily in the kitchen. Puzzled, she looked at Mr. Brediger and then looked back toward the kitchen door. They both dropped their suitcases on the hall floor at the same instant and walked rapidly to the kitchen.

Steam was boiling from the spout of the kettle as it danced on the red-hot burner of the stove. The kitchen was empty, but the curtains were drawn open, letting in the warmth of the late afternoon sun. A bright sunbeam fell across the kitchen table, glinting off the edge of Mrs. Brediger's favorite teacup and saucer, set neatly in her place at the table. In the teacup was a fresh tea bag—Earl Grey.

No one else was in the Brediger house that day, and all the doors and windows were securely locked. No one had been in the house while they were gone. Although this was an extreme experience, Mrs. Brediger was not completely surprised that a cup of tea appeared to be preparing itself for her, prompted by a psychic suggestion from one hundred miles away. The Bredigers had had other experiences that led them to believe that they did not live in their house alone. They had become convinced that they shared the house with a ghost. The tea-making episode only served to confirm that conviction.

Who the ghost was or why it was there remained a mystery. Legend holds that an English woman came into the house and stayed with Mrs. Brediger while Mr. Brediger was in the hospital one time. She was supposed to stay for awhile to help out while Mr. Brediger was ill, but she left after only a few days. Incidents and things that happened while she was in the house convinced her that the structure was possessed. She became so uneasy that she was compelled to leave.

The Bredigers' ghost was not generally noisy or intrusive, but occasionally it was heard on the second floor, which was used only for storage. The first time the ghost began rummaging around upstairs, Mrs. Brediger thought Mr. Brediger was up there looking about for something. Next thing she knew, Mr. Brediger came around the corner and asked her what she had been doing upstairs to make all the racket. Mrs. Brediger informed her spouse that indeed she had *not* been upstairs and that it must have been the ghost. What *it* had been looking for, they couldn't imagine.

It became obvious that their tea-making, attic-rummaging ghost was not threatening; in fact, the phantom was something of a helpful presence in their lives, anxious to assist anytime its help was needed. One winter evening the Bredigers had plans to go out. Mrs. Brediger was still in her dressing room putting the finishing touches on her hairdo and pinning on her favorite brooch. Mr. Brediger was in the hallway outside her room, his coat folded over his arm. When Mrs. Brediger said, "I'll be ready to leave in just a minute," Mr. Brediger began putting on his coat. He slipped one arm in one sleeve and then reached behind himself to grasp the other sleeve. An unseen someone behind him kindly helped him with the other sleeve, lifting it up and sliding it onto his outstretched arm. Mr. Brediger looked around expecting to see his wife, but she was not there. She was still in her dressing room, gathering her purse, gloves, and coat. "Thanks," Mr. Brediger mumbled sheepishly, to no one in particular.

This kindly ghost also knew how to go to great lengths to help itself, even to the point of treating itself for a toothache. The Bredigers both knew an old and effective remedy for toothache: oil of cloves. One day Mrs. Brediger noticed the distinct odor of oil of cloves when she walked by her husband's bedroom. She wondered if he was having trouble with a tooth. When he came home from work that evening he went to his bedroom to change. Appearing at the supper table a short while later, he asked his wife why he had smelled oil of cloves in his room—did she have a toothache? No, she answered him, but then she wondered aloud: Do ghosts have teeth?

The Skirt-Tugging Ghost

Quite a few years back, Grandpa lived in a house on Ninth Street with his son, daughter-in-law, and four granddaughters. Grandpa was a lovable old galoot who loved his custom-made cowboy boots and wore them night and day, except when he was in bed. His favorite spot in the house was in the kitchen next to the heat stove. All day long he would sit there, smoking his pipe and admiring his cowboy boots.

Whenever one of his granddaughters would walk by his spot next to the stove, he would lift the pointed toe of one of his cowboy boots and snag the hem of the girl's skirt, giving it a tug. At first this annoyed the girls, who didn't care to have their clean frocks snagged and hitched by Grandpa's boots. But as time went on and he continued to delight in this game, the girls grew accustomed to Grandpa's harmless pursuit.

More time went on, and Grandpa eventually passed away. His wake was held in the house, and friends and relatives were invited over to share food, drink, and memories of Grandpa. All four daughters assisted in preparing the food for the wake and spent much of the day in the kitchen helping their mother. Later in the day, each of the girls came to the mother separately and described being in the kitchen and feeling something hooking or snagging her dress hem, "just as Grandpa had done when he was alive." "Mother," they said, "it was just as if Grandpa was back, sitting by the stove, waiting for us with a little smile on his face, reaching out with his cowboy boot to snare us and tug on our skirts!"

For many years after, the daughters insisted that every time they walked by the old kitchen stove in the house, Grandpa, or something, would tug at their skirts.

A few years ago, a local fund-raising group was searching for a vacant house to use as a Halloween haunted house. The old house on Ninth Street was settled on, and frightening vignettes of ghosts, ghouls, and monsters were set up throughout the house. The house was a success and many people toured it, but members of the sponsoring group were perplexed when several women dressed in skirts asked them how they had managed to rig up something that tugged at their dress or skirt hems each time they passed through the kitchen!

Quite recently, another group wanted to utilize the house as a funeral parlor, but these people were discouraged from proceeding with their plans when chilling noises were heard issuing from the interior walls of the house each time work commenced on reconstruction. They left the house vacant again—vacant, that is, except for Grandpa.

The Ghost of Anna

Anna's father was a German immigrant who built a cozy three-room house in northwest Atchison back in 1897. The house, enlarged and remodeled over the years, remained in the family for several generations. Anna remained in the house, too, and is said to have died there of natural causes. She was laid out for her wake and funeral in the family room.

Younger members of Anna's family eventually sold the house and moved out of Atchison. But Anna wasn't about to give up the family home, and she evidently decided to stay behind and maintain the family presence in the house. She even announced her rightful place in the house the very first night of the new owners' residence in their newly purchased home.

Unpacking and arranging the furniture had proven to be exhausting, so the new occupants headed for bed early. The husband and wife were in the master bedroom downstairs, their daughter and son in their bedrooms upstairs. The house was dark and quiet. In the dark, the husband realized their unfamiliarity with the house might pose a problem, or a hazard, for any of the family members who might have to get up in the middle of the night. He decided to get out of bed and turn on the hall light so the path to the bathroom and kitchen would be illuminated. After flipping the light switch on in the hall, he returned to bed and settled in. His wife, clearly worn out from the day's frenetic activity, was sound asleep. The children had been asleep in their rooms for some time.

As the man adjusted his pillows and leaned forward to pull the covers up over himself, a sudden movement in the hallway caught his eye. Focusing on the lighted area beyond his bedroom door, he was amazed to see the figure of a woman walking down the hallway away from the stairs to the second floor. He could see her clearly enough to ascertain her approximate age (mid-forties), hair color (brown), hair type (long and flowing), and apparel (white nightgown). Frozen into inaction for several seconds, the man finally was able to extricate himself from the bedclothes and begin pursuing what he thought was an intruder. He gained the hallway and looked quickly in both directions. He saw nothing. He quickly searched the bottom level of the house, turning on all the lights and checking the locks on the doors and windows. Everything was secure. As he started up the stairs to the second level, his wife joined him, awakened by this time by the lights and noise. When her husband informed her of what he had seen, she immediately ran past him up the stairs to check on their children. They were still sleeping. The man awakened his son and together they spent another hour searching the yard around the house and rechecking all the windows and doors. Nothing was found.

Several weeks later, the man had occasion to see an early photograph of Anna's family. The slim figure of a woman in her mid-forties with long brown hair jumped out at him. Startled, the man realized that he recognized this figure from the past as the woman he had seen walking purposefully down his hallway that first night in their new home. This first experience with Anna was certainly the most vivid for the family, but it was not to be the last. Anna was not a bothersome ghost, but just about the time they thought she had finally gone away, she would quietly but firmly reassert herself so that it could never be forgotten who was the "real" mistress of the house.

Some years after they had moved in, the family had reason to believe that perhaps Anna was not the only spirit from Anna's family to inhabit the old house. One evening, the wife was chatting with her daughter in the girl's bedroom. The conversation had turned to the ghost and some recent events that they suspected might be a reminder from Anna that she was still around. Out of the corner of her eye, the daughter caught a movement by the door to her bedroom. Turning her head, she found herself staring into the pale eyes of a young boy leaning out over her threshold. The boy's feet were firmly planted in the hallway outside of the room, but his body was slanted at an unnatural angle, almost hovering above the floor. It was almost as if the boy was intent on eavesdropping on the conversation but unable or unwilling to wholly move into the room. With a shriek, the girl jumped up from the bed and rushed toward the intruder, who turned and ran. Her startled mother had not seen this apparition, but alarmed by the girl's behavior, she joined in the chase and followed her daughter out of the room.

The girl lost sight of her quarry in the hallway, but she continued running on down the stairs, and then out of the house. No boy was in sight anywhere. Turning around, she confronted her confused and understandably concerned mother. "I saw a boy," the girl said, "a boy wearing the strangest clothing." She described the boy and his knee-high pantaloons, lacy shirt, and bowl haircut. Once again, shortly after this strange sighting, the current residents had the opportunity to see an old photo of Anna's family—this one of a fiftieth-anniversary celebration. Anna's family was posed in front of the house, smiling and wearing early-twentieth-century dress. The daughter gasped when she saw the picture—sitting on the lawn close to Anna was a young boy with pale eyes and a bowl haircut, dressed in pantaloons hiked over his knees and a shirt with a long, lacy collar.

Anna tolerates the new family that has moved into her house, but she is not tolerant of strangers. Just a few years ago the home was on the Atchison Fall Homes Tour. A volunteer tour guide was taking visitors through the house pointing out decorating details and architectural points of interest. Upstairs, as the tour group was admiring one of the bedrooms, a full set of keys on a keychain evidently "flew off a pegboard, slapped against the wall on the opposite side of the room, and cascaded down to the floor." The stunned visitors took a moment to recover and then beat a hasty retreat from the house. Anna obviously was not happy being disturbed inside her home by strangers. As an October 21, 1995, article in the *Atchison Globe* succinctly phrased it, this was "a 'take the keys and go' statement if there ever was one."

The Suitcase-Throwing Ghost

Although the ghost of Anna has learned to coexist peaceably with the people who share her house, another ghost in another house in Atchison is not quite as accommodating. The ghost in the house on Riverview Drive has the wizened face of a kindly old woman, but in this case appearances are definitely deceiving.

Although the ghost keeps to herself in the attic most of the time, she definitely doesn't like it when it gets stuffy up there. Time and again when the family living in the house has returned from an outing or a trip, all the windows into the attic are found open. For the umpteenth time they patiently shut, latch, and lock the windows, only to find them all flung open again the next time they come back from an expedition away from the house. This fresh-air phantom manages to duplicate this trick repeatedly without ever forcing or breaking any of the windows or locks.

The ghost also likes to spook the occupants, particularly in the middle of the night, by causing the television or stereo, or both, to come on spontaneously at high volume, literally blasting the family out of bed. Other strange noises are also heard at times throughout the house, sounds that can't be satisfactorily explained except by attributing them to the grumpy old woman ghost in the attic.

Alone in the house one night, the woman who lived there heard noises in the room next to her bedroom. She sat up abruptly in her bed and listened intently. Finally, she decided that the family dog must have come upstairs and was snuffling around in the room on the other side of the wall, making the odd noises that she was hearing. The woman called to the dog and told it to "come here." Something then entered her room, but it wasn't the dog. The glow from a streetlight just outside the window dimly illuminated a dark, shrouded figure shuffling across the floor, casting a murky shadow on the bedroom wall. It passed in front of the terrified woman in her bed and went around to the empty side of the bed. It stooped over, patted and smoothed a place on the bedspread, and sat down. Not keen on the idea of sharing her bed with this unearthly wraith, the woman let out a piercing scream and turned on her bedside light. Evidently no longer so keen on crawling into bed with this now-shrieking mortal, the dark spectral creature hoisted its form off the bedcovers and shuffled quickly from the room. The woman, nearly swooning from fright and revulsion, heard the shambling footsteps recede down the hallway and ascend the stairs leading to the attic. She then heard the attic door creak open, then close with a resounding bang.

The ghost in the house on Riverview has gone to even more extreme measures to rid itself of what it must see as unwelcome boarders. The occupants travel frequently (no wonder!), and their suitcases are kept stored in the attic. Occasionally, when the old woman in the attic gets especially cranky or frustrated, she pitches all the suitcases out the attic door and down the attic stairs. One can almost picture her, brushing the dust off her noncorporeal hands, muttering toothlessly under her nonexistent breath, "There! Maybe they'll just all pack up and get out of my house." Then she shuffles back to her corner in the attic, the edges of her long black tattered shroud dragging slowly through the dust behind her.

The Ghost of the Bride Trapped in the Trunk

No faces are seen in the attic window at the house on Seventh Street. No doors bang shut, no windows fly open, no ghostly footsteps are heard. No phantoms fly through the rooms, and no ghouls gibber or play snooker in the basement. The only ghostly presence in this house is kept well contained—confined in an old antique trunk in a bedroom on the second floor. The trunk is large and commodious: big enough to hold a body.

Most of the time the trunk just sits like a normal piece of furniture. Its designated place in the decorating scheme of this bedchamber is against a wall at the far side of the room. There it looms—solid and heavy, with an old-fashioned metal latch and lock securing it closed. The trunk seems to be perfectly innocuous. Innocuous, that is, until it begins to drag itself across the floor. Rasping and scratching across the floorboards, lurching and thumping through the room, the old trunk hauls its wooden frame into the center of the room, and then it is still once more.

The first time this sound was heard, the alarmed owners of the house and trunk rushed upstairs to investigate. They were perplexed to find the ponderous piece of furniture square in the middle of the room. They also were puzzled by a concentrated sweet smell—a potent perfume that was not recognized, or worn, by any member of the family. The heavy concave lid was lifted and the interior of the trunk was examined, but nothing was in it. No trapped animal jumped out, no giggling child hopped out to reveal a prank. The dark, musty interior of the trunk was empty except for a lingering scent of perfume. The trunk was shoved back in place, and there it stayed—for awhile.

Months later, the family members were once again assembled in the living room. The rasping, scraping sounds began, just as before, over their heads. Again, they hurried upstairs only to find the restless trunk resting in the center of the room, yards away from its customary place against the far wall. The essence of flowers—a heavy, creamy bouquet—hung in the air. Again, the trunk was pushed back over to the wall. The next time it happened, the family didn't even bother to run upstairs and investigate immediately. They knew what was making the noise, and they knew it would stop—when the trunk reached its destination in the center of the room.

The trunk had been a find at a yard sale during an excursion to Kansas City. It was a beautiful old antique trunk, and it had been a real bargain, sold for a ridiculously cheap price. The purchasers had been ecstatic over their good fortune and had loaded the massive piece into the back of the car and returned to Atchison with it. It had been shortly after the placement of the trunk in its new home in the second-story bedroom of their house on Seventh Street that the strange unfurniture-like behavior of the trunk had begun.

A year or so after the purchase of the trunk, the son of the owners got married. He decided to take the trunk with him to his new home. Perhaps, he said jokingly, it will like my house better. After just a few months he returned the trunk to his parents' house. His new wife was fed up, and not a little frightened, by the intermittent movements of the trunk. Even in its new house, the trunk had continued to migrate from the wall to the middle of the room.

Finally, the family decided to investigate the history of the trunk. They went back to Kansas City and contacted the people living at the house where they had purchased the trunk. According to them, the trunk had originally been owned by a wealthy family in town. Several stories had been told about the trunk, but they all centered around the daughter of the family and how she came to die on her wedding day.

Everyone knows that a bride must wear "something old, something new, something borrowed, and something blue" to her wedding. Some tales about the trunk said that on the morning of her wedding, the bride went up into the attic of her parents' home to look for something old to go with the new, borrowed, and blue items she had already collected. Spotting the old family trunk in a corner of the attic, she decided to look inside for something suitable. She lifted the skirt of her bridal gown up off the dusty floor and walked to the trunk. She hoisted up the heavy lid and pushed it back, the chain guards on the sides holding it in place. It was dark inside the trunk, and the attic was poorly lit. The girl leaned over and into the trunk, straining to see what might be tucked away at the very bottom. Unwittingly, she caught a piece of lace from the bodice of her gown on the metal edge of the trunk lid. Suddenly, the ponderous top of the trunk, pulled forward by the snagged fabric, crashed down on top of the bride, the metallic edge striking her in the back of the head. Knocked unconscious, the girl tumbled into the trunk, and the lid crashed shut, the lock snapping into place.

Locked in, the trunk became the bride's tomb. No one could find her, although they searched and searched. They didn't think to search in the corner of a third-floor attic inside a dusty old trunk. Perhaps the blow on the head killed her instantly; perhaps she suffocated inside the airtight trunk, her moans and screams unheard. Regardless, the bride died in the trunk, her anguished groom, family, and friends thinking she had just vanished into thin air.

Other versions of the story told of a beautiful wedding and of the happy bride and groom joining in songs and dancing and games at the reception in the bride's parents' house. Finally, a high-spirited game of hide and seek was initiated and the groom was "it." The bride, gathering up her skirts, slipped away up to the attic. Spying the old trunk in the corner, she ran over to it, pushed with all her might to lift the heavy lid, and climbed in. "He'll never find me in here," she said. As she strained to lower the top gently, it slipped from her hands and crashed shut, the hasp dropping and latching. As in the other version of the story, the hapless bride is trapped in the truck, unable to get out or to be heard calling for help.

Although the scenario changes for the alternate versions of how or why the bride is trapped in the trunk, the ultimate outcome is the same. Years later, so both versions go, someone—a maid, the mother—goes up to the attic to find something. Noticing the trunk in the corner, the person decides to look in it. The latch is unlocked, the clasp is unhooked, and the lid is lifted. There inside is the long-missing bride: a skeleton dressed in a wedding gown.

The story of the trunk that moves across the floor in the house on Seventh Street is an Atchison ghost story. The secondary story of the bride in the trunk is a rendition of an old traditional tale from English and American folklore. The ballad "The Mistletoe Bough" by Thomas Haynes Bayly is based on similar variants of the legend, and the last verse of the ballad goes:

> At length an oak chest that had long lain hid,
> Was found in the castle; they raised the lid,
> And a skeleton form lay mouldering there
> In the bridal wreath of the lady fair.
> Oh, sad was her fate; in sporting jest
> She hid from her lord in the old oak chest;
> It closed with a spring, and her bridal bloom
> Lay withering there in a living tomb."

A Quartet of Ghosts

THE REDECORATING GHOST

One house in Atchison was purchased by its present owners fully furnished. Even the pictures on the walls came with the house. Although the owners liked the furniture and most of the decorating touches, a few things were not to their taste, so they spent some time rearranging pictures and furniture. One painting in particular was not to their liking; they took it down from the wall, wrapped it up in newspaper, secured the paper with twine, and stored it in the basement. The next morning, the painting was back up on the wall right where it had been before. The newspaper and string that had wrapped the painting had vanished. Some other pictures that had been rearranged by the tenants of the house were also back in their original locations.

One new item installed by the owners was a large hanging clock that they placed in the dining room. The morning after it had been hung on the wall, it was discovered perched on the floor in the middle of the room. The owners rehung the clock; the next day the clock was back on the floor. After many replayings of this scene, the owners gave up and donated the clock to a relative who lived elsewhere.

The ghost in this house evidently fancies itself an interior designer, or else it emphatically likes things to remain the way they were before the arrival of the new occupants. Other than its redecorating binge, the ghost has not bothered the owners.

GRANDMA'S GHOST

A parapsychologist was shown a picture of an old house on Second Street. He was able to discern the image of an elderly woman peering from a window on the second story. This was disturbing to the owner of the house because he was the grandson of the original owners of the house, and he remembered that particular window on the second floor as his grandmother's favorite. She had spent a lot of time when she was older sitting in front of the window and looking out to the street.

The grandson was planning on moving into the house until he found out his grandmother might still be there, at least in spirit. He contacted a priest and discovered that an ancestral blessing could be conducted in the house to help free the structure of his grandmother's presence. The priest arrived and passed out candles to the grandson and other family members present. They lit the candles and made a procession through the house, blessing each room and every nook and cranny in the house.

In spite of the blessing, the grandson still never did feel comfortable in the house. Although he never saw or heard from his granny, other people said that she was still there, sitting up at her window, rocking and watching the street. Although the house remains in the family, it remains largely vacant, except for Grandma.

THE GHOST OF NELLIE AND THE CIRCLE OF LIGHT

Nellie was a schoolteacher who never married. She lived and died in a house on Third Street. Nellie still frequents her old house but in a very unusual form. Construction workers remodeling and renovating the house saw Nellie. So did the woman who owns the house now. It didn't look like Nellie, but they knew it was her.

What they saw was a strange circle of lights—bright multicolored lights that appeared all around the house. Sometimes the light circle was only about a foot in diameter, but other times it expanded to two feet or more. Almost like a tiny UFO, the flashing light disc hovered in the air and, sensing movement and proximity, glided away as someone approached it.

The owner now has trouble getting construction workers to stay on the job because of Nellie. The lights have appeared upstairs, downstairs, and on the stairs. No one likes to be in the house alone, although Nellie has done nothing other than appear in her bizarre illuminated form—a phantasmic will-o'-the-wisp whirling through the house.

THE GARGOYLE HOUSE

Rumors swirl around the so-called gargoyle house in Atchison. The builder of the Gothic-style house and original owner was a railroad lawyer and politician in the late 1800s. Legendary stories about the man and the house tell a Faustian tale of a man who bargained with the devil to buy himself success. The visible marker of his dark deal with the prince of darkness was to be the placement of the malevolent winged gargoyle figures on the highest points of his house.

Legend also holds that the second owner of the house suffered a crushing and ungainly death when he fell from his roof attempting to move the glowering stone gargoyles from the house. Obviously, the devilish curse, like the gargoyles, isn't so easy to remove.

ATCHISON'S HAUNTED PARK

The Legend of Molly's Hollow in Jackson Park

Molly's hanging from her tree. Hanging and twisting, her body is moving ever so slightly in the breeze. The rope creaks on the bark of the tree branch. The midnight moon rising behind Piano Cliff casts an eerie glow on Molly's Hollow and spotlights Molly's poor body suspended by its neck. A mournful moaning sound begins to rise like mist from the river, slowly building, increasing in intensity and pitch. Louder and louder, closer and closer, until, at the stroke of midnight, the scream bursts forth in full voice, the sound shattering the stillness in Jackson Park. The piercing sound cuts through the wind like a knife, slicing through the air and the tree and the rope until, abruptly, Molly falls and disappears.

Molly's tree is gone—cut down—and Molly's Hollow is gone, too— filled in. But the legend of Molly and Molly's Hollow is still very much present in the tangled interior of Jackson Park alongside the Missouri River. Molly's legend is a complicated one, with at least three distinct story lines and numerous versions. The time frame of the story depends on the teller, but the setting is always the old hollow in the park. Who Molly was and why she was in the park differ from version to version, but Molly's ultimate end is also a constant. She either hangs herself or is hanged by others, her body left to sway in the breeze in the hollow.

The legend of Molly's Hollow is a very good example of a durable multigenerational legend that mutates and changes to fit the concerns and realities of each succeeding generation or group of tellers. Molly's story started out as one of Civil War–era racial tensions and ended up a modern tale of a suicidal or murdered coed. Even though the landscape has changed culturally as well as physically in regard to the legend, the story lingers on as a fixed feature in Atchison's folkloric scenery.

Cindy Jones-Blanton is the assistant director of the Atchison Library, the children's librarian, and a self-described "teller of tales." Cindy first heard the tale of Molly before 1960, when she was in elementary school in Atchison. It was told to her as a slavery story, a story dating back to the very earliest days of Atchison. According to Cindy, Molly was a black woman who was hung because she was caught with her master in a compromising situation and was hung from a tree in what is now Jackson Park. "At midnight," Cindy said, the story is that "you can hear her scream near where she was hung."

Similar versions of the legend are more specific as to who was directly responsible for Molly's death. Molly, a young slave girl, was thought merely to be "spending too much time with her master" and was rounded up in the park by the white women of the town. The following morning, young Molly's body was "found hanged in a tree overlooking the Missouri River."

Cindy remembered going to Molly's Hollow as a child: "You could look up the road and see the tree and the branch she was hung from. The bluff is right there—there is an opening in the bluff, right by the pond. The hollow and the tree are gone, but you can still see the area and go up to 'Piano Cliff,' right behind Molly's Hollow." Cindy also remembered hearing sounds that convinced her she was hearing Molly's screams. She recalled that it was "always a Halloween thing at Jackson Park" to go out and listen to Molly "holler" at midnight in the hollow. In fact, she said, some people refer to the site as Molly's Holler instead of Molly's Hollow.

According to Cindy, the 1950s- and 1960s-era legend she heard about was always a slavery-based legend, and Molly was always a black woman. The legend hearkened back to a time when Atchison and other Kansas towns were part of a bitter war between antislavery and proslavery forces in Kansas and Missouri, a time when Kansas was known nationally as Bleeding Kansas. Cindy interpreted the legend of Molly as functioning as a cautionary tale to remind us of the horrors of slavery.

Another vivid element of the legend portrays the sound of the anguished Molly screaming, a sound that can be heard in the vicinity of the hollow only at the stroke of midnight. Cindy revealed that an industrial factory located a short distance downriver from the hollow used to sound a midnight whistle to designate a shift change, and she believed that was the sound that she and others heard and mistook for Molly's ghost's unearthly screams. "By the time the sound of the whistle drifted up there to the park," Cindy surmised, "you heard [or thought you heard] a high, shrill voice."

A more contemporary version of the legend of Molly centers around the hollow as a local lovers' lane for teenagers and college students well into the 1970s. Molly and her boyfriend, both teenagers, are parked on the road under Piano Rock ledge. The couple quarrels and breaks up, or perhaps the young man informs his girlfriend he is no longer interested in her. The distraught Molly gets out of the car and tells the boy she wants to walk home. He drives off and leaves her in the park. The next morning she is found hanging from the tree, a suicide, "swinging in the breeze in Molly's Hollow." Again in this version, on moonlit nights the body of Molly is visible swaying below the branch of the tree, and the sounds of her tormented screams are heard in the hollow and down the river. Many versions assert that those screams "have been heard throughout Jackson Park over the years."

A thirty-two-year-old waitress at a local restaurant in Atchison recalled her memories of Molly's Hollow: "When I was in Girl Scouts, about sixteen or seventeen years ago, we would go on hikes around there, around Molly's Hollow. You could listen, and you could hear a scream. I don't know if it was because we thought we should, or we wanted to, but we could hear a scream."

A different contemporary account placed a slightly older Molly, a coed from an Atchison college, at the park one night with a group of friends. For a prank, her friends left her there alone in the hollow, in the dark. When they came back later to find her, they discovered that she had been murdered by an unknown assailant and left hanging by a rope from a tree. This version was told by a woman in her mid-forties who grew up in Atchison. In her account, anyone who went out to Jackson Park at night could go to Molly's Hollow and see "her shadow hanging from a tree." If her name was called out, the story said, she would scream in response. The woman who told this tale took her nieces and nephews out to the park to tell them the story. According to one of her nieces, Myra Innes, who lives in Topeka, "She took us there [to Jackson Park], and she scared us to death."

Molly's Hollow was filled in toward the end of the 1980s by a local foundry, and the legendary tree was cut down. A small park area over the filled-in hollow now buries the site of Molly's supposed demise. Whether some core of truth exists within this legend is unknown. Another story indicates that many years back a man named Marlow lived in the hollow in a little house, and the hollow came to be called Marlow's Hollow. Perhaps "Molly's" is just a corruption of "Marlow's," and the entire legend was created to explain the naming of the hollow for a girl called Molly.

For whatever reason, the legend of Molly's Hollow is the dominant legend in the Atchison area, one of a handful of quite complex and ever-changing legends in the state. (See the stories of the Albino Woman of Topeka and Theorosa's Bridge in this book.) The ghost or the figure of Molly takes on different forms, different eras, and different story lines, but it remains a legendary character rewoven into contemporary stories that still serve a purpose in the present-day culture of the city.

Molly as a slave woman or girl murdered in a horrible way that was all too common in times past points up the injustice of prejudice and the inhumanity of slavery. As Cindy Jones-Blanton remarked, the legend does remind us of the horror of that barbarous system. Molly as teenager or coed left behind alone in a dark and isolated place is a cautionary against teenage parking on lovers' lanes and a warning against a reckless foolhardiness that abandons a vulnerable individual to the diabolical forces that lurk in the shadows.

Epilogue

*Throughout history, the comforting story runs, people have loved
to sit around the flickering fire, chilling one another's blood with tales
of monsters and the vengeful dead.*
—Walter Kendrick, *The Thrill of Fear*

A native of Hutchinson, a former resident, remembers from his childhood a house in his hometown that was deserted but, weirdly, always remained the same: curtains open, rooms full of furniture and personal possessions. For years, this man says, "things were sitting on the coffee table and wouldn't be moved. In the kitchen, the spoons and other silverware were set and always neatly in the same place. It looked," he recalls, "as if someone was just ready to sit down to breakfast, but no one ever did."

He remembers a Volkswagen Beetle parked in the driveway, and a 1962 or 1963 Corvette sitting in the garage. Nothing was ever moved or changed, and no one was ever there: Everything stayed the same for years.

He and his friends would go there to look in the windows. Eventually, he says, it became quite "spooky" and provoked endless speculation as to what had happened to the occupants, why they had left, and why they had never come back. The most prevalent story, he recalls, was that the people who had lived in the house had gone on vacation to Yellowstone National Park sometime in the 1960s. They had perished in a flood there, and none of the family had ever come back home. Distant relatives (so the story went) kept paying the taxes on the house but didn't want to deal with it or disposition of the contents.

So it remained the same, month after month, year after year. Eventually the Volkswagen in the driveway was stripped. The man doesn't know what became of the Corvette. He wonders if the house is still there—and is it still the same? A time capsule from the 1960s, a Twilight Zone house on a quiet street in Hutchinson, the ghostly abode of a drowned family always sitting down to breakfast in 1963.

Encountering the ghost stories in this book can be a bit like entering the dream world of the house that time forgot, particularly if the stories are from our own hometowns, from our own childhoods. We can recall a story we shared years ago with our friends, remember a time when the frights and fears of the real world may have been distant, but the adventure of visiting Theorosa's Bridge or Witches Hollow was a cathartic experience that could hold us in the thrall of terror, but then release us to easily return to the safety of our homes. We can allow ourselves to slip back into the world of legendry, back to a place that is always the same, year after year, in our memories.

Like the haunted house in Gaylord, where the same scene is replayed each night, and the house that time forgot in Hutchinson, where history is static, Haunted Kansas is a place we can visit in our imaginations any time we want. As, in reality, things *must* be changing at the house in Hutchinson—the cars are being stripped, the house is deteriorating—so too the stories of Haunted Kansas are changing over time, with each retelling of the legend. But for each of us as individuals, our own unique version of a hometown ghost or story remains the same, a place to be visited whenever we like.

In this book many reasons and functions for the telling of these stories have been given, and they are all valid. But in the end, the main reason for telling and preserving these stories (the sole reason for many people) is to allow us to suspend our disbelief, release our modern skepticism, and draw around the collective campfire of legendry and folklore. As the author Roald Dahl has said, "Spookiness is, after all, the real purpose of the ghost story. It should give you the creeps and disturb your thoughts."

Notes and Sources

Introduction

Brunvand, Jan Harold. *The Vanishing Hitchhiker.* New York: W. W. Norton, 1981.
————. *The Study of American Folklore.* New York: W. W. Norton, 1986.
Degh, Linda. "The 'Belief Legend' in Modern Society." *American Folk Legend: A Symposium.* Berkeley: University of California Press, 1971.
Enright, D. J., ed. *The Oxford Book of the Supernatural.* Oxford: Oxford University Press, 1994.
Mitchell, Pat. "Things That Go Bump . . . in the Night." *Kanhistique* 15, no. 6 (October 1989): 2–3.
Ryden, Kent C. *Mapping the Invisible Landscape: Folklore, Writing, and the Sense of Place.* Iowa City: University of Iowa Press, 1993.

The Old Stone House

In a 1994 book, *Ghostwatching,* authors John Spencer and Tony Wells group ghosts into several categories; among these are "ghosts that ignore you," "ghosts that interact with you," and "ghosts with attitude." The ghosts that the Cummings family lived with for ten years seem to fit in the category of "ghosts that ignore you." Seemingly oblivious to the very real family living in their midst, what one supposes to be former occupants of the old stone house carry on continual conversations, pitched just low enough to be unintelligible to the living residents; tend to a crying baby that seems to be in the buffet (was the original nursery in the room that served the Cummings family as a dining room?); and trudge up the stairs to the bedroom at night, perhaps weary after a long day of ghostly work in the realms of the not-quite-granted-eternal-rest.

Mrs. Cummings found evidence that the house was remodeled, possibly in the 1880s, sometime after the original, much smaller, house was constructed. Additions enlarged the house for later residents, but the ghostly family that evidently never completely left may have continued to live in the original rooms of the stone house until the entire thing went under the wrecking ball. Mrs. Cummings also at some point talked to a man who had lived in the house as a boy before the Cummings family purchased it. He said that "strange things" had happened in the house when his family had lived there as well, but according to Mrs. Cummings, "he would not elaborate."

SOURCES

Interview with Mrs. Marcella Cummings. Eureka, Kansas, December 12, 1996.
Cummings, Marcella Benson. "The Old Stone House SE of Neal, Kansas."
    Eureka, Kansas. March 1996. (Handwritten account available at Green-
    wood County Historical Museum.)
The Greenwood County Historical Society. Mrs. Helen Bradford, volunteer.
    Eureka, Kansas.
Spencer, John, and Tony Wells. *Ghostwatching.* London: Virgin Books, 1994.

The Haunted Farm

This is a frightening story because of the particularly violent and gruesome behavior of this ghost. Not only does the Koett farm ghost exhibit poltergeist-like behavior with its noises and thumpings and moving of furniture, pictures, and other items, but it punches people in the nose and delivers a horrible death to the family pet with the dreaded farm implement—a pitchfork. This particular ghost seems somewhat satanic in its behavior and its perceived form as a dark, thin wraith. Add the element of the pitchfork, and the picture is complete. One wonders if an exorcism might have been helpful in the Koetts' war with their resident demon ghost.

A variety of recognizable standard elements, or motifs, peculiar to hauntings exist in this story. One common element not present in many stories included in this collection is that of a peculiar or strong odor that is associated with the ghost or a haunting.

SOURCES

The Folklore Papers of William E. Koch. Courtesy of Dr. James Hoy, Emporia
    State University, Emporia, Kansas.
Moore, Kim. "Night of the Supernatural." *Hutchinson News.* October 26, 1980.
"Prankish 'Ghost' Causes Koett to Leave His Home." *Great Bend Tribune,* 1927.
Scott, Beth, and Michael Norman. *Haunted Heartland.* New York: Warner
    Books, 1985.

The Blue Handkerchief Ghost of Carey House Square

Stories of the Carey House ghost incorporate numerous motifs and images that are classic ghost legend material. The color blue is often associated with ghost legends, and the gauzy, hazy appearance of the ghost is typical of many apparitions. This ghost is mischievous rather than malevolent, and its actions, too, are predictable: walking (or tromping) overhead, ascending and descending a staircase, floating down a hallway, flinging items off shelves and off walls, rearranging items, playing pranks such as taking the phone off the hook, and so on. This ghost appeals to all the senses as it manages to induce the smell of roses, change the temperature in a room, and provoke dizziness. It is not very vocal but has managed to call out the name of a close human ally, Rose.

Publicity has enhanced the legend of this ghost, added new elements to it, and introduced the story to an audience beyond the walls of Carey House Square. But the ghost of Julie served a definite function, beyond that of just a good scary story, for some former employees. During an extended interview after hours at the building with several women who worked there at the time, it became obvious that tales of Julie and her pranks had served as a bonding experience between the women. Those who had not actually "seen" Julie seemed to be anticipating the experience, certainly as an initiation into the exclusive club of people who spend a part of each week coexisting with a ghost that they have personally met.

SOURCES

Bower, Beth. "Beth Discovers Real Find in Dine & Roses Cafe: Warm Atmosphere, Delicious Food, and the Carey House Ghost Doesn't Bother Anyone!" "Beth's Best Bets" column, *Wichita Old Town Gazette* (October 1995).

Interview with Rose Mason, building manager of Carey House Landing and owner of Dine and Roses Restaurant. Wichita, Kansas, September 7, 1995.

Interview with Rose Mason, Marnie Fagerberg, and Sami Barry of Carey House Landing. Wichita, Kansas, October 15, 1995.

Interview with Beccy Tanner, *Wichita Eagle* newspaper. Wichita, Kansas, October 16, 1995.

Tanner, Beccy. "Eleven Ghostly Tales from Kansas." *Wichita Eagle,* October 31, 1993.

Herbie the Bakery Ghost

Herbie is a typical house or building ghost, except for his one odd trick of blowing on the backs of people's necks. Amorous neck blowing is somewhat of an unusual behavior pattern for a ghost. The owner of the bakery expressed his wish that Herbie would help him fry some doughnuts sometime, but doughnut making as a ghostly activity is even rarer still.

SOURCE

"Friendly Ghost Haunts Local Bakery Basement." *Kansas State Collegian*. Manhattan, Kansas, October 31, 1985.

The Ghost of Ida Day

Ida Day was a legendary character when she was alive, and the stories and anecdotes about her stern visage and strict rules and demeanor qualify her as a subject of interest as a local character kept alive through legend. The ghostly element to her legend simply adds "luminosity" and further interest to the stories of Ida Day as a fabled personality.

A contemporary pop-culture element added to this legend is the similarity between the description of the ghostly figure of the stern Hutchinson librarian floating between the stacks and an opening scene in the 1984 hit movie *Ghostbusters,* in which the human appearance of a prim (but somewhat luminous) librarian shelving books metamorphoses into a macabre and ghastly ghost—the prelude to the entire city of New York's being temporarily (thanks to Bill Murray, Dan Aykroyd, et al.) overrun by ghosts and goblins.

SOURCES

Martinez, Karen. "Hamburger Man and the Library Ghost Live On." *Hutchinson News,* October 27, 1996.
90th Anniversary: Hutchinson Public Library—1901–1991. Hutchinson Public Library, 1991.
Peirce, Larry. "Oyler: 'I Loved the Growth, the Books—Hutchonian Closes Book on Library Career." *Hutchinson News,* October 8, 1992.
Staff and archives, Hutchinson Public Library, Hutchinson, Kansas.
Williams, Judy. "Ida Day Returns to Hutch: Does a Ghost Haunt the Library?" *Hutchinson News,* October 31, 1975.

The Emporia Country Club Ghosts

The stories of a ghost or ghosts at the Emporia Country Club have been kept alive in part by the tradition employees and members have of sharing the tales with one another. This tradition functions as something of an initiation rite, or bonding ritual, to bring a new member or employee into the "family."

Ghostly revelry and ghosts eating, drinking, and partying are ghostly activities that are uncommon but not unheard of as elements of ghostlore. According to Gail White's *Haunted San Diego,* visitors to the Whaley House in San Diego, a historic house that is widely recognized as "one of the most actively haunted houses in the country," routinely report hearing the sounds of music and laughter and smelling perfume and cigar smoke. Sounds and smells like these hearken back to the mid-1800s when the wealthy Whaley family hosted elaborate parties for their friends.

SOURCES

Interview with Don Blaylock, general manager of Emporia Country Club. Emporia, Kansas, December 6, 1996.

Rainwater, Gretchen. "The Emporia Country Club's Ghost." Student paper written for Dr. James Hoy's American Folklore class, Emporia State University, May 2, 1991.

White, Gail. "The Whaley House." *Haunted San Diego*. San Diego: Tecolote Publications, 1992.

Interview with Gayle Woods Gardner, historian, Emporia Public Library. Emporia, Kansas, September 28, 1995.

The Haunted Duplex

Like the ghosts of the old stone house, the ghost in the haunted duplex is a personal ghost. Many local ghost legends are historical, and most are told for fun—for what author Edith Wharton in *The Ghost Stories of Edith Wharton* called "the fun of the shudder." Any actual sightings of ghosts in these legends is usually by what folklorist Jan Harold Brunvand has termed an FOAF—the seldom identified, but always ubiquitous, Friend of a Friend. Rarely does one talk to an individual, in the context of collecting local ghost legends, who has had an actual experience with the supernatural. But in a very few instances, rational individuals with believable stories relate unexplainable encounters with the paranormal.

Are these ghosts real, and not just stories? If *any* ghost in Kansas is real, it just might be the ghost in the haunted duplex.

SOURCE

Interview with anonymous female informant, south-central Kansas, August 9, 1996.

The Watching Widow

The theme of the "ghost of a tragic lover who haunts the scene of tragedy" is very recognizable and prevalent in worldwide ghost lore. Even though, in this instance, the ghost has evidently only "appeared" to one individual, the implication is that the watching widow is always in that room, looking out that window, forever compelled to haunt the place where her lover died. The only surprising aspect of this story is that it has remained so self-contained and utterly unknown outside the confines of the old fort.

SOURCES

Kansas Department of Commerce and Housing. "Historic Forts and Trails in Kansas." 1996.
Interview with Arnold Schofield, National Park Service fort historian, Fort Scott National Historical Site, Fort Scott, Kansas, August 28, 1995.
U.S. Department of the Interior. National Park Service. *Fort Scott—National Historic Site, Kansas*. Washington, D.C.: GPO: 1994.

The Ghosts of Fort Riley

The phantoms at Fort Riley are almost exclusively frontier ghosts. Other ghost stories or ghosts may lurk in other places on the base—haunting a hall or a residence, gliding across the grounds—but if so, they aren't as prevalent or as well known as the stories recounted here. Bill McKale has not heard any new stories, or new variants of old ones, since the early 1980s.

Stories of Custer's ghost abound in many places where he lived or stayed (see "The Ghosts of Fort Leavenworth"). But the haunted toys in the story of the Haunted Teddy Bear are unusual and make this legend particularly vivid and scary.

SOURCES

Bloomfield, Gary. "Whether You Believe in Ghosts or Not, Fort Riley Is Definitely . . . Haunted!" *Fort Riley POST*. October 26, 1979.
Caroll, Nan. "Ghost of General Custer Seems to Live at Fort Riley." Unidentified newspaper. 1955. The Folklore Papers of William E. Koch. Courtesy of Dr. James Hoy, Emporia State University, Emporia, Kansas.
Childs, Gaylynn. "Ghosts Haunt Fort for Decades." *Junction City Daily Union*. October 29, 1995.
"The Custer House at Fort Riley, Kansas—History and Tradition." Student paper. The Folklore Papers of William E. Koch. Courtesy of Dr. James Hoy, Emporia State University, Emporia, Kansas. 1976.
"A Haunted House." *Junction City Union*. October 8, 1887.
"Historical Homes Yield Stories." *Junction City Daily Union*. October 7, 1989.
Interview with Bill McKale, museum specialist, U.S. Cavalry Museum. Fort Riley, Kansas, August 15, 1996.

Pride, Captain Woodbury F. *The History of Fort Riley.* N.p., Cavalry School
    Press: 1926. Reprinted by the Fort Riley Historical and Archaeology Soci-
    ety, September 1987.
"Shocking Suicide!" *Junction City Weekly Union.* October 18, 1863.
Synovec, Dan. "Haunting of Fort Riley." *Manhattan Mercury.* January 13, 1980.
Wright, Carol. "Haunted Houses Aren't Fun for Some—They're Fearsome."
    Kansas State Collegian. October 31, 1979.

The Ghosts of Fort Leavenworth

Some of the Fort Leavenworth ghost stories are excellent examples of how
legends evolve and change or how simultaneous versions of the same story can
differ vastly. They also illustrate how two legends that may be similar in some
respects or share common elements can begin to merge or how a single incident or legendary individual can spawn different stories. Could the Lady in
Black and the Ghost of Catherine Sutler be one and the same, or do these two
different stories simply share similar motifs of a mother-ghost or mothering
ghost dressed in black? It seems unlikely that the stories of Father Fred who
died in a fire and the stories of the Face in the Fire who may have been a priest
are not derived from the same source or at the very least are legends that draw
from each other. Custer, of course, is a legendary figure of national stature, and
one would assume that Custer's ghost makes appearances at numerous forts
and locations throughout the West, not just Fort Leavenworth and Fort Riley.

SOURCES

Bingham, Joan, and Dolores Riccio. "A Distraught Mother at Fort Leaven-
    worth." *More Haunted Houses.* New York: Pocket Books, 1991.
"George Armstrong Custer." *The New Encyclopaedia Brittanica.* 15th ed.
Ghost Stories of Fort Leavenworth. Compiled by Musettes of the Fort Leaven-
    worth Museum, Fort Leavenworth, Kansas, 1988.
Hauck, Dennis William. "Fort Leavenworth." *Haunted Places: The National
    Directory.* New York: Penguin Books USA, 1996.
McConnell/Millert, Sharon. "Post Ghosties." *Star* magazine, *The Kansas City
    Star.* October 31, 1982.
Interview with John Reichley, publicist, Fort Leavenworth Historical Society.
    Fort Leavenworth, Kansas, October 25, 1995.
Reichley, John. *The Haunted Houses of Fort Leavenworth.* Fort Leavenworth,
    Kans.: Fort Leavenworth Historical Society, 1995.
Richmond, Robert W. *Kansas: A Land of Contrasts.* Arlington Heights, Ill.: The
    Forum Press, 1980.

The Oxford Middle School Ghost

Billie is not the true name of the girl who was killed in a school-bus accident in Oxford in 1943. But the incident is real and the stories that have sprung up about the haunting of the middle school building by the girl's ghost are very real, even upsetting, to those who claim to have experienced them.

SOURCE

Phyllis Hege, librarian, Oxford Public Library. Oxford, Kansas. Correspondence: June 24, 1996. Interview: December 16, 1996.

The Ghostly Trumpeter of Paola High School

The Ghostly Trumpeter is an excellent example of a multiple-version legend that changes elements and motifs, even characters, as rapidly and as fluidly as a trumpeter plays up and down the scale. Even if a perfectly logical explanation could be made for any trumpetlike sounds reported inside the school or emanating from its front door, odds are the stories would continue about the ghostly trumpeter, because these stories are an integral part of the school and the town's folklore and folk heritage.

SOURCES

"The Ghostly Trumpeter." Student paper, 1972. The Folklore Papers of William E. Koch. Courtesy of Dr. James Hoy, Emporia State University, Emporia, Kansas.

Hauck, Dennis William. "Paola High School." *Haunted Places: The National Directory.* New York: Penguin Books USA, 1996.

Death Takes a Holiday: *The Salina Central High Stage Ghost*

The stories of the ghost of Joyce at Salina Central might be distressing to some people—family and friends—who knew her when she was alive. When the stories began to circulate and become common knowledge in Salina, some former classmates expressed chagrin that their friend would be remembered in this way. Joyce was a very real person who died nearly fifty years ago in a terrible accident. Oftentimes a tragedy similar to this one involving a student or a teacher will be the impetus for this type of legend. (See "The Oxford Middle School Ghost" in this chapter.)

The legend of Joyce and *Death Takes a Holiday* is of such long-standing duration and so widely known (and documented through newspaper articles, yearbook and student newspaper articles, a student scrapbook, and so on) in the Salina area that it would be an oversight to ignore it in a collection of Kansas ghost legends. One would hope that this story and any other dealing with real, historical individuals would not cause anyone discomfort or distress.

After an article appeared in the *Salina Journal* in October 1996 mentioning the legends of Joyce and her ghost and retelling some details of her life and tragic death, Salina Central High School received several phone calls regarding the story. Many were from former students mentioning that they remembered the legend well. According to the Salina Central director of theater, Brad McDonald, "Most of the phone calls I received were from people who knew of the legend. None of the calls were negative."

SOURCES

Clouston, David. "Ghost Stories: Salina Central's Ghost Among Spooky Tales in Book to be Published." *Salina Journal.* October 28, 1996.

"The Ghost of Central: A Memory of Elegance." *Salina Central High School Yearbook,* 1982.

Houston, Velina. "Ghosts: The Dead May Still Be with Us." *Kansas State Collegian.* May 10, 1977.

"Joyce's Pink Phantom Lurks in Salina School." *Kansas State Collegian.* October 31, 1984.

Interview with Brad McDonald, director of theater, Salina Central High School. Salina, Kansas, December 5, 1996.

Morrow, Barbara. "Student Actors Bring Back Ghost for Decades of Curtain Calls." *Salina Journal.* October 28, 1984.

Nashawaty, Chris. "Deja View." *Entertainment Weekly.* December 6, 1996.

Interview with Jeff Travis, special education teacher, Salina Central High School. Salina, Kansas, August 15, 1996.

George and the Night Nurse: Kansas State University

The sharing of stories of George and the Night Nurse functions as a bonding ritual between members of the fraternity and between potential members and active members ("we mention the ghosts during rush"). Alumni of the fraternity also enjoy telling ghost stories from the days they were in the house, an activity that not only is entertaining but also serves to reinforce and prove their ties to this particular social organization.

SOURCES

"Ghost in Old St. Mary's Hospital." Student paper, 1978. The Folklore Papers of William E. Koch. Courtesy of Dr. James Hoy, Emporia State University, Emporia, Kansas.

Hauck, Dennis William. *Haunted Places: The National Directory.* New York: Penguin Books USA, 1996.

Interview with Kyle Klenke, Delta Sigma Phi Fraternity. Manhattan, Kansas, December 1996.

Scott, Beth, and Michael Norman. *Haunted Heartland.* New York: Warner Books, 1985.

"Spooked U." *Manhattan Mercury.* Manhattan, Kansas. October 27, 1985.

"Things That Go Bump In The Night." *Kansas State Collegian.* Manhattan, Kansas. October 31, 1978.

Virginia, The Ghost of Sigma Nu: University of Kansas

As with the George and the Night Nurse stories from the Delta Sigma Phi fraternity at Kansas State University, the stories of Virginia at the Sigma Nu house at the University of Kansas serve as a tradition and bonding ritual between members of the fraternity, both active and alumni. However, the particular longevity of this legend seems unusual. It has lasted over literally generations of men who have come and gone through the Sigma Nu house since 1922.

The almost Edgar Allan Poe–ish touch in the legend when the poor hanged girl's ashes are walled up behind the stones of the fireplace with the eerie plaque as her marker also marks this legend as something a bit out of the ordinary.

SOURCES

"Ghostly Tale Still Haunts Sigma Nu House." *Lawrence Journal-World.* October 31, 1982.

Norman, Michael, and Beth Scott. *Historic Haunted America.* New York: Tom Doherty Associates, 1995.

Richmond, Robert W. *Kansas: A Land of Contrasts.* Arlington Heights, Ill.: The Forum Press, 1980.

Interview with Ryan Smartt, president, Sigma Nu fraternity. Lawrence, Kansas, January 22, 1997.

The Musical Ghost of McCray Hall: Pittsburg State University

It is not unusual for a large public building or school building to be presumed haunted by more than one ghost. But in McCray Hall, one ghost alone is presumed to be responsible for many poltergeist-type activities as well as assuming at least three reported forms: a frightening faceless entity, an ordinary man dressed in khakis, and a woman in a red dress. All collected references to the ghostly activity in this building mention only "the ghost" in the singular, never "ghosts" in the plural.

A ghost rearranging chairs with or without an aisle or with a certain number of rows or a ghost straightening disordered chairs (or vice versa) is a common ghostly activity in a number of "haunted" auditoriums, theaters, or schoolrooms.

SOURCES

Fullerton, Beth, "Mysterious Music: Several Claim They Have Seen Ghost at McCray Hall." *Morning Sun*. Pittsburg, Kansas. October 29, 1995.

Interview with Dr. Gene Vollen, retired chairman of the Pittsburg State University Music Department, Pittsburg, Kansas. January 8, 1997.

Earl, The Brown Grand Theatre Ghost

Stories of Earl and his antics have circulated around the Brown Grand Theatre and among its staff, patrons, and performers for many years. The strong personalities of the Brown family and their important position in Concordia's history as a town as well as the theater's history have added to the size and scope of the legend. Earl Brown and his family members were legends in their own time, and the vivid instances of unexplained occurrences at the theater continue to add to Earl's own personal legend and the legend of the ghost of the Brown Grand Theatre.

Earl's legend has many vivid motifs and elements. The use of the Ouija board to communicate with Earl is an interesting aspect of the legend, as is the large bat that periodically flies around the auditorium, buzzing theater patrons and board members alike. In traditional ghostlore, the appearance of a flying bat is the sign of a ghost. Nowadays, bats are more commonly associated with the appearance of a vampire. Perhaps in his afterlife, Earl has become a *real* lady-killer.

SOURCES

The Brown Grand Theatre. Commemorative Program Book. Concordia Chamber of Commerce. Concordia, Kansas: Blade-Empire Publishing Company. 1980.

Interviews with Susie Haver, curator, and Susan Sutton, president, Brown Grand Theatre. Concordia, Kansas, July 30, 1996; Susan Sutton, correspondence, June 19, 1996.

Workman, Thelma. *The Best in Kansas: A History of the Brown Grand Theatre and Its Restoration*. Concordia, Kansas: n.p., 1980. (A compilation of previously published newspaper articles from Concordia newspapers, the *Daily Kansan* and the *Blade-Empire,* plus additional previously unpublished articles.)

Chapter Introduction: Graveyard Ghosts

Guiley, Rosemary Ellen. "Charms Against Ghosts." *The Encyclopedia of Ghosts and Spirits.* New York: Facts On File, 1992.
Koch, William E. *Folklore from Kansas: Customs, Beliefs & Superstitions.* Lawrence: University Press of Kansas, 1980.
Leach, Maria, ed. "Graves and Graveyards." *Funk & Wagnalls Standard Dictionary of Folklore, Mythology, and Legend.* San Francisco: HarperSanFrancisco, 1972.

The Albino Woman

One of the more interesting elements of the Albino Woman story is its link to the Hispanic legend of La Llorona. There are direct ties to the Mexican "weeping woman" legend in one branch of the Albino Lady legend, characterized by the shared motifs and descriptions of the central legend figure and her actions. This was characterized by an interview with a sixteen-year-old Hispanic youth from Topeka in which he shared his versions of both the La Llorona legend and the Albino Woman legend.

About La Llorona, he said: "I've heard she walks along the Rio Grande in Texas. I heard that she had an affair in the 1880s with a Mexican army person. She had his kids, he promised to marry her. He never did. So she was so hurt that she killed her kids. She died a few years later. They say God punished her for the murders and so her soul can't rest because she is being forced to search for her kids which she dumped in the river. So now she roams the Rio Grande at night crying or yelling—that's how she got her name—and looking for her kids."

His version of the Albino Woman was this: "What I heard—there used to be an albino chick, the community didn't like her, especially little kids. She finally died, I heard, in the 1960s. She is buried in Rochester Cemetery. That's when people first started seeing her—after she died. I heard she stays between Soldier Creek and Goodyear, and she walks around. . . . I heard that there's a house by the cemetery. One of the guys takes care of it, a guy by the cemetery, lived in a house by it with a big bay window. He saw somebody crossing right on the border of the cemetery and his yard, then started seeing her (the Albino Lady) every night. Every time he saw her, she would come a little closer to the house. Then it got so he expected to see her. One night he didn't. He got kind of worried, so he went to check on his kids, and saw her looking through the window at his kids. Then he didn't see her anymore."

Versions from other sources have related that the Albino Woman has "lost her kid or her kids and is looking for them" or "every night if there are kids around, she will try to catch them and eat them" and "her husband had left her for another woman, so she prowled the cemetery at night looking for young lovers to get her vengeance."

SOURCES

Broddle, Tom. "Topeaking." (Weekly column.) *Washburn University Review.*
    April 14, 1971; April 28, 1971; October 27, 1971.
Hauck, Dennis William. "Rockingham Cemetery." *Haunted Places: The National
    Directory.* New York: Penguin Books USA, 1996.
Heitz, Lisa Hefner. "The Albino Woman of Topeka: A Local Belief Legend as Cultural Prism." Master's thesis, American Studies, University of Kansas,
    1996.
Scott, Beth, and Michael Norman. "The Mad Woman of Topeka." *Haunted Heartland.* New York: Warner Books, 1985.

The Blue-Eyed Monster of Clearwater Cemetery

This is an amusing story but also a vivid illustration of some unusual and colorful motifs. A ghost is not unusual, a monster is not too unusual, but a ghost-monster is rare. Ghosts and monsters with glowing red eyes are commonplace, but a blue-eyed ghost *or* monster is in the realm of the eccentric. Glowing, mesmerizing, hypnotic: This must have been the Mel Gibson of monsters. Deer or not, it's quite a story.

SOURCES

" 'Ghost' Startles Clearwater." *Wichita Beacon.* Wichita, Kansas. May 17, 1965.
"Spooky Deer, Your Tale Has Wagged Before." *Wichita Eagle.* Wichita, Kansas.
    May 19, 1965.
Tanner, Beccy. "Eleven Ghostly Tales from Kansas." *Wichita Eagle.* October 31,
    1993.

The Demonic Church

The legend of Stull can definitely be seen as a cautionary, an example of a legend that grows out of control and threatens elements of the very community that has produced it or maintained the landscape that has drawn it.

One version of the legend mentions a witch who "was said to have been hanged from a tree in the graveyard." This element may be derived from an actual incident in the early history of the Stull community when a man, reported missing by his family, was found, "his body hanging by a rope from a tree limb." The odd, isolated reports of a "werewolf child" or "ghost child" in the graveyard might, again, have a connection to a real-life incident from the early days of the town. A small boy who lived in the Stull neighborhood wandered into a field of tall grass and weeds that was being burned off by his father. The boy died in the fire, and his body was later discovered in the ashes and stubble of the charred field.

One unexplained side note. In a history of the Stull community in *Soil of Our Souls*, mention is made of a certain road in the area: "A road leading to the north . . . was called Devil's Lane, and at one time it was shown on county maps. When the natural gas line was laid in 1905, the men working for the gas company used this old road." Why was a road leading north away from Stull, toward Emmanuel Hill and the church and cemetery, called Devil's Lane back at the turn of the century? Maybe the legends of Stull are older than we think.

SOURCES

Hauck, Dennis William. "Stull Cemetery." *Haunted Places: The National Directory.* New York: Penguin Books USA. 1996.

The History of Stull. Publication of the Stull Bicentennial Celebration. July 3, 1976.

Interview with Dr. Steven Jansen, director, Elizabeth M. Watkins Community Museum. Lawrence, Kansas, October 1995.

"Legend Tells of Haunted Cemetery in Stull." *University Daily Kansan.* October 28, 1983.

Martinez, Michael. "Tonight in Stull, the Law Meets the Legend." *Kansas City Times.* October 31, 1989.

Interview with Jill Maycumber. Topeka, Kansas, November 1994.

Mitchell, Pat. "Things That Go Bump . . . in the Night." *Kanhistique* 15, no. 6 (October 1989): 2–3.

Interview with Curt Oglesby. Topeka, Kansas, December 1996.

Parker, Martha J., and Betty A. Laird, eds. and comps. "Stull." *Soil of Our Souls: Histories of the Clinton Lake Area Communities.* Overbrook, Kans.: Parker-Laird Enterprises, 1976.

Penner, Jain. "Legend of Devil Haunts Tiny Town." *University Daily Kansan.* November 5, 1974.

Pittman, Bob. "Devil of a Story Clings to Stull Cemetery." *Lawrence Journal-World.* October 31, 1982.

Ramstack, Tom. "Equinox in Cemetery Is Devil's Night Out." *University Daily Kansan.* March 20, 1978.

Ramstack, Tom. "Devil Bypasses Cemetery." *University Daily Kansan*. March 22, 1978.

————. "College Students Give Halloween Legend a Hand." *Kansas City Times*. November 1, 1980.

Retzlaff, Duane. "Members Mark 125 Years of History for Stull Church." *Lawrence Journal-World*. October 28, 1984.

Schwalm, Maurice. "Occult Studies. An Exercise in Photographic Discrimination: The Haunted Cemetery at Stull, Kansas." *Mension*. September 1986.

Sodders, Lisa M. "Cemetery Peaceful Under Watch." *Topeka Capital-Journal*. November 1, 1989.

Interviews with Stull area residents. Stull, Kansas, December 1996 and January 1997.

"The Tale of Stull Cemetery." *Lawrence Journal-World*. October 31, 1982.

The Urge Overkill Stull EP (compact disc). Recorded by Urge Overkill. Touch and Go Records, Chicago, Illinois. Released in 1992.

Vogel, Steven. "Exploring Myths About Stull Cemetery Proves Interesting." *Shawnee Heights High School Totem*. Tecumseh, Kansas. April 15, 1981.

Vogel, Steven. "Adventure to Stull Cemetery Proves Bizarre to Staffer." *Shawnee Heights High School Totem*. May 1, 1981.

Worrall, Michelle. "Ghostly Tales Haunt Town's Graveyard." *University Daily Kansan*. April 16, 1985.

The Caretaker Ghosts

The motif of ghosts coming back from the dead to tend their own graves is an unusual one. Combined with the element of the "ghost light" or "spook light," this makes for an interesting legend and fascinating story. These ghosts are concerned not only with trimming the grass around their graves but also in righting any headstones that had tilted over time. In olden times, gravestones were not just markers but were considered to be shrines to the individuals buried beneath them. It then makes sense that these ghosts would be interested in straightening up their own shrines.

This story is also a good example of the idea of ghosts being used as scapegoats for weird occurrences that are difficult to rationalize or interpret. A light where no light should or could be makes no sense unless it is assigned some type of explanation, even if it is a paranormal explanation.

The story of the caretaker ghosts was found in the files of the Joan O'Bryant Collection at the Wichita Public Library. The original story was told by the real-life Miss Alma to her nephew in 1961. She actually did teach at the Flag School in 1909 and 1910 and did indeed see the ghost light several times. She was disappointed, however, that she must have scared the ghosts away when she went to the hilltop to find them.

SOURCE

"A Ghost Story." Joan O'Bryant Kansas Folklore Collection. Wichita Public
    Library. Wichita, Kansas. (Collection now housed at Wichita State Univer-
    sity, Wichita, Kansas.)

The Glowing Tombstone

If Atchison is the most haunted town in Kansas, Emporia comes in a close
second. Two tales from Emporia are included in this collection, but numerous
others exist. Emporia State University has several dormitory ghosts, and its
most celebrated haunt is the ghost in Albert Taylor Hall. The Praying Nun Tree
Stump, the ghost in the William Allen White house, and the Lake Wooster Monster all call the Emporia area home. The city also claims an unparalleled example of a "legend in the making" in the protolegend tales of Bird Bridge. These
stories must be saved for volume two of *Haunted Kansas*.

SOURCES

Heffley, Deborah Anne. "Haunting Tales of Emporia, Kansas." Student paper
    written for Dr. James Hoy's American Folklore class, 1983. Courtesy of Dr.
    James Hoy, Emporia State University.
Interview with Dr. James Hoy, Department of English, Emporia State Univer-
    sity. Emporia, Kansas. September 28, 1995.
Interviews with members of folklore class of Dr. James Hoy, Emporia State Uni-
    versity. Emporia, Kansas, September 28, 1995.

The Ghost of the Cimarron

A ghost carrying a lantern to light its way is a common motif and rationalization for unexplainable "spook lights" or moving lights where there should be
no lights. An unsolved murder is often reason enough for a restless ghost to
retrace the last path it took, locked into an unvarying pattern that changes or
stops only if and when the crime is solved and the true murderer named. This
unfinished business is believed to be one of the primary reasons a ghost is compelled to haunt.

SOURCES

Buchanan, Rex C., and James R. McCauley. *Roadside Kansas: A Traveler's Guide
    to Its Geology and Landmarks.* Lawrence: University Press of Kansas, 1987.

Fisher, James J. "Schoolmarm's Murder Sparks a Legend in Western Kansas." *Kansas City Star,* May 26, 1996.

McClure, Janice Lee, ed. *Haskell County, Kansas 1887–1987: A Historical Anthology—100 Years Beneath the Plow.* 1987.

Interview with Kim Pendergraft, librarian, Dudley Township Public Library. Satanta, Kansas, October 9, 1996.

The Hamburger Man

As mentioned, some versions of the Hamburger Man legend include narrative elements from the pervasive American urban legend of the Hookman. Numerous examples of the Hookman story exist in Kansas local legendry, particularly in areas near a prison, reformatory, or mental institution.

A vengeful ghost or monster (although given his impressive longevity as a legend, he most certainly must be a ghost by now), the Hamburger Man seems to be seeking retaliation for the slights and stares of a cruel populace by attacking just about anyone who gets in his way or invades his territory.

The Hamburger Man legend exemplifies the way contemporary culture insinuates its way into stories of this type. The comparison of the Hamburger Man's features to those of Jason, the deranged killer from the *Friday the 13th* horror movie series, indicates that for this particular teller of the tale, the Hamburger Man is very much a contemporary story, one with its brotherly counterpart found right up on the big screen at the local multiplex. The Hamburger Man becomes that much more frightening when his gruesome visage and garbled speech are imagined, right alongside that of Jason's, in bloody color and Surroundsound.

SOURCES

Interview with Valerie Hemphill. Hutchinson, Kansas, May 1996.

Interview with Candy Miller. Hutchinson, Kansas, August 9, 1996.

Mitchell, Pat. "Things That Go Bump . . . in the Night." *Kanhistique* 15, no. 6 (October 1989): 2–3.

Interview with John Stratton. Lindsborg, Kansas, September 1996.

Interviews with Barbara Ulrich-Hicks, curator, and Pat Garwood, curator of education. Reno County Historical Museum. Hutchinson, Kansas, August 9, 1996.

Interviews with participants, Reno County Ghost Town Tour. Sponsored by Reno County Historical Museum. September 21, 1996.

Theorosa's Bridge

The legend of Theorosa's Bridge includes elements and motifs that echo many other legends in Kansas as well as in other locations. Most striking is the wandering female ghost, searching along the water for her drowned child. This is highly reminiscent of the Mexican legend of La Llorona, the "weeping one"— the demonic ghost of a bereaved mother who eternally searches for her lost children along the banks of a river or stream, children whom she herself has murdered.

The ritualistic chanting process, the evocation, that visitors to the bridge must go through in some versions to summon the ghost of Theorosa is unusual for most Kansas ghosts. Many ghosts seem to appear quite readily on their own without Theorosa's preferred summoning-up ceremony. Theorosa's horseback-riding episodes are also quite unusual in Kansas folklore, although the motif of a ghost riding a horse, and even riding it to death, definitely has an established precedent in certain other areas rife with legends.

Theorosa and the bridge stand together as elements of equal importance in the tale. But whereas the character of Theorosa changes from one group of variants of the story to another (sometimes she is a woman, sometimes she is a child; sometimes she is white, sometimes she is Native American; sometimes she is a pioneer in the 1800s, sometimes she is a contemporary farm wife), the element of the bridge remains as a focal point in all versions. Even when the story being told predates the construction of the bridge, the bridge still serves as a way to ground the story to a particular place in south-central Kansas, in the here and now. Theorosa's Bridge ties the legend to the landscape around Jester Creek and figuratively bridges the time gap between the supposed date of the story's events and the time of the telling. It also serves as an anchor for a wandering ghost and an excellent and appropriately eerie landmark for active legend tripping by teenagers and others who have sought, and continue to seek, the ghost of Theorosa's Bridge.

SOURCES

The Folklore Papers of William E. Koch. Courtesy of Dr. James Hoy, Emporia State University, Emporia, Kansas.

Interviews with freshman/sophomore English and speech classes and their teacher, Nancy Hopkins. Valley Center High School, Valley Center, Kansas, May 8, 1996.

"Investigating the Ghost of Theorosa's Bridge." *Wichita Eagle Beacon,* October 10, 1980.

"The Legend Lives On." *The Hornet* (yearbook), Valley Center High School, 1974.

"Psychic Claims Theorosa's Bridge Is 'Haunted.'" *Wichita Eagle Beacon,* December 12, 1980.

Interviews with Sergeant Alan Sherry and Investigator Ron Farthing. Valley
    Center Police Department, Valley Center, Kansas, May 8, 1996.
"This Weekend Watch Out for Ghosts of Kansas' Past." *Wichita Eagle Beacon,*
    October 31, 1981.
Tanner, Beccy. "11 Ghostly Tales from Kansas." *Wichita Eagle,* October 31,
    1993.
"Theorosa Lost Her Home but Legend of Ghost Continues." *Ark Valley News,*
    June 18, 1975.
"Theorosa's Bridge Undergoing Repair." *Ark Valley News,* July 18, 1991.
"Valley Center Area Residents Say Strange Things Happen at Theorosa's
    Bridge." *Wichita Sun,* October 29, 1975.

A Ghostly Sisyphus

In this historical legend, the juxtaposition of Native American references, a vengeful lover, a lovers' triangle, a headless ghost chasing his head as well as a boulder down a hill, and distinct elements of Greek mythology make for an unusual and memorable story.

SOURCES

Geary County Historical Society and Museum.
"A Ghostly Sisyphus." *The Junction City Republican.* Junction City, Kansas. Janu-
    ary 24, 1890.
Heldstab, Marilyn. "Tale of Forlorn Indian and His Ghostly Task." "Museum
    Musings" column, *Junction City Daily Union,* Junction City, Kansas, Octo-
    ber 28, 1990.
Leach, Maria, ed. "Sisyphus." *Funk & Wagnalls Standard Dictionary of Folklore,
    Mythology and Legend.* San Francisco: HarperSanFrancisco, 1972.

Kate Coffee and Her Ghouls

The legend of Kate Coffee is fascinating because of its unusual evolution over a period of 120 years or so. First the story is a documented account (through newspaper articles and court records) of an actual person and an actual crime, the person already achieving legendary status in life because of physical characteristics and an unusual lifestyle. The story then evolves, after the central figure's death, into a fantastic ghost story of a haunted ranch and a high-spirited female ghost and her raucous band of ghouls partying around the countryside. Finally, within the last quarter century or so of the legend's life, the ghost figure has been reduced to a ghost light or fireball that is seen through the trees, among the hills, over the creek, and alongside or even on the highway in the vicinity of where the legendary figure lived and died.

Kate Coffee is just one in the widespread collection of American road ghosts, phantoms that flit alongside cars, appear in front of headlights, flash by as ghostly fireballs, or lurk in the underbrush alongside the road until an unsuspecting traveler passes by. The most famous road ghost is the utterly pervasive Vanishing Hitchhiker, a ghostly rider in human form that hitches a ride with a helpful driver, only to be revealed at some point in the story as a phantom. Numerous stories of the Vanishing Hitchhiker exist in Kansas as well as throughout the United States and elsewhere in the world.

SOURCES

Rush County Kansas . . . A Century in Story and Pictures. Compiled by the Rush County Historical Society Book Committee, La Crosse, Kans.: Print Press and the *Rush County News,* 1976.
Interview with Carolyn Thompson. McCracken, Kansas, October 12, 1996.

The Legends of Witches Hollow

This legend is another prime example of the phenomenon known as legend tripping—visits by young people to a locally famous site that is known to be haunted or a hangout for monsters and other supernatural creatures.

No information regarding this story explains "the legend behind the legends," the reasons why these malevolent spirits are in this particular place. This seems to be an instance where the inherent spookiness of a place has invited supernatural creatures and their resultant legends to reside there temporarily, until the place is altered. Then when the physical landscape and the mood are changed, the ghosts, witches, and monsters necessarily leave the vicinity, looking for "darker pastures."

SOURCES

Interview with Captain John Gagliardo, Crawford County sheriff's office. Girard, Kansas, January 6, 1997.
Wolkey, Laurel. "Legends of Witches Hollow Persist." *Pittsburg Morning Sun.* October 1979.

The Holmes Ghost Light

Five other stories in this book include reports of ghost lights or spook lights as a part of their legends: "The Caretaker Ghosts," "Kate Coffee and Her

Ghouls," "The Ghost of the Cimarron," "Mystic Cow Lights," and "The
Haunted Hayloft." In the "Notes and Sources" section of the "Mystic Cow
Lights," a summary of the baffling phenomenon known also as ignis fatuus,
corpse light, or "will-o'-the-wisp" is detailed.

SOURCES

Interview with Mike Baughn, undersheriff of Thomas County and past presi-
    dent of the Thomas County Historical Society. Colby, Kansas, January 6,
    1997.
Baughn, Mike. "The Holmes Ghost Light." *Prairie Winds* (a publication of the
    Thomas County Historical Society). September 1990.
Richmond, Robert W. *Kansas: A Land of Contrasts.* Arlington Heights, Ill.: The
    Forum Press, 1980.

St. Jacob's Well: The Cowboy Ghost and His Ghost Horse

Sinkholes are the source of many legends and fantastic tales in Kansas. St.
Jacob's Well and the Big and Little Basins are perhaps the best known, but other
sinkholes, water filled or dry, are part of the setting for numerous other stories.
A sinkhole near Inman is home to the legendary Sinkhole Sam, a sea serpent–
type creature reportedly sighted there in the 1950s. In Mitchell County, a story
tells of a man digging in a sinkhole who fell in and was never seen again. Tales
of people, tractors, cars, houses, and even a depot falling or disappearing into
sinkholes abound—some may be true, but many are embellished or exagger-
ated. Like St. Jacob's Well, Kansas sinkholes seem to be a bottomless source for
folklore and legendry.

SOURCES

Austin, Jackie. "Legends Surround Mysterious Well." *Dodge City Daily Globe.*
    December 28, 1991.
Buchanan, Rex C., and James R. McCauley. *Roadside Kansas: A Traveler's Guide
    to Its Geology and Landmarks.* Lawrence: University Press of Kansas, 1987.
Cloutman, Donald G. "The Geology, Folklore-History, Morphometry, and Biota
    of St. Jacob's Well, Clark County, Kansas." Final Report to the Kansas Fish
    and Game Commission, Pratt, Kansas. September 30, 1982.
Clute, Helen. "Saint Jacob's Mystery Well." *Dodge City Globe.* October 27, 1924.
Interview with Henry Alonzo Ford Jr. Ashland, Kansas, June 7, 1996.
McHenry, Eric. "Of Epic Proportion." *Topeka Capital-Journal.* June 9, 1996.
Meschberger, Alesa, and Sue Sprenkle. "The Legend of St. Jacob's Well." *Dodge
    City Daily Globe.* October 30, 1993.
"Murder Unsolved." *Notes on Early Clark County, Kansas.* The Clark County

Chapter of the Kansas State Historical Society. Volume II: August 1940–
September 1941. (Reprinted from the Clark County Historical Society column in the *Clark County Clipper.* Ashland, Kansas. June 13, 1889.)

Staff and archives, the Pioneer Museum. Floretta Rogers, curator. Ashland,
Kansas.

Sill, Carole. "Sinkholes of Kansas." *Ford Times.* August 1960.

Steele, F. M. *Kings and Queens of the Range: A Pictorial Record of the Early Day Cat-
tlemen of Clark County, Kansas from 1884 to 1904.* Mt. Vernon, Ind.: Windmill Publications. 1991. (Reprint sponsored by Clark County Historical
Society and the Pioneer Museum.)

Whittemore, Margaret. "St. Jacob's Well a Clark County Feature." *Topeka Daily
Capital.* September 14, 1953.

Winter, Ann. "The Mysterious Oasis." *Kansas!* 3d Issue. 1978.

Mystic Cow Lights

Ignis fatuus, or "foolish fire," is only one name for the phenomena commonly known as spook lights, ghost lights, corpse lights, jack-o'-lanterns, or
will-o'-the-wisps. Ghost lights are universally found in folklore and legend
throughout the world and have been seen in the air, on the ground, over water,
or on the ocean. The shapes and sizes of spook lights run the gamut from small
dancing flames to large glowing balls of light. Colors may vary but are commonly reported as white, yellow, red, orange, or blue. They may even change
colors as they are being observed.

The lights are usually perceived as erratic and jumpy, seemingly possessing
some type of awareness or intelligence in that they evidently react to observers
or pursuers by moving toward or away from them, chasing them, or fleeing
them. The lights have also been reported at times to be "playful," engaging in
games of tag or hide-and-seek with witnesses. They can flash, spin, dance, bob,
weave, split, fragment, hum, or buzz. They are generally found in remote areas.

In folklore, ghost lights are omens of death, moving from a churchyard to
the house of a sick or dying person or hovering over the roof of a building
where a dying person lies inside (see the story of the Haunted Hayloft in this
section). These types of ghost lights are also called corpse candles, fetch candles, or fetch lights when they resemble most closely a candle flame. Corpse
candles usually bob over the ground or float in the air and are always harbin-
gers of death.

Gases of all sorts, natural earth energies, strange atmospheric conditions,
electromagnetic energy, vapors escaping from faults in the earth's crust, and
extraterrestrial activity have all been advanced as answers to the mystery of the
source of these kinds of lights. When these phosphorescent lights are observed

over marshes, as they often are, they are usually attributed to marsh gas. But the most common explanation, although not necessarily the most rational, is one that incorporates local legendry and the supernatural. The ghost of a lost traveler, carrying a lantern to light his way; a headless phantom chasing after his severed head that continually rolls before him in the form of a ball of fire; a murdered miner searching for his murderer, finding his way through the dark of night by the light of his miner's hat—these are all ghosts that have been associated with luminous phenomena that defy natural explanation.

Attesting to the popularity of ghost light legends and research into them, there is even an organization that conducts investigations of ghost light sites and compiles data on them as part of its ongoing mission of inquiry into paranormal phenomena: The Ghost Research Society, headquartered in Oak Lawn, Illinois.

SOURCES

"Gas May Explain 'Spook.'" *Dodge City Daily Globe.* Dodge City, Kansas. November 29, 1922.

Guiley, Rosemary Ellen. *The Encyclopedia of Ghosts and Spirits.* New York: Facts On File, 1992.

Leach, Maria, ed. *Funk and Wagnall's Standard Dictionary of Folklore, Mythology and Legend.* San Francisco: HarperSanFrancisco, 1984.

"Morton County Has a Midnight Mirage." *Dodge City Daily Globe.* Dodge City, Kansas. November 29, 1922.

"'Mystic Lights': Wallace, Kansas." Joan O'Bryant Kansas Folklore Collection. Wichita Public Library. Wichita, Kansas. (Collection now housed at Wichita State University, Wichita, Kansas.)

The Phantom Cat

Interview with Bill Brooks. Ashland, Kansas, January 30, 1997.

Brooks, Bill. "The Phantom Cat." Ashland, Kansas. (Handwritten, undated account available at Pioneer-Krier Museum, Ashland.)

Cavendish, Richard. *The World of Ghosts and the Supernatural.* New York: Facts On File, 1994.

Leach, Maria, ed. *Funk and Wagnall's Standard Dictionary of Folklore, Mythology and Legend.* San Francisco: HarperSanFrancisco, 1984.

Poe, Edgar Allan. "The Black Cat." *The Complete Poems and Stories of Edgar Allan Poe.* New York: Alfred A. Knopf, 1982.

Quest for the Unknown: Ghosts and Hauntings. Pleasantville, N.Y.: The Reader's Digest Association, 1993.

Angel over Greensburg

In the realm of spiritualism in the nineteenth century and early twentieth century, mediums, most of them female, became the high priestesses of what became a religion in Great Britain and the United States. Frenzied interest in seances and communication with members of the spirit world peaked toward the end of the century and then gradually faded out (except for a brief revival during World War I) by 1920 or so.

The practitioners of spirit photography amazed their clients and supporters with photographs that might "reveal" the images of multiple spirits surrounding a subject. These spirits could be of deceased loved ones, unknown individuals, or famous deceased personages such as Abraham Lincoln or George Washington. Dummy heads, double exposures, and models posed as spirits in many of the fraudulent photos that were accepted by gullible believers as proof of the afterlife. Spirit photography as a fad declined in the twentieth century, but it continues in contemporary times to be used, in a different way, to find photographic evidence of ghosts and supernatural phenomena in investigations of supposed hauntings.

SOURCES

"Angel over Greensburg." *Kiowa County History Book: A History of Kiowa County, 1880–1980.* Kiowa County Libraries. Lubbock, Tex.: Taylor Publishing, 1979.

Guiley, Rosemary Ellen. *The Encyclopedia of Ghosts and Spirits.* New York: Facts On File, 1992.

Guiley, Rosemary Ellen. *Harper's Encyclopedia of Mystical and Paranormal Experience.* Edison, New Jersey: Castle Books, 1991.

Staff and archives, Kiowa County Library. Jean Kile, librarian. Greensburg, Kansas.

Randi, James. *An Encyclopedia of Claims, Frauds, and Hoaxes of the Occult and Supernatural.* New York: St. Martin's Press, 1995.

Wood, Frank, and Scott Daymond. *Reflections of Kansas: 1900–1930, a Prairie Postcard Album.* Wichita, Kans.: Daywood Publishing, 1988.

The Haunted Mattress

This humorous and all-too-true tale is legendary in the Wichita area. Various versions of the "haunted mattress" story can be found in print and from oral reports. Similar stories of haunted mattresses and haunted beds can be found dating back to colonial times in American folklore. This type of story is nearly a historical urban legend.

SOURCES

"Ghost Moves Along with the Mattress—Reports Funny Sounds Heard in the
    Window of Crook Furniture Store: Lucases Have Silence." *Wichita Eagle*.
    April 3, 1940.
"Spooky Deer, Your Tale Has Wagged Before." *Wichita Eagle*. May 19, 1965.
Tanner, Beccy. "Eleven Ghostly Tales from Kansas." *Wichita Eagle*. October 31,
    1993.

The Haunted Hayloft

This ghost story was collected from an unnamed informant in 1961 in
Axtell, Kansas. The source claimed that her aunt, when she was young, had
been to visit a relative of the Sullivan family at the house and had seen the barn
and met Mrs. Sullivan. The aunt told her niece the story. The time period of the
events at the Sullivan farm was indicated to be the late 1890s or very early in
the 1900s.

The original first-person account of this story is to be found in the folklore
archives of Joan O'Bryant, a native Wichita educator and active folklorist who
collected and preserved a large repository of Kansas folklore during the 1950s
and 1960s. Her specialty was folk music and songs, but a significant number of
stories and legends can be found in her collection as well.

SOURCES

"Ghost Story." Joan O'Bryant Kansas Folklore Collection. Wichita Public
    Library. Wichita, Kansas. (Collection now housed at Wichita State Univer-
    sity, Wichita, Kansas.)

The Singing Ghost

This story was found in a portion of the late William E. Koch's folklore
papers. Koch was a professor of English at Kansas State University for many
years and a well-known and respected folklorist. He was a former president of
the Kansas Folklore Society and author of two books on state folklore: *Kansas
Folklore* (coauthored with S. J. Sackett, 1961) and *Folklore from Kansas: Customs, Beliefs, and Superstitions* (1980). *Kansas Folklore* includes two chapters
concerning ballads and folk songs collected in Kansas. Many of these ballads
are variations on traditional English ballads, such as "Bonny Barbara Allen,"
that have been orally transmitted and adapted over generations.

At first the story of Bonnie, the Singing Ghost, seems to be a fairly familiar ghost story of a tragic death and a suicide and a ghost who lingers near a familiar place loved in life. But the oddity in this story is that the ghost happens to be not only a singing ghost, which is unusual, but a *ballad*-singing ghost, which is very unusual. This leads to the conclusion, given the facts of this particular legend, that this story is itself a prose variation of a traditional ballad, transformed into a local ghost legend. The plot, the description of Bonnie (even her name echoes the ballad of Bonny Barbara Allen), the repetition of what are known as commonplace elements—phrases and descriptive motifs that are common in ballads (references to "her lover," had "long, flowing hair," and so on), all indicate a genesis for this story in a narrative folk song or ballad that was circulated in the area or heard and then adapted into this ghostly legend.

The ballad excerpts quoted in the story are the only element not original to the Pleasanton legend—they are portions of traditional English/American ballads. But they seemed to fit quite well with the legend of Bonnie the ballad-singing ghost and to illustrate the connection between the two.

The informant for this story related the tale in 1972 but indicated that he had been told the story by an older gentleman who had lived south of Pleasanton, near the area where Bonnie had supposedly lived and died years before. This man had insisted that he had "heard the ghost sing many times" when he had lived there.

SOURCES

"Bonnie's Ghost." (1972 student paper.) The Folklore Papers of William E.
    Koch. Courtesy of Dr. James Hoy, Emporia State University, Emporia,
    Kansas.
Brunvand, Jan Harold. "Ballads." *The Study of American Folklore*. New York:
    W. W. Norton, 1986.
Koch, William E., and S. J. Sackett. *Kansas Folklore*. Lincoln: University of
    Nebraska Press, 1961.

Atchison's Haunted Houses

Each of the haunted house stories in this section is derived at least in part from *The Atchison Trolley Presents: Haunted House Tours* booklet distributed by the Atchison Chamber of Commerce for their annual Halloween trolley tour of local haunted houses. Other sources elaborated on the stories or supplied additional information.

SOURCES

The Atchison Trolley Presents: Haunted House Tours. Atchison Area Chamber of
    Commerce. October 1995.

Interviews with Cindy Jones-Blanton, assistant director, Atchison Public
    Library. Atchison, Kansas, August 1995; October 1995; November 1996.
Michaels, Susan. "Haunting in the Heartland." *Sightings*. New York: Fireside
    Books, 1996.
Schwartz, Alvin. "The Bride." *More Scary Stories to Tell in the Dark*. New York:
    Harper Trophy, 1984.
Interviews with Alan Shaver and Colleen Jaegle, Atchison Visitor's Center and
    Chamber of Commerce. Atchison, Kansas, August 1995.
Taylor, Chris. "Ghostly Doings Abound in Atchison." *Atchison Globe*. October
    21, 1995.

The Legend of Molly's Hollow in Jackson Park

The story of Molly's Hollow is a complex multigenerational legend that is particularly fascinating in view of the number of different elements of social concern reflected in its various versions. Racism, slavery, suicide, abandonment, teen sexuality—a lot of social issues are buried in the narrative of the legend of Molly.

SOURCES

The Atchison Trolley Presents: Haunted House Tours. Atchison Area Chamber of
    Commerce. October 1995.
Interview with Myra Innes. Topeka, Kansas, April 1995.
Interviews with Cindy Jones-Blanton, assistant director, Atchison Public
    Library. Atchison, Kansas, August 1995; October 1995; November 1996.
Interviews with Alan Shaver and Colleen Jaegle, Atchison Visitor's Center and
    Chamber of Commerce. Atchison, Kansas, August 1995.
Taylor, Chris. "Ghostly Doings About in Atchison." *Atchison Globe*. October 21,
    1995.

Epilogue

Dahl, Roald. *Roald Dahl's Book of Ghost Stories*. New York: The Noonday Press,
    1983.
Kendrick, Walter. *The Thrill of Fear*. New York: Grove Press, 1991.

Additional Resources

In this section, an asterisk denotes a source that I believe deserves a special recommendation.

General Background

Readers interested in learning more about ghost stories and legends might begin with several excellent reference books that define common terms and elements found in ghost lore and present an overall introduction to the variety of spooks, phantoms, ghouls, and ghosts that populate the world of supernatural legendry:

Cavendish, Richard. *The World of Ghosts and the Supernatural*. New York: Facts on File, 1994.

Guiley, Rosemary Ellen. *Harper's Encyclopedia of Mystical and Paranormal Experience*. New York: HarperCollins, 1991.

*Guiley, Rosemary Ellen. *The Encyclopedia of Ghosts and Spirits*. New York: Facts On File, 1992.

*Hauck, Dennis William. *Haunted Places: The National Directory*. New York: Penguin Books, 1996.

Leach, Maria, and Jerome Fried, eds. *Funk & Wagnall's Standard Dictionary of Folklore, Mythology and Legend*. San Francisco: HarperSanFrancisco, 1984.

Randi, James. *An Encyclopedia of Claims, Frauds, and Hoaxes of the Occult and Supernatural*. New York: St. Martin's Press.

State and Regional Collections

There are numerous state and regional collections of ghost tales. Books about New England ghosts, southern ghosts, Texas ghosts, and coastal-area ghosts predominate. There are a few collections of ghost stories from individual cities, typically large and/or historic cities such as Charleston, Chicago, and San Diego. Here is a sampling of some state and/or regional collections.

*Citro, Joseph A. *Green Mountain Ghosts, Ghouls and Unsolved Mysteries* [Vermont]. Shelburne, Vermont: Chapters Publishing, 1994.

Graydon, Nell S. *South Carolina Ghost Tales*. Beaufort, South Carolina: Beaufort Book Company, 1987.

Holzer, Hans. *Dixie Ghosts: True Recent Southern Hauntings*. Norfolk, Virginia: The Donning Company, 1990.

*Martin, MaryJoy. *Twilight Dwellers: Ghosts, Ghouls and Goblins of Colorado*. Boulder, Colorado: Pruett Publishing, 1984.

McNeil, W. K. *Ghost Stories from the American South*. Little Rock, Arkansas: August House, 1985.

Murray, Earl. *Ghosts of the Old West*. New York: Tom Doherty Associates, 1994.

Rhyne, Nancy. *Coastal Ghosts*. Orangeburg, South Carolina: Sandlapper Publishing, 1985.

*Scott, Beth, and Michael Norman. *Haunted Heartland*. New York: Warner Books, 1985.

Young, Richard, and Judy Dockrey Young. *Ghost Stories from the American Southwest*. Little Rock, Arkansas: August House, 1991.

National Ghost Stories

A number of collections present "true" ghost tales from across the entire United States, often categorized by region or by state. (The midwestern states are always underrepresented, and Kansas often is not represented at all.) A few books are more truly representative and present an interesting cross section of national ghosts, some even including tales from the Sunflower State:

*Bingham, Joan, and Dolores Riccio. *More Haunted Houses*. New York: Pocket Books, 1991.

Downer, Deborah. *Classic American Ghost Stories*. Little Rock, Arkansas: August House, 1990.

*Myers, Arthur. *The Ghostly Register*. Chicago: Contemporary Books, 1986.

*Myers, Arthur. *The Ghostly Gazetteer*. Chicago: Contemporary Books, 1990.

*Norman, Michael, and Beth Scott. *Haunted America*. New York: Tom Doherty Associates, 1994.

*Norman, Michael, and Beth Scott. *Haunted Historic America*. New York: Tom Doherty Associates, 1995.

Ghost Stories for Children

For younger readers, the *Scary Stories* set is a terrific series of ghost and monster stories based on traditional tales from folklore. The numerous illustrations are wonderfully creepy—nearly as scary as the stories.

*Schwartz, Alvin. *Scary Stories to Tell in the Dark.* New York: HarperCollins, 1981.

*Schwartz, Alvin. *More Scary Stories to Tell in the Dark.* New York: HarperCollins, 1984.

*Schwartz, Alvin. *Scary Stories 3: More Tales to Chill Your Bones.* New York: HarperCollins, 1991.

Ghost Stories on Film

For further *watching,* here is a short list of some of the most haunting ghost stories on film.

Carnival of Souls. (1962) Directed by the late Harold "Herk" Harvey, a University of Kansas graduate and former Lawrence resident. This cult classic, filmed in and around Lawrence and in Utah by Harvey for $30,000, was named by *Rolling Stone* magazine in 1992 as "one of the 10 scariest movies-you've-never-heard-of on home video." It's also been called "the best movie ever made in Lawrence, Kansas" (*VideoHound's Complete Guide to Cult Flicks and Trash Pics* [Detroit, Mich.: Visible Ink Press, 1996]).

The Haunting. (1963) Directed by Robert Wise. A chilling adaptation of Shirley Jackson's classic book, *The Haunting of Hill House.*

The Innocents. (1961) Directed by Jack Clayton; screenplay by William Archibald and Truman Capote. Based on one of the world's most famous ghost stories, Henry James's novella, *The Turn of the Screw.*

Poltergeist. (1982) Directed by Tobe Hooper. The 1996 *Golden Movie Retriever* describes this movie, cowritten by Steven Spielberg, as a "stupendously scary ghost story."

The Uninvited. (1944) Directed by Lewis Allen. A brother and sister buy a seaside house in England, only to find it is haunted by the mother of a young woman they meet. Described by critics as "one of the first films to deal seriously with ghosts."

Index

Readers interested in sharing stories with me
regarding any of the tales collected in this volume or
any other ghost legends or local legends from around
the state, or readers wanting additional details about
interviews or accounts described in this volume,
please write to:

Lisa Hefner Heitz
P.O. Box 4106
Topeka, Kansas
66604-0106